ADVENTURE ATHLETES

Climbers

Scaling the heights with the sport's elite

Steven Boga

STACKPOLE
BOOKS

Published by
STACKPOLE BOOKS
5067 Ritter Road
Mechanicsburg, PA 17055

Printed in the United States of America

Cover design by Caroline Miller

First Edition

10 9 8 7 6 5 4 3 2 1

Library of Congress Cataloging-in-Publication Data

Boga, Steve, 1947–
   Climbers : scaling the heights with the sport's elite / Steven
Boga. – 1st ed.
      p.   cm. – (Adventure athletes)
   Includes bibliographical references (p.   ).
   ISBN 0-8117-2415-8 : $14.95
      1. Mountaineers – United States – Biography.   2. Mountaineering.
   I. Title.   II. Series.
   GV199.9.B64   1994
   796.5'22'0922 – dc20   93-42349
      [B]   CIP

To my parents,
who were there at the start of the climb

Contents

Preface vii

Acknowledgments x

PROFILES

Peter Hackett: Mountain Medico 2

Lynn Hill: Vertical Gymnast 20

Galen Rowell: Lens Master 38

Mike Corbett and Mark Wellman: The Hard Way 59

Sharon Wood: On Top of the World 86

John Bachar: Rock Star 105

David Brower: Mountain Guardian 123

RESOURCES

Tips to Improve Your Climbing 144

Safety 152

Climbing into the Past 161

Climbing Oddities 176

Quotations and Inspirations 183

Glossary 193

Organizations 210

Bibliography 211

Preface

Climbing may be
hard . . . but it's easier
than growing up.
———T-shirt philosophy

Climbers belong to a club with a diverse, ever-expanding membership, no dues, and very loose entrance requirements. The sport itself is elastic enough to include bouldering, big-wall climbing, expedition work, ice climbing, peak bagging, free soloing, free climbing, and aid climbing. It has room for the likes of John Bachar, who climbs nearly naked, without ropes, on sun-drenched vertical walls; it includes Sharon Wood, who has spent months at a time wearing the same clothes at ridiculous heights in the frigid Himalaya; it embraces Lynn Hill, a sport climber who can usually be found indoors on man-made walls with artificial holds; it welcomes paraplegic Mark Wellman, whose ascent of El Captain was a remarkable feat of mechanical engineering; it reveres David Brower, who pioneered routes in the thirties and forties when friction-soled boots weren't even a twinkle in a climber's eye.

A climbing rat, as one empassioned with the sport is called, might come from anywhere on the socioeconomic spectrum. In this volume alone, there is scruffy Mike Corbett, who spent ten years living in a Yosemite campground, climbing big walls, and shoplifting from the local store, as well as Galen Rowell, whose success as an outdoor and climbing photographer places him considerably higher on the food chain.

Nor is age an obstacle to membership in this amorphous club. My four-year-old daughter, who loves to scramble up slopes, and Hayley Sequoia Yager, who at 3½ years has her own harness and practices on a climbing wall at her Yosemite home, both qualify. At the other end of the spectrum, Fritz Wiessner was still climbing when he was eighty-six.

Once a climber, always a climber. David Brower is an honorary member, even though his last noteworthy climb was more than forty years ago. Even at age eighty, there's nothing he'd rather talk about than climbing.

The fraternity includes people who don't even recognize their membership, their essential kinship. John Bachar once told me, "Everyone free solos. When you walk to the store, you're free soloing. The only issue is degree of difficulty." It occurs to me that what's really important, then, is to maintain some degree of difficulty in your life — even if it's a Class 1 walk to the store.

Climbing, though not without standards, has few rules except those self-imposed. It can be a competitive, financially rewarding sport, as it is for Lynn Hill; a shared activity with a seldom-seen husband, as it now is for Sharon Wood; a challenging romp with friends, as it often is for Galen Rowell; a scientific study, as with Peter Hackett; meditative gymnastic moves as for John Bachar; or an empowering recollection of youthful accomplishment, as with David Brower.

Unless you climb with those who compete for prize money in a sport-climbing event or seek bragging rights to a rated climb, you won't keep score. For most, climbing is a do-your-own-thing sport, with the climbing bum its poster boy.

The extent of the climbing explosion is difficult to fathom. Until last century, only a handful of people ever climbed much of anything just to get to the top. And not until forty years ago — less than an eye blink in the context of human history — did anyone climb an eight-thousand-meter peak. Now all fourteen of them have been climbed every which way but naked; there's a ten-year waiting list for Everest; and on a single day in 1992 thirty-two people, some led by a professional guide, reached the top of the highest mountain on earth.

After interviewing heaps of climbers, I have learned that the sport is about doing what you love in spite of, not because of, the risks. The serious climbers I have met are joy seekers, not thrill seekers, though at the world-class level the connection between the two is obvious. In the past sixty years, seventy-five people have died on Mount McKinley alone. Just recently, Derek Hersey, a world-class climber, died while free-soloing a 5.9 route — well below his capabilities — on Yosemite's

Sentinel Rock. Maurice Herzog, leader of the 1951 French expedition that summitted the first eight-thousander, Nepal's Annapurna, sacrificed most of his fingers and toes to that "successful" expedition. Reinhold Messner, who has climbed every eight-thousander, wonders whether his increasing forgetfulness is a result of brain damage brought on by a plethora of hypoxic nights at high altitude.

And yet back they go, these climbers, to take their stab at the mountain. That is, the Mountain. For someone like me, whose climbing goals do not include topping out on Everest or playing Spiderman on a big wall, the question *why* is never too distant. Talk to climbers and you will hear many superficial reasons why they do their thing – the views, the exercise, the chance to go where few can follow – but it really boils down to an irrepressible love of moving freely over rock. More than any of the athletes I have known and interviewed, climbers' motives are as pure as giardia-free snow.

Acknowledgments

I am, as always, grateful for the tireless aid, counsel, friendship, and editorial advice of Bruce Maxwell; also for the assistance of Alison Osius; for the quality photo work of Rachel Johnson, Ingo Kalk, Bruno Engler, John McDonald, Galen Rowell, Gwen Schneider, Chris Falkenstein, Dwayne Congdon, John Roskelley, and Virginia Renfro; for historical photos from Phoebe Adams and the Sierra Club; for the unrelenting support and guidance from my editors, Duane Gerlach and Sally Atwater; for the loving support and willingness to read rough drafts from my wife, Karen; and most of all for the climbers themselves and their willingness, some would say need, to continually push the proverbial envelope.

PROFILES

PETER HACKETT

Mountain Medico

Everest is a harsh and hostile immensity. Whoever challenges it declares war. He must mount his assault with the skill and ruthlessness of a military operation. And when the battle ends, the mountain remains unvanquished. There are no true victors, only survivors.

———Barry Bishop

A sudden cold wind swept down the south face of Mount Everest, bringing swirling eddies of snow and ice. Peter Hackett, alone at 28,000 feet, felt his nerves tighten. He was standing on the edge of a sheer drop, staring up at a formidable barrier of rock and ice, a 900-vertical-foot fang that pierced the blue sky. He breathed rapidly through his mask until he could do it without gasping. Near the top of the world, it was what passed for "catching your breath." Although he could see the powdery plumes from countless small avalanches in the valleys below, all he could hear was the wind. He watched a bird, a lammergeier with its long, narrow wings and diamond-shaped tail, floating effortlessly on invisible pillows of air.

"He's having a much easier time of it than I am", thought Hackett, wondering what the Big Adventures are for birds? What do they do for kicks? For his part, he climbed mountains and studied the effects of high altitude on the human body. Right now he was both subject and object.

Alone at great heights, he realized, contradictory pressures were at play. On the one hand, he seemed raised to a higher pitch of awareness. In the rarefied air, with no one to talk to, he tuned in with every fiber to the Voice of Nature. He identified with Her, felt intimate with

Her. On the other hand, working at an altitude more than five miles above sea level created a mental numbness and a sapping of the will that could be fatal. Cowardice, it seemed, came easily at great heights. He could imagine himself just sitting down on the ice and becoming one with nature.

Hackett wasn't much of an athlete as a kid: the kind who gets picked last for baseball, then shunted off to right field. His mother, who had given up a promising career as a concert pianist to marry his father, inspired him to take violin lessons. Though he was better with a bow than a bat, he still lacked the tools of greatness.

The oldest of ten brothers and one adopted Bolivian sister, Hackett grew up in a strict Catholic household in the Chicago suburbs. His father was a physician, a general practitioner with a large middle-class practice that kept him away from the house much of the time. As a young boy, Peter was cast in the role of surrogate head of household to an ever-growing brood of younger brothers. "So much is expected of the oldest child," he says. "I'm sure all that responsibility made me an overachiever."

After graduating from Marquette University in Milwaukee in 1969, Hackett decided to go to the University of Illinois Medical School. Like his father he would be a doctor, but his motives ran deeper than a mere desire to follow in Dad's footsteps. As a teenager, he'd watched helplessly as doctors labored over his best friend, who had struck his head on the edge of a swimming pool. The friend died, and Hackett remembers wishing that he'd known enough to help.

As a college student in the sixties, Hackett was radicalized by the times. He grew his hair long, dabbled in experimental behavior, and became attached to the radical notion that health care was a right, not a privilege. "I was committed to delivering health care to those who were normally bypassed by the medical establishment — that is, those who didn't have money. I didn't read Marx or Lenin and wasn't into the Daily Worker, but just like any student of my day I saw the inequalities. It was a time when you felt like maybe you could make a difference."

He interned at San Francisco General Hospital, a one-year stint that thoroughly soured him on the idea of a conventional urban medical career. "Every knifing and gunshot victim in the city came through here," he says. "I got sick and tired of all the violence." So the day after his internship was over, he fled to Yosemite Valley. He bought some hiking boots and dehydrated food, and went backpacking in the High Sierra.

After a couple of weeks in the wilderness, it dawned on Hackett that he had no desire to go back to the city. He asked at the Yosemite Rescue Center if they needed a doctor. "Never had a doctor," was the reply, "but can you teach an EMT (Emergency Medical Technician) course? We sure need one of those."

Although Hackett had never taught such a course before, he said he could do it and got the job. As there was officially no such position, he was hired as "fireguard" at $4.47 per hour. In addition to teaching EMT classes, he participated in helicopter rescue missions.

"The whole summer was great," he says, with a slight smile, about as animated as he ever seems to get. "Before I started work in Yosemite, I went back to Chicago to see my family. My mother had recently died and my father was remarrying. After the wedding, I took eight of my brothers on a 212-mile canoe trip through northern Minnesota."

The combination of Yosemite and Minnesota cemented his love for wilderness. " For the first time in my life, I was working outdoors, doing physical labor, putting on muscle. I lived in a tent cabin in Yosemite, and my next-door neighbor was an owl. I learned about geology, ecology, botany. I spent a lot of time in the Yosemite library, reading up on soils, rocks, and trees."

It was in Yosemite that Hackett was first introduced to rock climbing. He became friends with Beverly Johnson, the first woman to solo Yosemite's El Capitan, who taught him the rudiments of climbing. From the beginning, he was drawn to multiple-pitch routes. "It wasn't just getting to the top," he says. "I loved pitting myself against the mountain. Climbing is a sport that provides immediate results. Either you make the move or you don't. I also loved the concentration it requires. You can't be doing a move and thinking about work undone. And it's a sport that is essentially noncompetitive: there's no scoring system. It appeals to me as an individualist, plus it's done in a gorgeous setting!"

At the end of the summer, Hackett wrote his father that he wouldn't be returning to Illinois to become a partner in his medical practice. He had, he explained, found a home in the mountains.

Most climbers, at one time or another, dream of doing Everest. Even if they harbor no realistic hopes of ever seeing its slopes, let

Peter Hackett's three passions

1. Yak obstetrics
2. Wolf orthopedics
3. Virginia Renfro (five-time fiancée)

---

alone summitting it, the foreboding thought will visit them; they will see themselves on her icy flanks, testing their mettle against the harshest elements Mother Nature can conjure up. Unless they are among the few who will act upon this vision, the question will haunt them: "Could I do it? When the crunch comes would I hold up?"

Peter Hackett knew first-hand about that dream. And about Mount Everest:

In 1852 a clerk rushed into the office of the surveyor-general of India shouting, "Sir, I have discovered the highest mountain in the world!"

The 29,028-foot peak, located in the Himalaya on the Nepal-Tibet border, was later named for Sir George Everest, but the people of the region continued to call it Chomolungma—"Goddess Mother of the Earth." The yeti, or abominable snowman, half-human, half-ape, was said to inhabit the lower slopes.

From 1921 to 1952 eleven expeditions, most of them British, made serious attempts to put a man atop Mount Everest, at a cost of ten lives. Although none of the expeditions succeeded, individuals climbed to more than 28,000 feet, doing the footwork and gathering the information that would be needed by the 1953 expedition on which New Zealander Edmund Hillary and Sherpa Tenzing Norgay made the first successful ascent of Everest.

Peter Hackett first laid eyes on Everest in 1974. Mountain Travel, an adventure-travel organization, needed a trekking doctor for the summer. "They offered all expenses paid," he says. "It was an offer I couldn't refuse."

Three months later, when his job as trekking doctor was over, he was still in Nepal and out of money. So he worked on more treks, satisfied to make only expenses.

It was in Nepal that Hackett was first introduced to mountain sickness. On his first trek to Everest Base Camp, he was amazed to discover that half of his group had flulike symptoms: headache, nausea, and vomiting. Only later did he realize that it wasn't flu but mountain sickness, a spectrum of maladaptions at high altitude, of which edema is the most severe.

While in Nepal, Hackett met John Skow, a Peace Corps volunteer who lived and worked in the Khumbu region near Everest. Alarmed by the number of deaths among high-altitude trekkers, Skow had finally persuaded trekking outfitters to finance a primitive medical clinic, which became known as the Himalayan Rescue Association.

Hackett was hired as the association doctor, or as he puts it: "I became the Himalayan Rescue Association. The clinic was a little yak hut with a dirt floor, an open-pit fire, and a lot of chinks in the stone walls – one of those nonmortared little buildings the dust blows right through."

He still remembers his first patient. "I was having breakfast when the doctor of a group headed for Everest Base Camp dumped a guy off with me and said, 'The man has bronchitis and can't travel with us. . . . We'll pick him up on our way back.' I said, 'Uh, okay,' but when I finished my *tsampa* (barley meal mixed with yak butter) and went out to check on him, I could hear the gurgling sound before I opened the tent flap. He had pulmonary edema, an abnormal accumulation of fluid in the lungs. His skin was the same blue-gray as his parka. He promptly coughed up blood and went into a coma. I radioed for a helicopter and two days later got a message back saying, 'The king is using the helicopter. Could you use something else?' The guy made it, though. He walked out of there."

Hackett used the yak hut for the clinic and at night slept in a tent in the front yard. The locals, good-humored Sherpas, loved having him around because he took care of them and their families and because he made an effort to learn their language. They started slipping him food from the kitchens of the trekking groups. "God, the Sherpas are great," Hackett says. "They would carry extremely ill trekkers or Sherpas down to the clinic and I'd literally save some of their lives. The Sherpas would be so grateful that they would give me a flashlight or a wool hat – something they knew I needed. The trekkers had no idea what kind of conditions I was living under. Finally I put up a sign: 'The doctor needs a new pair of pants,' or 'The doctor needs long underwear.'"

Winter arrived, closing out the trekking season. As usual, Hackett was broke. "At that time I didn't even know if I wanted to become a doctor," he says. "I was thinking of becoming a Sanskrit scholar, of joining a Buddhist monastery, of getting into Tibetan medicine. Anything could've happened."

What did happen was that Mountain Travel once again offered

him a medical job with a group trekking into the Karakoram, the Pakistani arm of the Himalaya. He describes his memorable journey to Pakistan: "I took third-class trains all the way, slept on the platforms with the beggars, had people die next to me during the night. When I finally made it to Pakistan and met the group leaders, they were appalled by the sight of their trip doctor. At that time I was probably about a hundred and twenty pounds, with straggly long hair and a beard. I looked like a Hindu ascetic. The first thing they did was buy me a beer."

In 1979 word reached Hackett that there would be an American Medical Research Expedition to Mount Everest in 1981. It would be the first climbing expedition onto that mountain to have as its primary goal the collection of scientific data. Climbers were to be tested to measure the pressure of carbon dioxide in their lungs as a function of barometric pressure, which decreases as altitude increases. They would also be tested for MVO_2, or maximum oxygen intake. Their "hypoxic drive to breathe" would be determined. Such studies would

Having climbed, worked, and studied among them for years, Hackett has developed a unique appreciation for the Sherpas of Nepal. (Courtesy of Peter Hackett)

contribute greatly to the understanding of how climbers can perform work and survive at extreme altitudes, despite available oxygen that is less than one-third that at sea level.

When Hackett learned that John West was heading the expedition, he was anxious to go. West, professor of medicine and physiology at the University of California San Diego, had been with Sir Edmund Hillary on the Himalayan Scientific and Mountaineering Expedition of 1960-61. "I knew working with scientists of West's caliber would be great. I also knew I was perfect for that expedition. I had lived at fourteen thousand feet. I spoke Nepali. And I knew the Sherpas. I offered the leaders my services, and eventually they agreed. I found out later they were hesitant because they thought I might side with the Sherpas on difficult issues."

There was reason to think so. Having spent five of the last six years in Nepal, Hackett knew and understood the Sherpas. And his appreciation for these short, sturdy mountain people was more than an intellectual one. As medical director of the Himalayan Rescue Association, he had spent most of a winter huddled around a potbellied stove with a Sherpa couple as his only company. He became close with the couple and later with their three children.

Returning to Nepal with the West expedition, he was shocked to discover that the couple had recently died. The story circulating in the village was that the mother, on her death bed, told the neighbors, "I'm not going to be around to take care of my children. Please make sure that Doctor Peter takes care of them."

Hackett searched for the kids as he trekked into Everest Base Camp, finally locating them in the village of Khunde. As he describes it: "I found two of them in a second-story room about six feet by eight feet with an open-pit fire and no bed. There was only one tiny window and it was very dark. I was flabbergasted. The boy was eight and the girl was ten. She was doing all the cooking; they were trying to make it on their own."

Hackett found a better home for the kids and paid for their boarding and school. In effect, he became their adopted father. To this day, he visits them as often as possible and continues to support them financially and emotionally. He intends to send them to college, if they want to go. And even though he's never been married, when he refers to them as "my kids," he makes it all sound perfectly ordinary. When he celebrated his fortieth birthday, he had the party in Kathmandu; "Gotta see my kids," he said.

As West predicted, Hackett's affection and respect for the Sherpas prompted him to take their side before the American Medical Research Expedition even got out of base camp. "I felt very strongly that we had a responsibility to put the Sherpas through some maneuvers, to make sure that they knew how to take care of themselves on the mountain. I talked the leadership into putting all of our Sherpas through a brief climbing course. Amazingly, we had Sherpas who had been on the mountain six times – some of them quite high up – but they didn't know how to use an ice ax, or didn't know how to stop themselves if they fell over backwards. At first the older Sherpas said, 'Oh, we don't need this, we've been on this mountain many times, we know what we're doing.' But it soon became painfully obvious to them that they never should have been up there without knowing the things we were teaching them. In the end, they appreciated the skills we helped them gain."

On September 1, 1981, they started climbing the mountain via the South Col route. They made it through the dangerous icefalls in three days – very good time – and established Camp II in six days. Camp III was also established quickly, but then progress was halted by the twin high-altitude bugaboos: bad weather and sick climbers.

It was well into October before Camp V (25,000 feet) was operational. In punishing winds, teams of climbers eventually secured fixed ropes to the camp, but the camp itself remained defiantly inhospitable.

The first summit team went up and was buffeted down by the wind. Hackett was part of the second attempt, which got as far as Camp V. The first night all three climbers and their equipment jammed into one tent because the other had been destroyed by wind. The second night, they managed to put up another tent. But they weren't able to attempt the summit because of violent wind that nearly blew them off the mountain. The storm ripped open the tent doors and filled the tent with snow, burying their scientific gear and forcing them to retreat down the mountain.

Another summit team tried, but they too were blown off the mountain. With three summit teams repelled, it looked more and more like they weren't going to make it. Every time a team went up, they consumed food and fuel and oxygen, which meant the upper camps had to be resupplied from lower down. The Sherpas were getting discouraged, and the climbers were beginning to think that maybe they had missed the window period between monsoon and winter winds. Supplies were running out. Morale hit bottom when the expedition got pinned down back in Camp II.

Although the scientific phase was going well enough, expedition leader John West still wanted to get somebody to the summit. He and John Evans, the climbing leader, decided to pick the strongest people for a mad dash for the top. The strongest were Chris Kopczynski and Sherpa Sundare, who had summitted Everest in 1979. A doctor had to go with them to collect data. They decided upon Steve Boyer, who was a superbly conditioned athlete but who'd already had pulmonary edema.

Off they went, going directly from Camp II (21,000 feet) to Camp V (25,000 feet) to try to save time. Because of their fast ascent, Boyer again came down with pulmonary edema. He was able to descend on his own power, leaving Kopczynski and Sundare up there. Back at Camp II, the consensus was that they still needed someone to take measurements up high on the mountain.

Chris Pizzo, a strong climber, volunteered. He hadn't been bothered much by the altitude and was still in fairly good shape. But he needed someone to go with him. Hackett had just come down a little while ago after getting blown off the South Col (26,200 feet), and few climbers had ever descended from that height and then turned around to go back up. But Hackett felt the same way as Pizzo, that they had to make a last-ditch effort. On the other hand, he had to face the fact that he had frostnip, was vomiting, had lost a lot of weight, and had bronchitis. Still, Pizzo needed someone to go back up with him, and Peter knew that he was the last hope.

As Kopczynski and Sundare had done, Pizzo and Hackett and two Sherpas went straight to Camp IV without stopping at III. To their amazement, Kopczynski and Sundare were at Camp IV after having summitted that afternoon. They had gone from the South Col to the summit in four and a half hours, a remarkable feat. Unable to recover any of the scientific equipment buried at Camp V, however, Kopczynski had taken no measurements on the summit. Pizzo and Hackett, committed to trying to advance man's ability to function at high altitude, felt obligated to push on and try to get those measurements.

The next day they moved up to Camp V, and during the night they tried to do sleep studies with tape-recorded EKG monitors. But Hackett resisted sleep. Huddled in a fetal position in his sleeping bag, he experienced intense longings for things he couldn't have. He thought of lamb chops . . . chardonnay . . . Susan . . . "Hypoxia at first sight," he mumbled, smiling sadly.

Arising at 2:00 A.M., they worked in the frigid darkness, melting snow for water, changing the batteries in the tape recorders, calibrating instruments, and adjusting crampons. Gasping for breath as an icy wind tore at them, they worked slowly. In that extreme cold their muscles were rigid and unresponsive, and it was hours before they were ready to climb.

Then Pizzo remembered that he had lost his ice ax when he abandoned Camp V during an earlier storm. Down lower on the fixed ropes he hadn't needed it; but above Camp V, where no such ropes existed, it was essential equipment. Ascending Everest without an ice ax was akin to a kayaker descending a whitewater river without a paddle.

One of the Sherpas had lost his ax, too, so they decided they would go in two roped teams, one ice ax to a team. Chris and Sherpa Yong Tenzing, got off about 6:30 A.M. Hackett was having trouble with his crampons and didn't get off until 7:30, with Sherpa Nuru Zonbu, a young, inexperienced climber. About half an hour out of camp, Zonbu stopped and said, "Doctor Peter, my feet are freezing. I have to go back." At that point it was very cold and windy. Thinking it might get warmer, Hackett persuaded him to go a little farther. But fifteen minutes later, he really got cold feet and said he would have to go back. Since Hackett would no longer have anyone to rope to, Zonbu took Hackett's climbing harness, the rope, and the extra bottle of oxygen and went down.

Hackett was physically doing well, but he was low on oxygen, and it didn't seem likely he would get to the top. He tried to catch up with Pizzo. Climbing rapidly, he wore himself out, then crouched behind a ridge to rest. The wind stopped, and suddenly it was warm enough for him to take off his down parka.

But at 27,000 feet, stopping is not synonymous with resting. At that altitude, the body burns more fuel than it takes in, no matter what it's doing. It begins to live off its reserves, which are limited. Hackett knew he was fighting a war of attrition – on the losing side. Not wanting to deplete his reserves, he went on, climbing with slow, plodding resolve. He considered stopping to make a couple of scientific measurements, but decided it was more important to catch up with Tenzing and Pizzo. They could use another ice ax, and he needed the safety of roped partners. Besides, he doubted he had the strength to do anything "extra." Just climbing and breathing were challenge enough.

As he approached the crest of a ridge, at about 27,800 feet, he suddenly came upon the body of a dead woman in a narrow couloir. She was facing into the slope as if struck down in midclimb, a frozen study, totally intact: clothes, boots, crampons. Doctor Hackett had seen a lot of dead bodies before, but this was the first time he'd ever had to climb over one. He would later learn that she was Hannelore Schmatz, who died in a fall in October 1979.

Near the south summit he met Pizzo and Tenzing on their way down from the summit. The Sherpa was leading. When he saw Hackett he said, "What are you doing here alone?" When Pizzo came down, he had an ice ax. He had found it a couple hundred feet below the woman's body. It had probably been hers. He told Hackett that when he picked up the ice ax, he knew he was going to make it to the top. He called it divine providence that an ice ax should materialize out of nowhere at 28,000 feet on Everest.

They discussed whether or not Hackett should try for the top. He knew it would be dangerous, but the weather was fine and he was going okay. Pizzo assured him that the route up to the Hillary Step—the most difficult part between the South Col and the summit—was in pretty good shape. Then he looked at Hackett and asked a question that needed no answer: "When's the next time you're going to be this close to the summit of Everest?"

Hackett dumped some excess gear from his pack, forgetting to take out two and a half pounds of frozen water. He and Pizzo each took a dexedrine tablet in hopes of increasing alertness and allaying fatigue. Pizzo assured Hackett that he'd wait for him down at the old Camp VI site.

It was 2:00 P.M. and still a fine day: windy, cloudless, with good visibility. Hackett swapped Sherpa Tenzing his two-thirds-full oxygen bottle for his own nearly empty one and took off. For the first time in his life, he thought he might actually get to the top of Mount Everest.

When he neared the south summit, a cold wind reared up. Hackett ducked behind a ridge and slipped on his parka. Huddled there against the wind, he thought to himself, "God, I could just hide here for a little while, then go down and say that I made it, that I summitted Everest." He was abruptly awakened from that dishonorable thought by the realization that if he stayed there he'd freeze to death.

He started moving again. The route from the south summit to the main summit was there before him. He thought it was the most beautiful ridge he'd ever seen. Very narrow, vertical on the Tibetan side, and extremely steep on the Nepalese side. The most ominous-looking feature was the Hillary Step, a formation of rock and snow about forty feet high at an angle of eighty degrees. It was the main technical barrier to the summit.

Moving slowly along the ridge, steadying himself against the wind, he was meticulous about placement of his ice ax and his feet. One fall and it was all over.

He reached the bottom of the Hillary Step, gulping air like a man dying of thirst gulps water. When at last his eyes and mind cleared, he stared at the formation before him, awestruck that something so difficult was so close to the top. This was supposed to be the easiest route up Mount Everest, but facing him was a very difficult section of climbing. Only forty feet high—but if he fell, he would bounce and roll all the way to base camp, two vertical miles below.

Seeing tracks starting up the step, he tried to go that way. But the snow wasn't consolidated. It was sugary and wouldn't hold the weight of a bird. Then he saw tracks going to the left, where it wasn't as steep and where there was some rock. He found better footing and began to climb. He still had his crampons on, but couldn't stop to take them off because his fingers couldn't function in the extreme cold. He could see sparks flying as his crampons scraped rock.

Near the top was a big boulder and a little snow-covered ledge. He had to put both hands up on the snow and hope the whole precarious piece wouldn't slide off. Clawing the rocks madly with his crampons, he pushed himself up and flopped onto the top of the boulder, like a beached fish.

For a while he just lay there hyperventilating. He realized he had made a total commitment. He would either get to the top or die. Then it occurred to him that he might get to the top and still die.

Progress was painfully slow: take two steps, stop, lean over the ice ax, breathe twenty times. He would come to a high point and think, "This is the top." But it was only a cruel visual trick of nature. There would be another high point, then another, and each time he would be fooled. Yet somehow, through the pain and the disappointments, there was discipline. While the shrieking wind pummeled him, he plodded on, a leaden body encasing a flickering spirit. At this altitude there was no grace in his climbing, only willpower. Finally it was down on all sides; he was on top.

The summit was a tiny plateau about three feet wide by six feet long. It was scary standing on that windswept piece of snow, but of course he had to do it because it meant standing on top of the world. He was higher than any earthbound human. A wonderful feeling of fulfillment, of satisfaction, washed over him. Visibility was amazing; it seemed to approach infinity. He took pictures to prove that he had been there. Then he said a word of thanks to the mountain for letting him get up, and prayed that she would let him go safely down.

Total time at the top: fifteen minutes.

Snowmass, Colorado. Dr. Peter Hackett is speaking before the Wilderness Medical Society, an organization of mountain climbers and wilderness doctors that he helped found.

"Acute Mountain Sickness shows extreme and unpredictable individual variation," he is saying. "It can come on and kill in a very few hours, and if you're genetically predisposed to getting it, no amount of training will prevent it. Scientific maladaptions like pulmonary edema and cerebral edema are really a matter of poor water-handling by the body, water getting to places it shouldn't."

Outside magazine recently ranked Hackett among the "Fifty Who Left Their Mark," calling him "the principal authority on the mysterious, deadly ailments that afflict high-altitude alpinists." The Colorado audience is extremely attentive to Doctor Hackett, who, besides being the preeminent expert in his field, is an articulate, thoughtful speaker. But it staggers the imagination that this man has summitted Mount Everest. He seems so . . . well, ordinary. He certainly appears to lack the indomitable vigor necessary to climb the highest mountain in the world. Dressed casually in blue jeans, Nikes, and a canvas shirt, he is slight of build at five-foot-ten and 150 pounds. With Brillo-pad hair and a scraggly beard, he looks to be more scientist than climber.

After his lecture, he moves to an outdoor cafe for lunch, where he speaks informally about his life on and off the mountain. As he approaches his fortieth birthday, he says, he is a more temperate person than he once was. Though proud of his climbing accomplishments, he sees, perhaps with greater clarity than ever before, that he has been lucky. "So many of my friends who have been killed climbing had more skill than I have," he says.

"In most cases it was just bad luck. Being at the wrong spot at the wrong time. One of the two women with us on a recent hang-gliding expedition to Everest – the one who had the best chance of becoming the first American woman to summit Everest – was just killed a month

Climbing an icy slope, Hackett is acutely aware of the limitations of his body and his equipment. (Courtesy of Peter Hackett)

ago on Mount Logan. A cornice fell off, taking her with it. Now, there's no way to have predicted that."

Despite a greater appreciation for his own fragile mortality, Hackett is not yet a member of the staid milk-and-cookies set. "I still do, and will always, spend time on mountains. Chris Pizzo is arriving tomorrow and we're going climbing. I'll always maintain a skill level that will allow me to survive and enjoy it out there."

Just then a sleek young blond in an electric-blue halter top strolls by, and Hackett's eyes follow her, his voice temporarily trailing off into a distant monologue. "You know," he says sadly, after she has passed, "there are about three hundred beautiful women here for every one in Anchorage, where I live." Then smiling wryly: "Yeah, I have a tendency to be self-destructive if I stay too long in an environment like this. It's a lot healthier for me in the wilderness."

That helps explain Hackett's willingness to fly into a base camp on Alaska's Mount McKinley every spring, set up his portable lab at 14,000 feet, and live there for the two-month (May-June) climbing season, measuring the blood oxygen level of prospective climbers. "That's the essence of what we need to know to determine how well a climber has acclimatized, how well his lungs are working. If he tests low, I'll tell him that he should stay down another couple of days. Of course, he can do whatever he wants, but at fourteen thousand feet on McKinley he'll tend to believe me. At sea level, he might be a bragging fool, but up there it's 'Doctor Hackett, would you check me out and tell me whether I'm adjusting okay?'"

Hackett can measure acclimatization all right, but he admits there is no sure-fire way of predicting whether someone will make it to the top of the mountain. Extreme altitude causes physiological stress for everybody, but with varying degrees of intensity. Ironically, though, Hackett refers to altitude as "the great equalizer."

"Someone who is not necessarily a great athlete at sea level may do very well at high altitudes," he says. "The best predictor is the hypoxic drive to breathe, which we can measure in a lab. We make the subjects hypoxic (underoxygenate their tissues), then see how much breathing it stimulates. On our expedition, the three non-Sherpas with the highest hypoxic drive were Kopczynski, Pizzo, and me, the same three who made it to the top."

Besides the physical skills, one must factor in the intangibles, like drive, judgment, and experience. "I'm a perfect example," he says. "How did I make it to the top of Everest? I wasn't supposed to. I was emaciated, vomiting, had bronchitis and a broken rib from coughing so hard. But at some crucial point, I made a commitment."

In climbing—perhaps more than in any other sport—it is that ability to commit that determines success. Psychology supersedes physiology. Austrian climber Reinhold Messner is a case in point. In 1980, Messner soloed Mount Everest without the aid of supplemental oxygen. He was widely regarded as the world's greatest climber, yet he tested only slightly above average in the lab. "He's been climbing since he was about four," Hackett says, "so he certainly has the experience. He's technically superb, knows his limitations, takes well-calculated risks, and is highly familiar with the environment."

Well-calculated risks? Like soloing Everest without oxygen? "For Messner it was," Hackett insists. "On the other hand, Roger Marshall, who tried it and died, probably thought the same thing."

From the top of the Hillary Step, Hackett looked down and didn't know what to do. His first thought was to jump, but he realized that he

would have to land on an angled slope and that the chances of breaking an ankle were good. Alone and more than five miles above sea
level, a broken ankle would be fatal. He didn't want to down-climb the
side he'd come up, because if he fell, a not unlikely prospect, there
would be no stopping. He considered going down the Tibetan side, but
that too was nearly vertical.

There was only one thing to do: turn around into the slope, face
the crumbling snow, and try to kick his way down, one step at a time.
With full realization that he might fall, he tightened his pack and made
sure his oxygen bottle was secure. Then he checked his gloves and
oxygen mask. Turning into the slope, he kicked the first step down,
kicked the second step down . . . suddenly all three points of contact
broke loose, and he started falling.

"I remember my thoughts very clearly. I'll never forget them. First
was, 'Oh, my God, I'm falling. This can't be happening. Now is not the
time for this to happen.' Second was, 'It's unbelievably easy to die. I'm
not even going to feel any pain.' Third thought was, 'Holy cow! I've
stopped falling. I'm not dead.'

"I was hanging upside down from my knees, with my lower legs
wedged behind a flake of rock. Facing away from the mountain, I was
looking down towards Camp II, a seven-thousand-foot drop. At that
point an incredible will to survive took over. I don't know what else to
call it. All my reactions became very automatic and extremely sharp. I
had to get upright, and to do so I had to sink my ice ax into a little
crack in the rock above me and pull myself up. This involved a series
of exhausting sit-ups. Every time I bent forward, I would try to wedge
the blade of my ax into the crack. After each failure, I gulped air for
several minutes. Finally the ax stuck.

"I pulled myself up, and there in front of me, where I had made a
hole in the snow from the fall, was a fixed rope from a previous
expedition. It was two feet under the snow. I grabbed onto it and was
able to lower myself until it went under some ice. I fell again, but only
a few feet this time, landing upright, feet stemmed against rock on one
side and ice on the other. The rope was exposed again at that spot, and
I was able to get to an eighteen-inch ledge at the bottom of the step."

By this time Hackett was totally drained. He didn't know if he had
the energy to make it back. It was about 4:30 P.M. The sun was low,
and it was getting colder. He had no bivouac gear, no stove, just one
frozen water bottle. If he didn't make it back to camp, he would die.

He decided his best chance was to go out on the Tibetan side and traverse around the mountain. It was steep with lots of loose rock and snow, and Hackett knew he was nearing his physical and emotional limits. He imagined that he looked like a dying animal.

Then Pizzo saw him. He'd been waiting at the old Camp VI site for three hours in deteriorating conditions. He had run low on oxygen, but had found a cache of bottles abandoned by a previous expedition, one of which had a little oxygen left.

"It was a real hero's move," Hackett is fond of saying. "If he hadn't waited, I might never have made it. Chris Pizzo and I will be friends for life. Camaraderie is a big reason I climb. My companions mean everything to me. . . . Climbing mountains provides a unique combination of solitude and deep companionship. I usually feel lonelier in Anchorage or San Francisco than I do in the wilderness. In the city there's alienation. In the mountains I feel intimate with the forces of nature. It's a very spiritual place for me."

When Pizzo got on the radio to say that Hackett had made it, everyone at base camp was relieved. They all thought he was dead, which was a notion that had crossed Pizzo's mind as well. In fact, he'd already made a tape that said, "This is Chris Pizzo speaking. If you find this tape it means that I have perished. On this tape is some very important data. I was waiting for Peter Hackett when it became clear that he must have perished up above. I am leaving this tape because my chances of survival are also very slim."

Hackett and Pizzo made it to Camp V that night well after dark, startling their Sherpas, who had also given them up for dead. A few days later they were all in base camp. And a few days after that, having finished their experiments, they were moving down the mountain. As they approached the first villages, the Sherpa residents came out and greeted them with gifts and chang, the local brew. For Hackett it was "local boy makes good." He was emaciated, with bronchitis, a broken rib, and frostnipped fingers and toes that would plague him for the next six weeks—yet he was a happy man.

Peter Hackett was the 111th person and the eleventh American to stand atop Mount Everest, and the first to solo from the South Col. Yet such a distinction has brought him little financial reward. Nor is there much money in his high-altitude research. Consequently, he works in an Anchorage hospital emergency room to finance his other pursuits.

He is often asked why he wasn't felled by mountain sickness on Everest. Why was he able to make it to the top when so many others have failed? "For one thing, I was lucky," he admits, "because in addition to a high hypoxic drive to breathe, you need big-time luck to succeed on Everest. You need, above all, good weather and good health. The meteorological moods of Everest can be vicious. The South Col, where merciless winds blow all the time, is one of the least hospitable places on earth. Swirling snow often reduces visibility to near zero. The extreme cold of Everest has cost climbers their fingers and toes, others their lives."

There is no question that Hackett's decision to go to the top of Everest was a courageous one, but was it also foolish? "I don't think so," he says. "I was going well and the conditions were perfect. There were risks, of course, but a life without risks is a life hardly worth living. Taking risks reaffirms the joy of living.

"Every time I've taken a risk, I've come out of it with a stronger feeling about being alive. It's that reaffirmation of life that makes climbing so refreshing, so rejuvenating. Living on the edge – the narrow line between life and death – improves everything in life. As we say in climbing, 'The higher you get, the higher you get.'"

Peter Hackett Update. Peter Hackett still lives in Anchorage, still earns most of his living by working in the hospital emergency room, and is still the reigning expert on wilderness and high-altitude medicine.

He occasionally hires on as a lecturer for an adventure-travel company, a job he loves. In that capacity, he has rafted down the Bio Bio River in Chile and joined group climbs in Russia, Nepal, and Antarctica.

He continues to be unofficial dad for three Nepalese children, one of whom he is now putting through college. Hackett has lived for several years with Virginia Renfro and her three kids, and he and Virginia are a serious item. Today, she says, Peter spends more time on "personal growth" than he does on climbing. "At the moment I'm probably his biggest risk," she says, with a laugh.

LYNN HILL

Vertical Gymnast

Stone is to Lynn Hill as marble was to Michelangelo. A vertical wall of granite, limestone, or schist is the medium through which she gives full expression to her creative urges. Climbing rock satisfies her need to be outside, to be physical, to compete, to be challenged by nature.

She grew up in Fullerton, California, in Orange County, part of the Los Angeles megalopolis, where nature is more a rumor than a fact. From her earliest memory, she was scrambling up telephone poles, shimmying up lamp posts, cavorting on monkey bars. As a kid, climbing came to her as naturally as running comes to a foal. Since she also liked to catch lizards and frogs and preferred pants to dresses, she was quickly labeled a "tomboy," a term she accepted but never embraced. At the time, she thought, "If catching frogs and climbing things means I'm a tomboy, then I'm a tomboy." Today, she is less forgiving. "It's discriminatory," she says. "The qualities of a tomboy are energy, vitality, a love of play. Those are not just for boys."

Her vitality was never questioned. At five she was swimming competitively. "I didn't even know what competition was," she says. "They just put me in the water and I'd go." When she was nine, already growing bored with swimming from one end of the pool to the other, she discovered gymnastics. She went into the YMCA one day to retrieve one of her four brothers (she also has two sisters) and stopped to watch some college gymnasts working out on the rings. "Want to give it a try?" one of them asked. So while her mother fidgeted in the car, Lynn took her first gymnastics lesson.

As she got older, climbing continued to be an outlet. But that wasn't even a sport, was it? To most people it was just kids at play; to Lynn it was much more. "Ever since I can remember, I got pleasure from climbing trees and building forts in the high branches," she says. "Climbing has always been the most natural expression and liberation of my energy."

Hill was fourteen the first time she scrambled on serious rock. On a family camping trip in Yosemite Valley, she played around on "erratics," huge boulders torn loose from the rock mass by glaciers grinding through the valley thousands of years ago. "In Yosemite I scrambled on some low-angled boulders," she remembers, "but I kept looking up at El Capitan and Half Dome. What *I* was on seemed like nothing compared to the big walls towering above me. I knew people climbed those walls, and that fascinated me. How could any human being climb what appeared to be blank wall?"

It wasn't long before curiosity and talent (fourteen pull-ups as a sixth-grader) met opportunity. Her sister Kathy had a boyfriend, Chuck, who had caught a serious case of climbing fever. He had infected Kathy and two other Hill siblings, Trish and Bob. Lynn heard about it and wanted to be included, so one day Chuck and the four Hill kids drove east to a granite slab near Riverside. Chuck and Bob went off on their own adventure, leaving the three sisters to fend for themselves. Kathy, the climbing veteran (Chuck had given her a couple of lessons), showed Trish and Lynn how to tie into a harness. But she was too intimidated to lead the climb and sent first Trish, then Lynn, up the low-angled slab to work it out for themselves in a trial by fire. "That first time I was dealing a lot with the fear of falling," says Hill. "But even then, climbing seemed more than just the physical act of hauling oneself up a sheer rock face. I was intrigued by the sensual side of the sport."

She credits her parents with a tolerant, if not openly supportive, attitude toward their kids' climbing. "They had affection for the outdoors," she says, "and took us on lots of camping trips where we swam, hiked, waterskied, sailed, and explored nature. They also had an appreciation of sports as a good outlet for kids. But they didn't understand climbing at all. 'Is it crazy?' they wondered. 'Do they know what they're doing? Will there be drinking on the overnighters?' They were uncomfortable with it, but they didn't try to stop me—except one time when I was all set to go without asking permission."

The climbing parties moved to Joshua Tree National Monument, a climbing mecca on the edge of the Mojave Desert. "Joshua Tree was my weekend playground," Hill recalls. "With friends I often explored the desert at night, especially during the full moon. Occasionally we would solo easy routes at night."

In junior high, Hill dropped out of gymnastics. "I liked the play of gymnastics but not the work, the learning but not the repetition. And I hated the compulsories. After quitting, I went through a period of not doing any sports except a little climbing on the weekends. Mostly, I was into being a bad teenager."

To prod Lynn back on route, her parents sent her to summer school: Typing 1A. During a break one day – "an escape from the interminable click, click, click of the typewriter keys" – she wandered into the gym and began doing some gymnastics routines. The high school gymnastics coach spotted her talent from across the gym. "Hey, you!" she shouted. "You're on the team!"

Throughout her high-school years, Lynn focused on gymnastics on weekdays and climbing on weekends. She lied about her age to secure a job flipping burgers at Carl's Jr. so she could buy a climbing rope and help pay for gas. "Climbing offered adventure, but also the opportunity to escape L.A. and get into nature," she says. "Already I was struck by the natural beauty of Joshua Tree. I can still see the golden rays of the late-afternoon sun striking a reddish-orange face, highlighting the features and form of the rock."

Inspired by the books of Reinhold Messner, Kathy's boyfriend Chuck developed a passion for mountaineering. He longed to climb a Himalayan peak in fast, light alpine style. Hill's passion remained rock climbing, but Chuck's enthusiasm persuaded her to accompany him on a spring ascent in the Palisades, in the Sierra Nevada range. They completed a new route but ran into trouble on descent, reaching a point where they had to down-climb the last two hundred feet to a small snow bridge between the rock face and an adjacent bergschrund. Lynn belayed Chuck while he descended the icy slope using their only ice tool: a rock hammer with a curved pick. After Chuck was safely down, they realized that a belay from below to protect Lynn would be ineffective. Instead, Lynn opted to down-climb by stemming between the rock face and the wall of ice formed by the bergschrund. "I placed my bare hands and the slippery soles of my shoes on the ice and wet rock, and straddled the dark abyss. My mind kept flashing on horrifying images of slipping and falling into the cold, dark gap between the rock and the ice."

Lynn Hill's seven reasons to climb

1. For the diversity
2. For the creativity – tying together the external and the internal
3. For the challenges – mental, physical, and emotional
4. For the spontaneity
5. For the feeling of being attentive, sensitive, and perceptive to yourself and the environment
6. For the love of it
7. For the sake of doing it

She made it, but a few months later Chuck was lost in a blizzard near the summit of Aconcagua (22,834 feet), the highest peak in the Andes. "Chuck's death and that experience in the Palisades convinced me to stay with the 'fun in the sun' atmosphere of free climbing rather than mountaineering." With no sign of tongue in cheek, she adds, "Mountaineering just seemed too dangerous."

At eighteen, she got her first car, and one could almost hear the doors of freedom clicking open. Now the world – or at least the West – was her playground. After high school, she spent the better part of two summers in Yosemite, where she climbed most of the big walls in the valley. "Yosemite Valley was the hotbed of free climbing during the seventies," she remembers. "Those were the golden years, when people from all over the world came to try what most climbers considered to be the most difficult routes in the world. For me, it was a time of carefree squalor. I lived on about seventy-five dollars per summer, supplementing my income by scrounging aluminum cans and recycling them for cash."

If she was down and out on level ground, she was up, up, and away on vertical rock. Included in her climbing accomplishments were two routes on Half Dome, another on the south face of Mount Watkins, and four on the 3,600-foot polished-granite face of El Capitan. She raced up one El Cap route, the "Nose," in eight hours. She and Mari Gingery did the first all-female ascent of another route, the "Shield," in six days. "Mari and I had done plenty of free climbing together at Joshua Tree," she says, "but neither of us had much experience with technical aid climbing and no experience spending multiple nights on the rock. In one section I took a fall while nailing up an expanding crack the size of a knife blade. It was an exciting adventure."

In the seventies and eighties, technological advances in rock-climbing gear were expanding the sport's boundaries. New aids included, but were not limited to, mechanical, spring-loaded camming devices called Friends, soft-soled rubber climbing shoes, and small, strong micro-nuts called RPs. Says Hill, "Those products helped raise the standard of difficulty in free climbing and had a dramatic effect on my own ability. I made a huge jump from five-eleven climbs to hard five-twelves."

Hill was referring to the American rating system, in which the fifth class, followed by a decimal, means that the climb is a technical one – and that a rope is needed. Climbs are named and initially rated by the first person to ascend them, and adjusted, if necessary, by those who follow. Routes from 5.0 to 5.6 are for beginners; climbs of 5.10 and up, which are further delineated by a, b, c, and d, are for experts. Climbs rated 5.12, 5.13, and 5.14 often require many successive attempts over a period of days or weeks, as a climber works out a complicated and strenuous sequence of moves.

A climb's rating is more subjective than the numbers would suggest. One person's 5.12d is another's 5.13a. Trying to objectify it, Hill says that "difficulty depends on the steepness of the rock, size of holds, how hard they are to hang onto, how far apart they are, the kind of movements they require, if you have to jump to holds, how many holds there are before you get to a resting place, and how hard it is to stop and put in protection."

In 1980, with the aid of mechanical Friends and her main squeeze John Long, Hill achieved the first free ascent (using only the rock's natural holds and not resting on protection) of a climb called "Ophir Broke" (5.12d) in Telluride, Colorado. Still a teenager, she owned the hardest climb ever done by a woman. So unprepared was the climbing community that at first the accomplishment was credited to Long, a reputable climber himself. When credit was finally given to Hill, it established her as the best woman rock climber in the United States, maybe the world.

After Telluride, Hill and Long set up temporary household in Las Vegas to be near some great rock climbing. While Long concentrated on his writing, Hill took college classes and tried to bring in a little money. She waitressed and did odd jobs, the oddest of which was boxing another woman in a bar for twenty bucks. "We had big pillows for gloves," she says. "I won." She shakes her head. "It was desperate."

When she returned to Southern California, another door clicked open. She was offered money to climb, not rock but a rope ladder. The assignment was to scramble up to and over a grounded hot-air balloon for a television program called "The Guinness Book." She performed so well that she was asked to do a more daunting variation of that stunt for a TV series called "That's Incredible." This time the balloon was hovering six thousand feet above the ground, which caused some viewers to break out in vicarious vertigo sweats but left Hill unfazed. "That stunt was a piece of cake," she says with no real hubris. "C'mon, a rope ladder? Anybody can climb a ladder. Once you're higher than a hundred feet, what difference does it make how much higher? Actually, I was wearing a parachute in case the gas burners melted the rope ladder, so the higher the better."

With a burgeoning reputation, she was next recruited to compete on an adventure program called "Survival of the Fittest." A half-dozen top women athletes from a variety of sports went at it in four events that played to Hill's divergent strengths: an obstacle course over ropes and bridges, a survival run, a whitewater swim, and a speed climb and rappel. Hill won easily, just as she would the next three years. Unlike the balloon climb, which she thought silly, the survival-of-the-fittest contest appealed to her. "It was fun and interesting," she says. "They were unusual, spontaneous events, without rehearsal – like on-sight climbing." She also appreciated them for their financial rewards: the prize money – five thousand dollars the first two years, ten thousand the next two – paid her way through college.

She enrolled at Santa Monica Junior College in biology, targeting a career in physical therapy. Wanting to become a more complete athlete, she began running. While she was doing laps one day on the school track, she again caught the attention of a talent scout, this time the junior college track coach. "You!" he called, "Come to my office. I want to talk to you."

She joined the college track team, motivated more by a desire to use quality facilities and equipment than to become a quality runner. But she discovered that she was good; the better she became, the harder she worked. "Training for track demanded more than I expected," she says. "Running six or seven days a week, I didn't have the energy to drive several hours to Joshua Tree and climb. Besides, I was tired of doing the same routes on the same rock. From age twenty to twenty-two, I didn't climb much at all."

Instead, she worked on the mile and two-mile, running it fast enough to qualify for the state JC track meet. There, with two personal records needed from her for a Santa Monica team victory, Hill came through in the clutch, finishing third in the mile and fifth in the two-mile. Not bad for a climber.

By age twenty-two, Hill had used up her junior college eligibility, was weary of living in Southern California and climbing at Joshua Tree, and had run the gamut on her romance with John Long. In short, she was ripe for change. Thus, when a reporter called and asked if she would like to come to New York's Shawangunk cliffs to be interviewed for a magazine article he was writing, she jumped at the chance.

Shawangunk, affectionately known as the "Gunks," has long been the main rock-climbing area east of the Rockies. Mostly conglomerate quartz, the escarpment rises about three hundred feet above a sleepy valley west of the town of New Paltz, New York. When Hill first saw the Gunks, with all its luscious overhangs, her climbing career was instantly resuscitated. This time the conversion would be permanent.

She decided to move to New York. Returning to Southern California, she loaded up her Volkswagen van and drove back across the country. Settled in her new home in New Paltz, she began to climb with a dark-haired, handsome man named Russ Raffa. Soon they were romantic, and they eventually married. Hill took more college classes, taught rock climbing, and explored new levels of calculated risk.

"When I first moved to New York, I started taking greater risks," she admits. "The equipment wasn't as good as it is now, and the ethics of free climbing were stringent. No bolts, no top-roping, no hang-dogging. Back then, before sport climbing, risk was a big part of the formula. You had to be able to evaluate the risks, calculate the protection, and figure out whether you could do the move without dying."

She was egged on by Raffa, who was riveted by the subject of risk. "Russ couldn't necessarily do the hardest moves," she says, "but he was good at working close to his limit, at shaving that margin of safety down to almost nothing." Watching from the ground one time as Lynn did a bold lead on "Yellow Crack Direct" with iffy protection, Raffa was heard to say, "These are the moments that really stand out – when you see someone totally on the edge. Those are the most satisfying moments."

Hill claims she was highly focused while doing that first ascent of

In a casual workout session, Lynn Hill's grace and strength are still apparent. (Courtesy of Steven Boga)

"Yellow Crack Direct," but never in fear of losing her life. "I'm always aware of the potential danger," she says. "I take calculated risks. I decide whether a move is reasonable or not. If I decide yes, then I don't think about the consequences of a fall. Instead, I think positively about what I need to do to get through the move."

Her power of positive thinking has enabled Hill to overcome physical, mental, and emotional obstacles. The latter includes the sexism inevitably faced by women who go hand-jam to hand-jam against men. "My ability to believe in myself allows me to maximize my physiological potential." In other words, she doesn't give in to the doubters, who are disproportionately male.

One time at Joshua Tree she glided through a bouldering problem with balletic grace, only to hear a male onlooker exclaim, "Gee, even *I* couldn't climb that." "The nerve!" she thought. "You're fat, unfit, and don't look like a climber. Why should being male automatically allow you to do what I can do?"

In 1986 Hill and Raffa and a few other climbers were invited to tour the famous limestone climbing crags of France. Their French escort made the kind of remark that never failed to burn a branding-iron imprint in Hill's brain: "It is impossible for a woman to do a 7c (5.12d) climb on sight," he declared. Hill looked at the man as if he had just announced that the world is made of schist. Because she was a guest in his country and is polite by nature, she said nothing. But making that remark work for her, she soon proved him wrong.

"It was extremely sexist," she says. "He was so limited in his thinking that he couldn't conceive of women progressing to where we
would achieve that level." To an interviewer from *Climbing* magazine,
she would add, "Society's contrived image of what a woman should or
shouldn't be is something I've never agreed with. Developing muscles
is something people look down upon. . . . You look at the Miss America
Pageant, and all of them have pencil arms. There's just no definition.
The classic American beauty has no muscle tone. What does she do all
the time?"

The content, if not the tone, suggests wrestler Hulk Hogan raving
about "pencil necks." But Hill is the physical antithesis of the Hulkster.
She is tiny – less than five-foot-two – and lean – about a hundred
pounds. She has almost delicate facial features, with soft, compelling
blue eyes. Her shoulder-length brown hair is wavy, with blond high-
lights. Her body is as tight as a snare drum, as lithe as a snake, with
muscle tone that is impressive but by no means massive.

Tired of the predictability of the Gunks, Hill found the limestone
crags of Europe fascinating. "The rock was beautiful and interesting,
but it also offered a new type of climbing. Because it was totally bolt-
protected, you didn't have to worry about little pieces of protection
falling out, or about falling and dying. It was fun to be able to push
myself to do the hardest moves."

She was struck by the standards of excellence achieved by European climbers. It was apparent that Americans were no longer the
dominant force in free climbing. "It was painfully evident that techniques considered taboo in America had allowed some European
climbers to make dramatic improvements in free-climbing standards."

If Hill was impressed with the Europeans, they were no less taken
with her. While climbing one day in the Verdon Gorge, she was approached by one of the organizers of the international free-climbing
competition in Arco, Italy. Hill had just finished climbing a route
called "Take It or Leave It" (5.12d) when an Italian man walked over
and introduced himself. Saying he had never seen a woman do such a
hard route, he invited her to the second annual free-climbing competition. Says Hill, "They needed a woman who could challenge Catherine
Destivelle, the winner of the first competition."

That 1985 event had been awash in controversy. Many top
climbers, free-spirited by nature, had objected to the idea of formal
competition. Wasn't that, after all, the antithesis of climbing? By the
second competition, however, the idea had become more palatable,

and many top climbers showed up to compete. "My first experience at Arco was disorienting," says Lynn. "I didn't know Italian, I didn't understand the format or the judging. It was so different than going out with a friend and climbing on rock. . . . They keep you away from the competition until it's your turn, then bring you out in front of all these people, sound a buzzer . . . *okay, warmup time is over. Get ready, go."*

Hill was also shocked by what she has called "the flagrant alterations of the environment." Spectators can't see? Chop down a few trees. Rock not right? Glue artificial holds onto it (now they use artificial walls for climbing competitions). Got a message? Festoon advertising banners from cliff to cliff, then let thousands of people tromp around the base of the climb.

When Hill was alerted to the disparity in prize money for the men and women climbers, she asked why. An Italian friend with a sheepish smile translated an official's reply: "The women will be paid equal prize money if they climb without their tops on."

"The injustice didn't end there," says Hill. "I was the only woman to flash (unrehearsed climb without rests or falls) the final route, but through various rule changes and arbitrary decisions, Catherine Destivelle was declared the winner."

Despite the negatives, Hill found plenty of positives in competitive sport climbing. The events brought out the gymnast in her. Later that summer she returned to Europe and won a competition – and fifteen hundred dollars in prize money – at Troubat, France. That winter she weighed the alternatives: enter a master's program in physical therapy or become a professional rock climber. The latter meant giving up her little business – guiding and teaching rock-climbing neophytes – and her job working with her husband as a sales representative for Patagonia.

By the spring of 1987, she had decided to commit to the nascent European climbing circuit. "Though I had always loved climbing for the absence of coaches, rules, and planned routines, I realized that I could make money and have fun doing competitions," she says.

She had fun winning fourteen of her first eighteen competitions, finishing in second place in three and third place in one. How such dominance? Physically, she has brought a gymnast's sense of body alignment to rock climbing. Mentally, she employs a technique she calls "analytical visualization." "I learned it in gymnastics, and now it's just naturally the way I think," she says. "I'm a visual thinker. When I memorize a phone number, I see it in my mind. When I look at a climb from the ground, I see the holds and automatically associate those holds with the angle of my body." To demonstrate, she raises her arms above her head, reaching for imaginary holds; the sleeves of her blouse slide over her shoulders, revealing small but bulging biceps. "Meanwhile I'm thinking, 'When I get to that hold, my hands need to be in this position. My left hand needs to be over there because the next move goes that way. . . .' I love the problem-solving aspect of free climbing, the figuring out a sequence of moves, but it's a rough sort of figuring. You can't know precisely which way to angle your body until you're actually on the rock."

Her domination on the pro circuit established her in the late eighties as the best woman rock climber in the world. It was generally accepted that she ranked among the top five U.S. climbers – men or women – at a time when, according to climber Alan Watts, "there might not be another woman in the top hundred." It suggested the kind of domination Babe Ruth enjoyed when he hit more home runs than any *team* in the American League.

The high point of her professional career might have been the final round of the final event of the 1990 World Cup tour. Hill had long been lobbying for men and women to compete on the same route, and in Lyon, France, they did just that. Both sexes tackled the same difficult 5.13d route on a constructed indoor wall studded with fiberglass holds. The higher they climbed, the harder the moves. Climbers were scored by the highest handhold attained. No woman came close to completing the climb until Hill electrified the crowd by climbing to the top of the route, a performance equaled by only two of the top men in the world. Friend and superclimber Alison Osius calls it "the most exciting thing in sports I've ever seen. The hard moves kept coming at Lynn and she kept doing them, going higher and higher. Her body was so strong and flexible. It seemed telescopic, portable. And her mind . . . Lynn has such focus anyway, but that day she dug clear to China."

Osius, who has won three national climbing championships, says it's like she's on the B Team while Lynn is on the A Team. "There is a huge gap between A and B," she adds. "If I go to the world championships, I'm happy to make the top dozen. You can always count on Lynn to make the finals." Osius and Hill took a three-week climbing vacation together, which provided Osius with an inside view into the mind of a champion. "One time somebody asked Lynn what her long-term goals were," says Osius. "Without hesitation, she listed five things – build a

Even during one of her rare visits to the horizontal world, Hill exudes energy and confidence. (Courtesy of Steven Boga)

climbing wall in her basement, learn to speak French, have children . . . I was agog. I couldn't have come up with my goals that quickly."

Could a woman be, hands up, the best climber in the world? Hill, who has a unique perspective, believes so. "The obstacles for women are mainly psychological," she says. "Since women are new to the sport, their perception of what is possible is limited. And how we train—what we demand of ourselves—is dependent on how we think. Women need to be willing to push past fatigue to a point just before injury. If you stop as soon as you feel tired, you won't be well-trained. You won't be able to maximize your physical potential."

Physically, Hill concedes, men would seem to have the edge. They are usually taller, the better to reach those hard-to-get holds. And with lower body fat, they usually have a greater strength-to-weight ratio. On the other hand, women can match men's endurance and tend to have smaller fingers and toes, the better to grip those tiddly-wink-size holds. "Right now women can be the best at certain climbs," she claims. "There are so many subsports within climbing—bouldering, free, direct-aid—you have to be specific."

To be the best requires an interesting blend of physical, mental, and emotional strengths. Hill attributes her success to "a lucky combination of genetics, personality, and environment. It all starts with the brain," she says. "The brain controls everything, the emotions, the physical. But it's all intertwined. You have to be strong to accomplish what you imagine, but you have to imagine it first before you can accomplish it physically."

Concentration is essential for success in all sports, but none more than climbing. A momentary loss of focus in tennis, badminton, or horseshoes might mean loss of point; in climbing if you're not top-roped, it could mean you're maggot meat. "Climbing involves a level of concentration unavailable to most people," says Hill. "Not many people get it in their careers."

When Hill is operating near her limit, as she usually is, she is intuitively focused. Her mind is locked on her task like a Denver boot on the wheel of a car. Her only serious brush with death occurred on a route she was capable of doing with her climbing shoes tied around her neck. It happened one fine spring morning in the south of France. Hill, who had just beaten Destivelle, her main rival, in a climbing competition in Germany, was at the top of her game. She had been the best rock climber in the world for the past two years, and was well on her way to winning her third straight championship.

It was 6:00 A.M., with a chill in the air, so Hill put on a jacket. While Raffa talked with a spectator, she lifted the bottom of her jacket and looped her rope through her new nylon harness. Noticing her climbing shoes a few feet away, she interrupted what she was doing and went over to put them on. Her jacket inched down into place, concealing her harness.

When she got back to the base of the wall, Raffa already had her on belay. "Great," she thought, "all set to go." With that, she wiped off her shoes and began climbing.

The climb itself was uneventful, an easy, graceful ascent, elegance masking effort. At one point, feeling no tension on her harness, she yelled down, "Pull up the slack." When she got to the top, seventy-five feet above ground, she looked down at Raffa, who was still talking to the spectator. "You got me, Russ?" she called. Climbers always alert their partners before they put weight on their anchors and lower off.

"Yeah, I got you," he replied, tightening his grip on the rope.

With that assurance, Hill leaned back and — *Whoa!* — lost all four contact points with the rock. Raffa, hearing her blood-curdling scream, looked up in time to see his wife in midflight flapping her arms like a hummingbird. She was instinctively realigning her body to avoid landing on her neck. Looking down, she saw the whites of her

Lynn Hill's three best places to climb

1. Southern France
2. Italy
3. Germany

husband's eyes, the black hole that was his open mouth, and the brown branches of a tree. She covered her head, curled into a ball, and aimed for the branches.

They slowed her down – barely – but they also knocked her elbow out of joint. She landed butt first, more on one cheek than the other, then bounced and came to rest face down between two Buick-size boulders, near a jagged stump. "She's dead," Raffa thought. He had once seen a climber dead after a fall of only twenty feet. But Hill was not dead; she was unconscious for a moment, then semiconscious and in shock. When she came to, her head was in her husband's lap, and he was stroking her hair and picking dirt out of her eye, like a baboon grooming his mate. "What happened?" she mumbled, over and over, even as she was being hauled into a rescue helicopter.

What had happened, she soon realized, was a beginner's mistake – failing to fully tie her knot – the sort of mistake one never makes twice. Besides a dislocated elbow, she had a broken foot, an impaled pectoral muscle, cuts requiring stitches in her shoulder, nose, and under her chin, a little deformity on one buttock where the cell walls had been compressed like glacial ice, and massive bruises that caused visitors to her hospital room to draw back in horror.

And the lasting impact? Her left arm is slightly weaker than her right (though she can still do one-armed pull-ups with it), there is a little depression on her butt, and "I never fail to check my knot now."

Four weeks after the fall, Hill began serious training again. She has never had a problem putting in workout time, but her need for variety is so great that no two training days are alike. "Training requires discipline, and I respect that," she says. "But I need a high level of stimulus."

An atypical week – because all her weeks are atypical – includes biking, stretching, swimming, running, weight lifting, sit-ups, and pull-ups. (She can do more than thirty pull-ups, including the one-armed kind, but she disdains one-armed fingertip pull-ups as too detrimental to the fingers, which are, she says, "the most important connection to the rock.") A favorite workout, and one that epitomizes her free-spirited approach to training, is to turn on MTV and choreograph her own floor routine, complete with gymnastics and break-dancing moves. She likens it to a "horizontal version of climbing."

Seven weeks after the fall, Hill was again ready to return to the rock. At that point she cut back on weight training. Years before she had shown a real talent for pumping iron – no surprise there – but now it bored her. "When I first met John Long, he was working with weights," she recalls. "He got me interested in trying to break the world record in the bench press. For my weight class it was one hundred and fifty pounds, so that became my goal. I worked on it for six months and finally did one-fifty in practice. I did a competition, didn't make that weight, and lost interest. Looking in the mirror, I thought my arms were getting too big. I didn't like the way I looked, the way I felt, and I didn't like training for it. After that I only did weights a little during New York winters."

Less than two years after The Fall, Hill and Raffa were divorced. Hill, whom John Long describes as "never having a bad word for anyone," says only, "Russ and I weren't meant to live the rest of our lives together. All the time I spent climbing in Europe probably didn't help our chances."

Another possible aggravating cause, she admits, is that "climbers tend to be very much into their own worlds. To climb at the top, you have to be really in touch with yourself, which means being 'into yourself.' That's good for climbing, but probably not good for personal relations, where you have to be able to see the needs of others and not be so engrossed in yourself."

Hill may be a strong egotist, but she is not impervious to the outside world. Her divorce got to her, chipping away at her focus like a pick ax on a stone wall. Her climbing performance suffered, and after three years as the number-one female sport climber in the world, she had an erratic season in 1990. "To climb well, you have to be free in the mind. I wasn't." On one occasion, she suffered the greatest lapse of concentration of her competitive career, scoring zero points in an event. "I literally put one foot on the wall and slipped off," she says. "They said, 'Okay, that's it. No points.' I thought that was ridiculous. I got a bunch of people involved in the protest, but it didn't do any good." Even with that cipher, she tied with Frenchwoman Isabelle Patissier for the championship.

After the breakup of her marriage, in March 1991, Hill decided to move to France. "It seemed like my life was more oriented toward Europe," she says. "Most of the competitions are there, yes, but it was more than that. The European community is more appreciative of climbers. In the United States it's all baseball and football. You tell an American you're a climber and it's 'Oh, what are you? Some kind of daredevil?' In France, climbing makes sense to them. They've often been climbing themselves, and they have more respect for the individualism and the dedication that the sport requires. I like America too – I'm keeping one foot on each continent – but right now living in France works best for me. Who I meet and where my career takes me will decide where I spend most of my life.

"Climbing is a lifestyle for me. It's not like putting on a glove and playing baseball for a couple of hours. Competing at the highest level requires a commitment to a specific lifestyle. You have to eat a certain way (I undereat), and live in a certain part of the world. Of course, I'm an extreme example."

Hill, in her early thirties, says she plans to quit making her living at competitive climbing. "When I first started, I was trying to prove something," she says. "Now I'm always trying to defend something. As a champion I can't go into a competition without being 'up' for it. When you're champion, people expect great things from you every time. I still try to be professional, but there's not much left for me. I feel out of place. There's a whole new generation coming up who is into climbing, climbing, climbing. I'm not like that."

Imagine Lynn Hill in the job market. On the one hand, she has been successful at everything she's tried; yet, despite her unrivaled athletic versatility, her résumé would look rather "focused."

• First place in all four "Survival of the Fittest" competitions held for women.

• 1984 American Alpine Award for Outstanding Achievement in Mountaineering/Rock Climbing.

• Winner of dozens of international climbing competitions, including first place at the Gran Prix de France D'Escalade, Troubat, France, 1986 and 1987; first place at the World Championships at Arco, Italy, 1987 and 1988; first place at the World Indoor Championships at Grenoble, France, 1987; first place at the International Climbing Championships at Marseilles, 1988; first place at the Masters Competition in Paris, 1988 and 1989; and first place in the German Free Climbing Championships, 1989.

Actually, Hill plans to continue making a living in climbing. "I want to work on creative projects I can control, giving something back to the sport." She has been working with a camera crew on a climbing video, and she has been desultorily writing a book (working title: *The Art of Free Climbing*) for the past couple of years. She also has ideas for the invention of a climbing apparatus for kids. "It's like a jungle gym, only better, incorporating fantasy, play, and adventure. There's not enough of those elements in today's equipment."

She also hopes to continue her sponsorships, like Petzl (lamps, carabiners, harnesses), Beal (ropes), and Boreal (climbing shoes). She has even struck deals with companies outside her sport, a first for a climber, signing with Reebok, Timex, and a perfume called Dare. Timex took advantage of her fall by promoting a dress watch with a "very secure buckle." The Dare perfume magazine ads were the real eye-catchers, dramatically displaying another aspect of Hill's versatility. In a two-photo spread, the "before" shot shows her at work on the rock, biceps bulging, back muscles rippling, the definitive female athlete. The "after" has her decked out in a low-cut purple silk dress, flashy earrings, and makeup. Her hair is lacquered and she is lounging provocatively, elbow resting on what at first appears to be a floor pillow but is actually a rock. A rope is coiled seductively through her fingers.

The two faces of Lynn Hill? "I dress up once in a while," she says, chuckling. "Just because I'm an athlete doesn't mean I can't be feminine."

In Hill's best years, her income topped $100,000, split more-or-less evenly between prize money and sponsorships. But now, by doing fewer competitions and not always winning them, her overall income has dropped and she makes a greater part of her money pushing products.

Most people, advertisers included, still see climbers as scruffy low-life unfit for decent society, much less the glamorous world of magazine modeling. Hill has bridged the gap by being (a) the best, and (b) attractive. Take away either one and she is just another climber, with the mass-market ad appeal of, say, a demolition-derby champion.

As it is, she has attained a modicum of fame. Among the climbing cognoscenti, she has near maximum name recognition. Alison Osius recalls coming upon Lynn climbing in Colorado. "Lined up below her was an audience of backpackers and climbers, who, without pretext, had stopped just to watch her. When she completed the climb they all applauded. I felt sorry for her. But she said it didn't bother her."

Despite such hero worship, Hill can still walk through an airport without being hounded for autographs. Even climbing's recent growth spurt (*Climbing* magazine says there are about 150,000 technical climbers in the U.S.) has not made her recognizable to the masses. That's quite all right with her. "Early in my career, climbing in front of people satisfied my need for recognition. It felt good to show off a good performance. Now that I've done that, I don't need it anymore.

"It's fine that more and more people are into climbing. There's talk of it one day being an Olympic sport – that would be great – but what I still like best is being off climbing with friends. Being Lynn Hill, though, if people are there they will stop and watch me. That makes it kind of like going to work.

"The only negative side to popularizing the sport is that before you were part of a select group, and now you have to deal with trash, noise, and lines on routes. Joshua Tree is crowded with climbers as well as tourists. You have to go farther from a road to find solitude. But then, a lot of people don't want solitude.

"Even with the growth of interest in climbing, it doesn't appeal to most people. It will always be that way. The reason is that most people's lives are hard enough already. They don't want to go after such intense challenges. But I thrive on intensity. I'm a person who doesn't mind taking risks, for the benefits it brings. Climbing helps me live *more*."

GALEN ROWELL
Lens Master

This is the gentlest form
of competition I've ever
seen.

——A Buddhist man
watching rock climbing
with Galen Rowell

Camp I, 1975 American K2 Expedition. Galen Rowell and Jim Whittaker were jolted awake by a demonic roar clawing at the darkness outside their tent. An avalanche! At first the two climbers felt safe enough. Their camp was on a knoll hundreds of feet above the main basin on the flank of the second-highest mountain in the world. Odds were that any dumpage of snow would miss them. But the noise grew louder, like a jet plane you hear but don't see. Rowell and Whittaker lay in their sleeping bags, alert as wild animals but powerless to do anything to change nature's course. Both felt anxiety but no panic. Experienced climbers, they understood the futility of panic in the face of unmanageable danger.

Suddenly they felt it! As they gritted their teeth and tensed their muscles, a gush of air flapped the walls of the tent and snow fell all around them. It sounded to Rowell like a giant emptying a grain sack. Then, as suddenly as there had been sound, there was blessed silence.

Despite this and other close calls, Rowell has maintained an abiding appreciation for outdoor adventure, almost as if it were in his genes. Before he was even born – during the summers of 1923-25 – his mother and aunt explored the High Sierra from Yosemite to Mount Whitney, the approximate route of what is today the 212-mile John Muir Trail. "My mother always called it one of her great life experiences," Rowell says. "She and my aunt did a first ascent of a peak, using ropes but not knowing how. I grew up looking at scrapbook pictures of my mom scrambling up rocks, a rope tied around her waist. It got me pretty curious."

His curiosity was further piqued at age ten when his family began going on Sierra Club backcountry outings. From then on, when Galen composed school reports on "How I Spent My Summer Vacation," he described two-week backpacking trips camping with more than a hundred people. "You had a choice of activities," he remembers. "You could hike a trail, climb an easy peak, or climb a harder one. The 'amblers,' 'ramblers,' and 'scramblers.' I got even more interested in climbing from those trips."

When Galen was sixteen he was befriended on one of the outings by an older boy who offered to show him the ropes. Near the end of the trip, the boy asked Galen's parents if, instead of walking out seven miles with the group, Galen could accompany him sixty miles, most of it cross-country, to Yosemite Valley, where they would spend a week rock climbing. "My parents hemmed and hawed before finally saying yes. In Yosemite we met several of the kid's friends and climbed for a week. It was the first time I had ever used ropes and pitons. I decided it was pretty neat."

It was the summer of 1957, a time, Rowell says when "rock climbing was right on the cusp of breaking loose from the Sierra Club hold and taking off on its own." With few climbing schools or big-wall climbers to teach others, the Sierra Club had an outsized influence on the sport. "Climbing was held down for years by an excessive concern with safety," says Rowell. "I began to react against that way of doing things: rigid, ultra-concerned with equipment. I preferred the freedom of rambling through the mountains, using a rope when necessary."

Meanwhile a few good climbers were busy taking the sport to new heights. In 1957, Royal Robbins, Mike Sherrick, and Jerry Gallwas scaled the treacherous northwest face of Yosemite's Half Dome, a two-thousand-foot vertical wall of granite that other climbers had declared unclimbable. The following summer, Gallwas was a cook on Rowell's Sierra Club outing. "He was a nice, quiet guy," says Rowell. "He helped me see that there were climbers who valued life and yet weren't so overly concerned with safety that they defeated their own ability to excel."

K2. Galen Rowell lay in his sleeping bag in a base-camp tent 17,600 feet above sea level, consumed by the delusion that he had two heads attached to the same body. It was part fever, part drug-induced, part oxygen deprivation due to altitude. His bronchitis had deteriorated into pneumonia, and Rob Schaller, the expedition doctor, had pre-scribed Keflex, a powerful antibiotic. Schaller could do no more, for the latest three-day storm had him and some teammates pinned down in Camp II, three thousand feet above Rowell.

It was June 21, the solstice, but summer was not exactly bursting out all over the Karakoram. No birds chirped, no insects buzzed, no flowers bloomed. Base camp, pitched well above tree line on the broad Savoia Glacier, was all rock and ice, mostly ice. After the latest storm, it resembled nothing more than an Arctic outpost.

Eleven thousand feet below the summit of K2, base camp was the launching pad for the expedition's planned pyramid of seven camps on the mountain. In the middle of camp was the warehouse section, with its orderly rows of porter boxes and stacks of oxygen cylinders. Paths carved in the ice led to six private residence tents for the climbers and the HAPs (high-altitude porters). There were also two equipment tents, a cook tent, and a recreation tent complete with paperbacks and tape deck; also a garbage pit for burnable trash and a latrine cozily protected by a tent. The expedition's brightly colored tents and sleep-ing bags contrasted sharply with nature's muted hues.

Their goal was to summit 28,250-foot K2 in Pakistan's Karakoram Range. Of the seven previous assaults on K2 (so named because it was the second peak surveyed in the Karakoram Range), only a 1954 Italian team had made it to the top. The Americans intended to go by way of an unexplored northwest ridge that marked the border between China and Pakistan.

Although Mount Everest is almost eight hundred feet higher, K2 is by consensus more difficult and dangerous. The slopes are generally steeper and the weather is abysmal, with violent storms frequently pummeling climbers like nature's bullies. Yet despite all that snow, K2 is actually a high-altitude desert, with little moisture in the surround-ing atmosphere. The combination of dry air and the heavy breathing demanded by high-altitude exertion in rarefied air threatens climbers with potentially fatal dehydration. No wonder K2 is called the "savage mountain."

Though climbers are used to overcoming obstacles, the American K2 expedition had faced more than its share. The problems started even before they got within crampon distance of the mountain. The

Galen Rowell's four most interesting cultures

1. Tibetans – for their attitude of universal responsibility toward all life
2. Sherpas – Tibetan people living in Nepal
3. Hopi Indians
4. Baltis of the Karakoram

---

ten American climbers had flown from the U.S. to Rawalpindi, Pakistan, where bad weather and bureaucratic rigamarole prolonged their supposedly two-day stay into eleven. Only one scouting flight was allowed near K2, and it couldn't approach the Chinese border. Neither Pakistan nor China would let them land people or equipment closer than one hundred miles from the proposed base camp.

Then there were the porters. Six hundred and fifty Balti tribesmen had been hired to haul fourteen tons of food and equipment to base camp. (From there the American climbers and the HAPs, supposedly the cream of the porter crop, would shuttle loads from camp to camp.) Keeping a rein on that motley crew was like trying to lasso Jell-O. Repeated strikes for higher wages slowed their progress to a crawl. When they finally reached snow line, they were one month behind schedule.

Because Baltistan and the great group of peaks around K2 had been closed to outsiders for fifteen years, the Baltis, unlike the Sherpas of Nepal, lacked experience meeting the needs of expeditions. (They also lacked decent footwear.) With nineteen expeditions arriving in the area in the spring of 1975, and the government decreeing that expeditions must pay porters in full on their last day of employment, no matter why they left, it was truly a porter's market. Once an expedition reached the discomfort of snow line, it made sense for the Baltis to quit on the slightest pretext and return to the warm valleys to hire on with another expedition. Consequently, the signed contract guaranteeing portage to base camp had less value than the paper itself. That at least could be used for toilet paper.

The Balti way of doing business meant that some expeditions never reached base camp. They were left stranded in the snows with tons of equipment. In an attempt to avert a similar fate, expedition member Lou Whittaker devised a strategy for dealing with their fifth strike in ten days. Assembling the remaining 150 porters, he told them that if they refused to carry, the climbers would burn all the equipment and money, walk out empty-handed without paying them, and lodge a complaint with the Pakistani government. To add punch to this threat, Whittaker pulled a ten-rupee note from the money bag and casually set it on fire. There was a chorus of oohs and aahs from the Baltis. While they stared wide-eyed at the burning money, the climbers got up and left.

The porters agreed to carry to base camp.

Despite the unity temporarily forged by a common adversary, dissension had cleaved the Americans into two bickering factions. The Big Four, as they came to be called, included expedition leader Jim Whittaker, 46, the first American to summit Everest; Jim's twin brother Lou; deputy leader Jim Wickwire, 32; and Jim Whittaker's girlfriend, Dianne Roberts, 26. The others, who referred to themselves as the Minority Five, were Leif-Norman Patterson, 39; Fred Dunham, 34; Fred Stanley, 31; Dr. Robert T. Schaller Jr., 39; and Galen Rowell, 34. (The tenth American, cinematographer Steve Marts, was along to make a climbing movie and did not intend to climb the mountain.)

As the delays mounted, so did the tensions. The rigid tent pairings didn't help, preventing associations that might have healed wounds before they developed; instead they festered. In the eyes of the Minority Five, the disunity was caused by inflexibility, rampant egotism, and poor communication from the top, that is, from team leader Jim Whittaker. With few team meetings, information tended to circulate by rumor. One such early rumor was that Jim Whittaker had already selected the summit team, a demoralizing notion for those not picked. At one point, the two Freds, feeling as though they had no more say than the porters, threatened to quit.

In his diary, Rowell wrote of a typical miscommunication that surfaced while the expedition was resting in the village of Skardu. "After tea in a rest house on the shores of Satpara Lake, we (Rob Schaller and Rowell) hike back to Skardu, arriving at 6:30 P.M. In the congested courtyard of our rest house, Jim Whittaker explodes at me for being away all afternoon. Lou joins in with equal vehemence. I now understand all those rumors I've heard about their violent tempers. . . . Early in the morning I had asked Jim about the day's plans. I suggested moving ahead with the gear we had. He said no, we would wait at least two days more for the gear to arrive before considering moving. Rob asked if he could help with the radios and found the situation well in hand. Others sat around writing in diaries or doing wash. There was absolutely no forewarning that the afternoon would turn into a hard work session to repack boxes and load them for a move the very next morning. Leif was also caught by surprise. He used the afternoon to climb the fortress hill above Skardu and was scolded on his return. It is hardly coincidence that Jim chose Leif, Rob, and me to stay in Skardu while the others moved on. Truants staying after school. . . .

"In the morning I find that the events have definitely left their mark. I feel guilty taking pictures of others working, especially in the presence of Jim and Lou. I am too scared to photograph their departure from Skardu on jeeps. This is not a healthy attitude for a photojournalist."

In a separate entry: "Perhaps one of the biggest flaws in expedition mountaineering is that it can sometimes promote a ruthless brand of militant enthusiasm that runs roughshod over friendships, health, safety, and reason. . . . They (climbers) seek that one memory of

Friendships made while climbing are special ones. (Left to right) *David Wilson, Galen Rowell, and Michael Graber at the summit of Mount Fitz Roy in Patagonia. (Courtesy of Galen Rowell)*

standing for a few moments above everyone else, and in order to get there they constantly try to elevate themselves and lower others. It doesn't have to be so."

After high school Rowell attended the University of California at Berkeley on a physics scholarship. He soon switched to geology, then to general humanities. After six years, with a lot of time off for good climbing, he had been promoted to junior. Finally, he quit altogether. "In 1961 a group of us quit school to climb. We wanted to be out in the natural world doing hands-on things rather than theoretical things that seemed to have limited value." One day Rowell and three of his drop-out friends were sitting in a greasy-spoon restaurant swapping stories. "We realized that every one of us had been a National Merit Scholar, had gone to U.C. Berkeley, had quit to go climbing." Suddenly the scientist in him surfaces. "The odds of that were something like the odds of all the molecules in the glasses in front of us lining up and moving away from us at the speed of light. The lesson for me was that a lot of interesting people get involved in climbing. Even if they seemed normal, they weren't."

Rowell knows that the popular stereotype of a climber is of a scruffy scumbag as comfortable under a rock as on one, but he also knows that the public is wrong. He recalls the time the *Saturday Review of Literature* ran a story on national parks. Pictured on the opening left page was the all-American family in its touring car, beneath it the caption "Yellowstone, 1922." The photo on the right was of a group of young, raffish-looking climbers lounging in a gear-cluttered campground in Yosemite Valley. The caption read "Yosemite 1967: How Do We Get the Schlocks Out?"

Rowell eventually wrote a letter to the editor of the magazine. "You might be interested to know who the 'schlocks' in that picture are," he wrote. "One is a physicist for the United Nations in Geneva. Another is an award-winning BBC nature cinematographer. . . ."

To me, he adds, "Like so many climbers, those men became very successful once they applied that climbing energy to other fields."

K2. One day a runner brought the expedition its first mail in weeks. Rowell, who received ten letters from his family, was struck by the contrasts between the icy world he inhabited and the one described by his eleven-year-old daughter: "We have had three frogs from about fifty polliwogs," she wrote. "Two jumped out and died. We think the dog ate one." Still smiling, he opened the letter from his wife, which began, "Your mother just called. I don't know quite how to tell you. She said she was sitting with your dad, holding his hand, and he quietly passed away."

Rowell closed his eyes and sat quietly. His father, ninety years old, had been ill for some time. Still, as the only son (he has a half-sister), he felt guilty that he was not at home. He had long feared that something would happen to his father while he was far off on a climbing trip. Checking the postmark – the letter was a month old – he tried to determine exactly where he had been and what he had been doing at the moment of his father's death. It seemed sad not to know something so intimately important to his life. He asked his tentmates not to tell the others about his father's death. It was just too personal to share with people from whom he felt so distant.

Unless they inherit the ranch, climbing bums must eventually descend to financial reality. Rowell was no exception. After playing dropout for a while, he sought a job that would allow him maximum time in the mountains. He decided to open his own auto-repair business. As a kid, his interest in science, physics in particular, found an outlet in tinkering with cars. Besides income, it gave him long weekends for climbing and strong hands and arms from "wrenching cars."

Meanwhile, Rowell was improving as a climber about the only way possible in the early sixties. "I papered a wall of my room with topographical maps, then found places where the topo lines were close together (indicating steep terrain). I'd meet someone and climb with them. If I climbed with someone better than I was – like, say, Fred Beckey or Warren Harding – I learned faster. There were no climbing schools, to speak of. It was the era of stealing your mom's clothesline and practicing on boulders in your backyard."

By the late sixties, Rowell was married, with two kids. In the beginning of their marriage, the Rowells often vacationed together. While the family camped, Galen would go climb a rock. "It worked well for a while," he says. "Then not so well." Financially, he supported his family by fixing cars; emotionally, at least from the perspective of his increasingly disgruntled wife, he failed to support them by escaping too often to his vertical world. He and his wife eventually split up, a divorce so acrimonious that she tried to keep him from seeing their two children.

Still, Rowell climbed and trekked. When he tried to describe his wilderness trips to others, they would often ask, "Got any pictures?" As a kid he had taken a few snapshots with a Brownie box camera, but the pictures were disappointing, so he quit. In his twenties, he bought an Instamatic and resumed shooting. And shooting.

The biggest difference between Rowell and countless other amateur photographers was his need to ask questions. "Why did photography work?" he wanted to know. "Why did photographs look different from what the eye saw? Usually photos didn't look as good, but sometimes they looked better. Why? Now if I could figure out why and make that work for me. . . ."

He nurtured the idea of making a living as a wilderness photojournalist. There had to be a niche combining photography, writing, and outdoor adventure, he reasoned, so why shouldn't he fill it? One thing was certain: he couldn't fix cars all his life. So in 1972, at age thirty-two, he sold his car-repair business and bought better cameras. "I figured I had enough money for my family to live for one year, so that's how long I gave myself to make it."

The Rowell bank account bottomed out at fifty dollars before Galen started making more money than he was spending on film. Two big breaks coincided to boost his fortunes: *National Geographic* assigned him to do a cover story, with pictures, on big-wall climbing in Yosemite, and he received a book contract to edit an anthology on the same subject, called *The Vertical World of Yosemite.*

K2.   Still recovering from bronchitis, Rowell arrived at Savoia Pass (20,400 feet) with Lou, Wick, Rob, and Steve. As they were already in shadows, they immediately set about establishing Camp II. Rigging a winch, they managed to bring up one load of gear before dark.

For five people they had five sleeping bags and plenty of food, but only two tents and one stove. The two-man tents, with their low profile for stability in high winds, were cramped for two, much less three, people. Lou and Wick, the two broadest men, took one tent, while Rob, Steve, and Galen shoehorned themselves into the other one.

Melting enough snow for five men over one small stove took hours, and it was pitch dark before Lou passed Galen enough water to rehydrate his freeze-dried meal. After dinner, Rowell asked if they could relight the stove to melt more snow to fill their water bottles. Lou said no, and Rowell girded himself for a long night with no water. That was no great sacrifice at sea level, but up four vertical miles, one loses considerable water through normal breathing, as the cold air

Galen Rowell's two favorite places to travel

1. Himalaya
2. Patagonia – wild, low population, fantastic peaks, lotta wildlife

coming in has far less moisture than the warm air going out.

At midnight Rowell was still awake. His mouth was so dry he felt as though his tongue were swollen two sizes too large. "This is the thirstiest I've ever been," he thought. Finally, unable to stand it any longer, he crawled over his mates to the tent door. Opening it, he plunged his mouth into the soft powder snow. Relief was immediate but fleeting. With the air temperature near zero, snow provided only a few teaspoons of moisture before his mouth became so cold that the snow stuck to his lips. Returning to his sleeping bag, he lay there until first light, agonizing for dawn as never before. He felt like an ocean sailor driven to the edge of madness by thirst, all the while surrounded by a form of water that was useless to him.

The morning dawned clear and cold. After what seemed to Rowell an eternity, the stove was lit, snow was melted, and his body was rehydrated by precious water. But it was too little too late. He felt weak and told the others that he could not join them on the climb to establish Camp III. Rob and Steve decided to stay behind, too. Together they would remount the winch and haul up more equipment to Camp II.

The following morning Rowell felt even worse. He again announced that he couldn't climb.

"Why not?" Lou asked suspiciously.

"I feel too weak," said Rowell. "I've got chills, a headache, muscle pains, and my eyes are sensitive to light."

"I've got the same symptoms," Lou retorted brusquely, "and I'm going to climb the mountain. If you wanted to climb K2 as much as we do, you wouldn't stay back here for every little thing. . . . I think you're just scared of the mountain."

Lou's assault seemed both unreal and outrageous, but Rowell was too sluggish to defend himself. Under the best of conditions, high-altitude thinking is to the mind as underwater-running is to the body. And it was not the best of conditions. He mumbled that he was weak and feverish and couldn't go on, then retreated to his sleeping bag and lay silent while the others ate breakfast and packed gear. He knew he should descend to base camp, but there was no way he could make it by himself. The others were gearing up for an ascent of the ridge. Soon he would be alone.

Before his companions left, Rob stuck his head in Rowell's tent to convey his support. "If you still feel sick tonight you should go down," he said. "I'll go down with you if necessary. But today is a perfect day that we can't miss."

"I know that," Rowell said, adding, "You know, Lou is wrong about me. I'd like to be up there with you today, and I want to climb the mountain."

"I know."

Throughout the morning, Rowell's condition worsened. He tried to write in his diary but felt too weak to put down anything more than the date and temperature. When he stepped outside to urinate, he became dizzy and dropped to his knees. It was all he could do to crawl back to his sleeping bag.

Late that afternoon Jim Whittaker soloed a double-load up to Camp II. Rowell described his symptoms to Whittaker expecting another lecture in macho mountaineering. But Whittaker was surprisingly sympathetic, and with his help Rowell eventually made it down to base camp. For the next three days his temperature hovered above 101 while a blizzard raged on the mountain. Had he stayed in Camp II, he decided, he would not have survived. Jim Whittaker, he was forced to conclude, had probably saved his life.

Lou wasn't the only one who harbored suspicions about Rowell's work ethic. Jim Wickwire would write in his diary: "With one of the biggest reputations among us, Galen simply did not perform well on the main objective: finding a route up K2's west ridge. Admittedly his sickness played a major role in his nonperformance, but it doesn't account for everything."

Today, Galen Rowell's name is known more for photography and writing than for climbing. Every Christmas, thousands of nature calendars sporting Rowell's photographs change hands. His work has appeared in dozens of magazines and coffee-table books. And while fame is not something he has ever sought, he takes it in stride. Sometimes it even makes him laugh.

A few years ago he was put in touch with Robert Redford, who

Rowell, climbing next to California's Yosemite Falls, approaches photo opportunities as problems to be solved. (Courtesy of Galen Rowell)

wanted to go to Nepal to research a movie he thought he was going to do on Himalayan climbing. Rowell and his second wife, Barbara, guided Redford to Everest Base Camp at 18,000 feet. "He was a good guy, very fit, as nimble-footed as any climber," says Rowell. "And, yes, even in Nepal, people recognized him."

One day they were sitting in a tiny tea house in a remote Nepalese village, when a hippie girl walked in. She looked toward their table and her eyes lit up. "Hey, I know you!" she cried. Redford, appearing uncomfortable, stared at the dirt floor. Too late. She bounded over, then her eyes locked on Rowell. "I've seen you in my North Face catalogue."

"Yeah," he grinned, "I've been in the North Face catalogue." Then, unable to resist, he gestured to Redford. "This is my friend Bob."

"Hi, Bob," she said, giving him a cursory glance before turning back to Galen.

K2. The dozen HAPs were a great disappointment to the K2 expedition. Although they had all claimed high-altitude experience with other expeditions, few of them were able to make it even as far as Savoia Pass. Without their load-carrying help in the lower camps, the expedition was logistically crippled. Original plans called for 414 load movements between camps preparatory to the establishment of Camp VII at 27,500 feet. With twelve HAPs and a full crew of climbers carrying every other day, it would have taken forty days to move supplies into position for an attack on the summit. As it was, lashed by eighteen days of back-to-back storms, weakened by illness and conflicting notions of team dynamics, supplying those camps became all but impossible.

With a summit attempt looking remote, Rowell made this diary entry: "One part of me wants to give up and go home to family and loved ones. This side sees the futility of dealing with the powerful forces on this expedition. The other part of me is mountaineer. It wants to get together a few people who will get up early and give the ridge a full-scale try."

The final blow came when one of the two HAPs in Camp II, Akbar Ali, came down with what at first seemed like altitude sickness. Fred Dunham took Akbar down to base camp, where he soon began to vomit roundworms, passing enough to fill a quart jar, before lapsing into a coma. Dr. Schaller determined that Akbar's intestine was perforated, leaking poison into his abdominal cavity and causing peritonitis. Schaller administered massive doses of antibiotics and steroids and used sixteen of his total twenty-four bottles of intravenous fluids. At night, the fluids were apt to freeze, and only the constant vigilance of Schaller kept Akbar alive.

Akbar would eventually recover, but the 1975 K2 Expedition was down for the count. They would not get above 22,000 feet, more than six thousand vertical feet short of the summit. As the climbers retreated from K2, porters passing by to pick up equipment at base camp brought them mail. Rowell received a bulky envelope from his mother. It contained his father's ashes, with a note asking Galen to spread them around K2, "in the most beautiful place you can find." She described his father's look at death as one of peace and serenity.

At Concordia, which was directly below six of the seventeen highest peaks in the world ("the grandest meeting place of glaciers in the world," Rowell would call it), he took his father's ashes and walked east until he came upon a glacial moraine of blocks of white marble. He knew he had found the place. "I released the ashes into a gentle breeze and watched them settle into nooks between the boulders where wild primroses blossomed out of the glacial silt." He spent the next hour by himself on the highest rock of the moraine, thinking of his father, his life, and the end of the expedition.

Although his father loved hiking in the mountains, the rarefied world above timberline had never attracted him. A professor of speech at the University of California, his academic training had been in philosophy and theology. Yet he never became so immersed in metaphysics that he lost his connection with the natural world. Galen recalled an especially inspirational sermon his father would deliver to the multitudes on Sierra Club pack trips. Titled "Mountains and the Human Spirit," the theme was the powerful therapeutic effect mountains had on people. For the ancients, he would begin, mountains provided thrones for their gods and security from attack. Later people began to climb mountains for fun and challenge. "Montani semper liberi," his father would intone. "Mountaineers are always free." Mountain solitude clarifies and purifies motives, he went on. It shores up resolve, bolsters courage. People invariably return from the mountains with a new wholeness of personality that is nearly impossible to realize in the complex bustle of civilization.

Recalling those words in the shadow of K2, Rowell felt anything but whole. Quite the contrary; he felt like a jigsaw puzzle with a missing piece. He had achieved neither mastery nor enhancement of his personality on K2. Yet it was his nature to try to make the best of a situation. "Now that all chances for climbing the mountain are gone," he thought, "I will try to bring the team closer together, to help make it possible for us to return home as friends." It might have been easier to climb the mountain, for the rifts among team members rivaled the chasms of K2.

Seventeen years after his first Karakoram expedition, Rowell sits in his Albany, California, photography studio peering through a magnifying glass at slides of a red fox. "Not a very good shot," he says hypercritically, "but it's not often you see a fox in the Bay Area."

The walls of his studio are dotted with dozens of Rowell's international nature photographs, revealing an artist's command of lighting and creating the ambience of an art museum. Over there is his world-famous "Rainbow over the Potala Palace, Lhasa, Tibet"; there, the sheer rock face of Patagonia's Fitz Roy (upon which Rowell and three fellow climbers spent a harrowing night on a ledge about the size of a Ping-Pong table); there, "Cloud Cap on K2."

Rowell has had plenty of fodder for his photos. In his thirty-six years of climbing he has been on fourteen Himalayan climbing and trekking expeditions, plus nine more in Pakistan's Karakoram. He has climbed all over the world—from Argentina to Alaska to Africa, more than a thousand climbs in all, about 140 of them first ascents (doing a route never before climbed).

Although Rowell doesn't keep an exact count of first ascents, he touts their importance as "the creative part of climbing. Your ability to be creative depends on your ability to do new terrain, where nobody has ever been before. If you hold yourself to what's already been climbed, you're not fully expressing yourself."

At fifty-two, Rowell still looks quite capable of expressing himself. Like most people with larger-than-life reputations, he is shorter than expected. Five-foot-eight and 155 pounds, he is fifteen pounds lighter than he was at the start of the 1975 K2 Expedition. Lean, compact, and strong, he is ruggedly handsome, with a JFK haircut speckled with gray and a taut jawline that looks as if it were chiseled from Karakoram rock. His green-brown eyes are piercing, expressive, quick to smile.

Such a youthful, fit appearance is more than cosmetic. He stays in shape by running about thirty-five miles a week and climbing as often as his demanding schedule allows. Just the week before, he had logged another first ascent near 12,000-foot Bishop Pass in the Sierra before a freak July snowstorm drove him to lower ground.

To talk climbing is to talk risk, a subject Rowell doesn't shy from. "I've never even broken a bone climbing," he says with no hubris. "And I've never been on an expedition where anyone was killed." His worst injury and closest brush with death occurred at the same moment, 13,000 feet up Alaska's Mount McKinley (Denali). He and adventurer Ned Gillette were trying to do the first one-day ascent of the treacherous 20,320-foot mountain.

"We were on skis, roped together, on an ice slope covered with light snow," recalls Rowell. "I wanted to stop and put on crampons, but Ned tried it and thought it was fine. We went a little farther and I insisted I had to put on crampons. Ned said okay and started to come back to me. Then he slipped. He fell right past me and down the slope, headed for a precipice. I rammed my ski pole into the snow up to its hilt, but when the rope went taut I was popped out of the ice and now we were both flying down the slope. I thought we were done for. But I had slowed him down, and when an old fixed rope appeared he was able to grab it with a gloved hand. He came to a stop on his back with his skis up in the air. I landed face first on his skis."

Gillette has described what happened next: "It's five A.M., twenty below, and the wind's blowing. We're hanging there on the ice above a fifty-foot drop, which is just above a four-thousand-foot drop. Galen has sliced his face open on my skis (severed artery in his lower lip, front teeth knocked out), and blood is everywhere. He goes into shock, and I have to convince him to get off me and tie us in. After that I could build a little platform with my ice ax, and we eventually climbed down."

And back up. A month later, sufficiently healed in body and mind, they returned and completed a hellish nineteen-hour round-trip of McKinley.

Another time, climbing a comparatively easy 5.9 route in the High Sierra, Rowell let his mind wander. "It was windy and cold and I didn't put in as much protection as normal. I was doing a lieback when suddenly a hold broke off and I was spewed out of the crack backward. My partner held me and I came to a stop upside down, my head three feet from a pointed rock. I climbed right back up and finished the pitch, but inside I thought, 'That was close. If the protection had been any lower or there'd been any more slack in the rope, it would have been all over.'"

He returns to his photos, apparently unable to recall any other close calls. It is a testament to the selective powers of the mind, our tendency to recall the good and forget the bad. For Rowell has shaken hands with death on at least two other occasions. Attempting a first ascent of the south face of Half Dome with Warren Harding, they were hit by a cold, wet storm, which forced their rescue. Another time, soloing a "small" 20,500-foot peak in the Himalaya, he was avalanched and buried up to his waist in snow.

Although he has no more of a death wish than the most conservative suburbanite, Rowell accepts risk as part of the climbing game. He would endorse Royal Robbins's assertion that "risk is in the final analysis an essential ingredient." Yet he is no daredevil. "When I did a traverse of the Karakoram, Kim Schmitz and I competed for who could be the most chicken. One of us would say, 'I'm scared to walk that unroped.' Or 'I'm chicken to try that icefall.' It was a way of playing it safe, of making moves without our ego interfering.

"What climbers do is to manage risk," Rowell is fond of saying. "The joy comes from overcoming risk without killing yourself." Of course, that's exactly what friends and family fear the most – that climbing will kill him. But two things that Rowell has in abundance – spirit and experience – greatly increase his chances for survival. Besides, so much of what Rowell does in his life includes more than a trace amount of risk that it seems unfair to pick on climbing. He and wife Barbara recently flew to South America, a trip in which they had close brushes with death, first in Barbara's small plane, then paddling on the Amazon River. When they returned home from South America, they learned of the death of one of their closest friends. "He had spent more than half his life in the Himalaya," Rowell says. "But on this day he was near home, waiting on the sidewalk for his brother to pick him up. He passed out, hit his head on the curb, and died." Another Rowell acquaintance, climber and speed skier Steve McKinney, recently died in an even more unlikely manner. "I was on Everest with McKinney. He was a bold climber, seemingly indestructible. Last year his car broke down late at night. He pulled over to go to sleep, and a drunk driver hit and killed him.

"I definitely believe it's better to live a short life and push yourself and do what you believe in and want to do, rather than live a long life filled with fear that keeps you from the fulfillment and enjoyment of testing yourself."

Rowell figures to be taking some of nature's best shots for at least the next twenty years. "I may have to tone down the climbing a little, but I'll never give it up," he says. "I love being in a natural environment and challenging myself in a controllable way. There are exceptions, like avalanches, but most of the time I'm managing my own destiny.

"Wild places can tell you more about yourself than people can," he continues, singing a few more bars of his paean. "We all grow up in a social structure, with people rating us in intangible ways – good, shitty – but we don't really know in any solid sense how we're doing in life. I never liked team sports for that reason. If my baseball team won, was it because I did well, or was it because the other eight guys did well, or six did well and three screwed up? On the mountain, though, you know exactly how you're doing. You know absolutely whether you've made it or not. When you get to the deep questions, like 'What do I know?' well, you know those peaks you climbed. In school I only knew what I read in books, what other people told me. But it's direct knowledge from the environment that's incontrovertible.

"The friends you make through climbing are your best friends.

Galen Rowell's two most extraordinary animals

1. Grizzly bears – they are super animals.
2. Peregrine falcons – they live on the edge of risk. The animals closest to climbers, they seek the steepest cliffs for their nests; I feel a real kinship with them.

With them you share the risks, the joys. It's the type of friendships forged by people fighting together in wars."

The consistent thread running through Rowell's life, the tendency that drives him to climb mountains and chase photo-ops, is a love of problem solving. "Faced with a new problem, the questions just start coming," he says. "'I wonder if I could climb that? I wonder if I could climb it in a day? I wonder if I could do it free without any direct aid? Should I take a sleeping bag? Which rack of hardware? . . .

"When you do it well, when you go up a rock face previously untouched by human hands or feet, having scoped it from below, why, it's the best feeling. But even if it doesn't go the way it's supposed to go, you put that experience away and use it later. Meanwhile, the wisdom and confidence you get from going through all that benefits you in regular life.

"Climbing is a wonderful metaphor for life," he adds, waxing philosophical. "If you risk too much, you'll eat it and die; if you don't risk enough, you won't get anything out of it."

Although Rowell has climbed almost injury-free, more than a hundred friends and acquaintances have died climbing. No wonder insurance companies, like most of the public, view climbers as bad risks. "Ironically, insurance companies try to manage climbing risk by outlawing the very tools designed to reduce that risk," says Rowell. "The Sierra Club was told not to participate in activities that use crampons, ropes, and ice axes. Soon after that regulation went into effect, I was out photographing a Sierra Club outing. People were doing difficult climbs without ropes or hardware because those tools were prohibited by the insurance company."

From the Rowell perspective, risk is not just something to be avoided or endured, but a life-enhancing necessity. "As a human being, you can't know your real potential unless you test and discover your limits. Danger makes you focus more intently."

Though Rowell insists he won't join another expedition intent on climbing an eight-thousand-meter peak, his reasons have more to do with damage than danger. "The large expeditions consume vast amounts of resources," he says, "and have a huge impact on the land and the culture. In the Karakoram, government regulations force expeditions to camp in designated sites. On our march to the K2 base camp, wherever our six-hundred-plus porters stopped for the night, the hillsides looked like they'd been ravaged by giant locusts. A three-day porter strike meant two thousand turds in one place."

Rowell also takes issue with the use of supplemental oxygen as a breathing aid. "Ten or more years ago I was capable of climbing Everest or K2 without oxygen," he says. "Now I'm probably not. Or maybe I am, but I'd be risking neurological damage. The alternative – using oxygen – defeats one of the purposes in climbing a high peak. Compare Mount Everest, which rises about twelve thousand feet above its base camp, with Mount Shasta (14,162 feet), which does the same. The only real difference is the thinness of the air on Everest. But if you use something that artificially changes that air, what have you really accomplished? I just don't believe in compromising the natural environment, because that's what you're out there to test yourself against."

Rowell's physical and intellectual energy level is something to behold. When he is not climbing mountains, running, or shooting world-class photos, he's darting hither and yon giving talks and slide shows to those needing his special dose of inspiration. Adventure – doing it and describing it – has him traveling about 100,000 miles a year. "The more sophisticated the travel, like flying, the worse it is. Next week I'm driving with two friends to the Northwest Territories in Canada to climb. I'm really looking forward to that. Then I'm home for a week before leaving for Siberia. After that Barbara and I are going to the South Pole."

Steve Bosque, who used to climb with Rowell at Indian Rock in Berkeley, describes him as "a real renaissance man, a Sir Richard Burton kind of guy. He's very nice, not at all arrogant, but as driven as any climber I've ever met. There's an intense sort of undercurrent there, a bottled-up energy, though it's very much under control." Bosque, who owns more Yosemite big-wall first ascents than anyone, was surprised by Rowell's climbing prowess. "I thought he was probably photographer first, climber second, but no. He could do a particular move, an overhanging jam crack, so quickly and gracefully. I couldn't match it, even though I was in my prime."

Rowell is the envy of every person who ever hoped to make a living from his hobby. He has traveled to and photographed all seven continents, covered the highest war in history (India versus Pakistan over a parcel of Kashmir), and met Tibet's Dalai Lama. Much of the world's most pristine wilderness has been captured by one of his many cameras. Ever humble, he credits climbing for permitting him to mix art and adventure. "You can't photograph a football game while playing in it," he says, "but with climbing you can do just that. The wonderful alternation between leading and belaying, between extreme effort and kicking back, allows you to capture the experience while you are emotionally involved with it."

Rowell is often asked what is the most important element in a good photo. "Emotion," he answers unhesitatingly. "I always try to connect emotionally with my subject. I do that by asking questions: 'I like that,' I will say. 'Why do I like that? What's special about it? Where should I be to bring out that specialness? And how can I get rid of the other stuff so people can see that specialness?'"

Specialness. Special photographs, special places. It is that lust for the special that first took Rowell to Tibet. He led the first American trekking group allowed into the backcountry of Tibet. "It was 1981," he says, "a time when only a few non-Asian foreigners had ever seen the holy city of Lhasa, where we started. I became intrigued by Tibet's culture, its wild animals, how both are threatened. China's hold on Tibet, which was independent until 1950, is like the hold Iraq had on Kuwait."

Rowell took on Tibet as a personal cause and made it a cause célèbre. At first he was shocked by how little support he received. "I found out that the Western media was effectively censored, almost as though they were operating in China itself. Printing anything that might outrage the Chinese would have cut their access to other stories. It took me years to get my Tibet work published. I finally decided to go on the record, to bare everything I knew, even if I didn't get to go back. It was a risk, but it worked out. The response has been positive. And I got to meet and work with the Dalai Lama, another one of life's great risk takers."

Rowell allows that the Dalai Lama is on his short list of heroes. Only three others easily come to mind: John Muir, David Brower, and Heinrich Harrer. "Harrer was on the Austrian Olympic Ski team in the thirties," Rowell explains. "He made the first ascent of the Eiger and was later imprisoned in India by the British. He escaped and [crossed] Tibet."

Whew! What qualities, I wonder aloud, are needed to qualify for the Rowell hero list? He pauses only a moment. "An adventurous spirit," he says, "combined with a real compassion for wild environment and other human beings."

But wasn't it easier to exercise your adventurous spirit back in John Muir's day?

"There's still lots of adventure that hasn't been done," says Rowell, returning to his red-fox photo. "Take a flight from China to Tibet, look down, and you will see hundreds of unnamed, unclimbed peaks above 23,000 feet. They're just there, waiting."

One morning after returning from K2, Rowell received a phone call from Jim Whittaker, inviting him to return to K2 in 1978. Most of the 1975 team had agreed to give it another go. The plan was to assail an alternative unclimbed ridge on the west side. Without hesitation Rowell said "Count me in."

As it turned out, Rowell was not included in the 1978 K2 Expedition. "Jim Whittaker never acted on the invitation," he says. "The expedition went to the top of the mountain (K2's third successful ascent), but I was not among the climbers. We've never talked about it, but it's obvious to me what happened. In between the invitation and the expedition, my book *(In The Throne Room of the Mountain Gods)* came out. Jim Whittaker, who is pretty thin-skinned, was not happy about the way it portrayed him."

When asked why he would go back to K2, after all the hassles in 1975, Rowell replies, "It was a chance to make things right."

MIKE CORBETT AND MARK WELLMAN

The Hard Way

If we don't hang together,
we'll hang separately.

—Ben Franklin

Nothing contributes more to the grandeur of Yosemite than the 3,600-foot off-white monolith, El Capitan. The Captain. Aptly named, for this noble rock commands the attention and respect of all who gaze upon it.

Enter Yosemite Valley from the west and the vistas are cropped until suddenly you gain a clearing in the pine forest and *whooaaa,* thar she blows! Piercing the sky like the prow of a ship of unimaginable size, El Cap fills your field of vision, even though it's more than a mile away. About two-thirds of a mile high, it is taller than three Empire State Buildings stacked end to end. But it is El Cap's girth, its sheer mass, that holds you in awe. It is the largest unbroken piece of granite in the world.

When Mark Wellman and Mike Corbett first set eyes on El Capitan, their jaws no doubt dropped just as far as everybody else's. And just like everybody else, they must have thought, "How in the world could anyone climb that?"

July 19, 1989, Day 1. The alarm went off early in Mike Corbett's dorm room, causing him to roll over and groan. A moment later, when he remembered what day it was, a knot of butterflies invaded his stomach. He was scheduled to start climbing El Capitan today, an enterprise he had undertaken many times before, but on this day his partner would be twenty-nine-year-old Mark Wellman, a paraplegic who had lost the use of his legs eight years before in a climbing accident.

No paraplegic had ever climbed one of Yosemite's big walls, a fact that greatly magnified the hype and pressure of the Mark and Mike Climb. It was not lost on Corbett that if Mark were killed, a lot of folks would blame him. And vice versa.

Corbett and his girlfriend, Gwen Schneider, had been up only minutes when the tension inside Corbett spilled out like lava. An argument ensued, alternating periods of heated silence and raised voices. In the heat of battle Corbett thought to himself, "It's six A.M. on the morning of the climb of my life and I'm fighting with my girlfriend. Great! And now Gwen's not going to carry a pack for me to the base of El Cap. This sucks!"

More disappointed than angry, Corbett left for Wellman's cabin in Yosemite Village. Mark was already up and darting about in his wheelchair. Like Corbett, he was anxious to get going. Before they could leave for the base of El Capitan, however, Gwen arrived. She and Mike quickly made up, prompting sighs of relief all around.

Thirty minutes later, a gasping, grunting Mike Corbett was piggybacking his partner the last quarter mile to the base of El Capitan. Though the sun had not yet risen above the rim of the rock amphitheater, Corbett was already sweating profusely. At five-foot-seven and 150 pounds, he weighed the same as Wellman, whose broad, buffed shoulders were in sharp contrast to his withered legs. Though Corbett carried a few extra pounds around his midsection ("I'm a couch potato kind of climber"), he was, at age thirty-five, a lot stronger than his unpresupposing appearance would suggest. He needed that strength to hump Wellman over uneven terrain littered with loose rocks while dodging a gaggle of reporters and fielding their questions.

"How long are you planning to take?"

"A week."

"Are you scared?"

"No, relieved to get going."

That was true for both climbers. Their rallying cry was *"We're finally doing it."* Yes, after six months of planning, of seeing the other guy every day, they were finally doing it.

At the base of the rock, about thirty friends and reporters surrounded them while they got ready. They had agreed that Mark would go first up the fixed rope that Mike and Gwen had set the week before. Mark could get a head start on the two thousand pull-ups needed to reach their first bivouac (bivy), Mammoth Terrace, one thousand feet

Mike Corbett's eight things to take on a big-wall climb

1. Camera. On El Cap, I had a camera maybe only five times out of fifty and regretted it every time I hadn't brought one. I could have had a hell of a slide show.

2. Pocket knife with can opener.

3. Toilet paper.

4. Water – more that you think you'll ever need. Water can become an issue pretty quick.

5. Sweets. It's the only treat you'll get unless you make the summit.

6. Silverware.

7. A good, positive attitude and . . .

8. . . . A partner who thinks likewise.

---

up the wall. Meanwhile, Corbett would stay behind to arrange gear, tie on haul bags, and answer questions.

The complicated system they had fabricated for Wellman took some rigging. It included three mechanical ascending devices – two Jumars and a Gibbs – as well as harnesses, an etrier, and the heavy rock chaps he wore to protect his legs. They hooked the upper Jumar to his swami belt (waist harness), the Gibbs to a chest harness and the swami belt, and the lower Jumar to a homemade etrier (portable ladder). The two Jumars were linked by an elastic cord. When Wellman pushed the highest Jumar's pull-up bar upward, the cord brought up the lower ascender, drawing his legs up into an "L." When he did his patented bent-elbow pull-up (a short power move, easier on the joints than a full-stretch pull-up), his legs dropped back down below him.

The system was effective in keeping his legs from flapping around on the rock. But it did create a lot of friction. Besides his chaps, Wellman wore elbow pads for protection. Turned ninety degrees to the face of El Capitan, one arm would almost always be rubbing against the rock. He would try to compensate for this unwelcome resistance by pushing off the rock with his arm. With a violent grunt and expulsion of air, Wellman cranked out the first pull-up, advancing six inches.

When he was just a few feet off the ground, a reporter asked him,

"How will you go to the bathroom?"

"We'll just let gravity do its thing," he replied.

A moment later, someone else asked Corbett, "Why have you climbed El Cap so many times?"

"'Cause it's different every time. I learn something new every time. I could do the same rock two consecutive days with the same partner and it'd be different both days. What I'm thinking, what I'm feeling—that's what it's all about."

"How many ledges up there big enough to sleep on?" There was a collective tilting of heads; eyes wandered up the rock. Up close, imperfections of the massive face were evident. Although El Capitan was polished rock, it certainly wasn't blank rock. There were plenty of flakes, cracks, and dents; but ledges large enough for camping? It didn't seem possible.

"Let's see," Mike said, adjusting his headband. He had a mop of dark hair that could be unruly. "If there are eighty routes on El Cap, just about every one has at least one ledge. The 'Nose,' the first route climbed, has six."

"Do you wear a helmet?"

"Nah. I probably should. Closest call I've ever had was on El Cap when a loose rock broke my finger. Yeah, if it'd hit my head, it could've killed me."

"Who do you look up to?" Laughter flitted about as people involuntarily looked up at Wellman, who was now a hundred feet above them, cranking out pull-up after pull-up with Sisyphean consistency.

"Yvon Chouinard, Royal Robbins, Warren Harding," Mike replied. "Early Yosemite climbers like those guys paved the way. They let others know it could be done. They built the road, I just drive the car."

Thirty minutes later, Corbett was behind the wheel, Jumaring (jugging) up the fixed rope. When he was high enough to drop a basketball through a hoop, a *Fresno Bee* reporter raised her microphone toward him and called out, "Any last words?"

"Yeah," he said. "Bye."

Mammoth Terrace is about the size of three picnic tables laid end to end and, according to Corbett, "about as comfortable a place as you'll find on a big wall." Most people, however, could never get comfortable in such a lofty aerie, for the exposure can be petrifying. The earth seems to fall away beneath your feet, leaving one feeling as vulnerable as a newborn.

Wellman and Corbett, feeling "good tired," had lots of company their first night. Three friends and two NBC cameramen also bivyed on Mammoth Terrace. The friends hauled up a celebratory case of beer and, although neither Wellman nor Corbett drank that night, everyone stayed up late talking, laughing, yodeling, and howling at the moon.

Day 2. The next morning, they awoke late, about 8:00 A.M. "The party's over," Corbett thought, with a sinking feeling. "No more fixed ropes. Now the real work begins." Wellman woke up sore but excited. He was enthralled by the endless sea of granite and anxious to get going.

Their friends, wishing them well, rappelled (rapped) down to the valley, leaving the two climbers to sort and pack gear. They were shocked by the bulk and heft of their haul bags. Besides clothing, sleeping bags, and Portaledges (lightweight, state-of-the-art cots), they had thirteen gallons of water, which alone weighed more than a hundred pounds. Their food, mostly perishables, added another hundred. It included cheese, salami, beef jerky, Pop Tarts, granola bars, cookies, canned fruit, hard candies, bagels and cream cheese, canned beans and franks ("beanie weenies"), and PowerBars. They also had four ropes, forty-five pitons, two hammers, 175 carabiners, twenty-five camming devices, twenty wired stoppers, and sixty short nylon slings. Most of that hardware – thirty-nine pounds in all – would be harnessed to Corbett's shoulders when he climbed.

They took more than two hours to break camp and get themselves ready. Despite the heavy loads and the prospect of triple-digit heat, they began the second day with high hopes. Optimists by nature, they fully expected to knock off three pitches and reach Gray Ledge by late afternoon. But they badly underestimated the obstacles. By midafternoon, the ambient air temperature was withering, the rock hot to the touch. Drenched in sweat, the climbers' eyes burned from the salt. After inching along the rock like ants up a hot skillet, they quit early. "It was so hot and the haul bags were so heavy," says Corbett, "we were cooked after two pitches."

Because of the public's interest in the Mark and Mike Climb, they had brought a walkie-talkie. That evening, Gwen radioed to Mike that the day's high had been 105 degrees and that tomorrow was supposed to be another scorcher.

In his sleeping bag that night, Corbett critiqued the day. It had been uneventful but enlightening, he concluded. He had learned that Mark was going to be a huge help with the haul bags. "They were rigged to a pulley and cam device that allowed them to be pulled up but not fall down," says Corbett. "The system worked pretty well, but the heat and the two hundred and twenty-five pounds of gear made it a nightmare. Without Mark, it would've been even worse. It was a great morale booster having someone else pulling on those suckers."

Consumption of food and water would lighten their load by about fifteen pounds a day. But fifteen pounds out of 225 seemed like spit in the ocean. At that rate, five days into the climb they would still be hauling 150 pounds, more than either of them would weigh at that point (Corbett would lose ten pounds on the climb, Wellman five). "Maybe seven days to reach the top isn't realistic," Corbett thought for the first time.

Day 3. With Wellman belaying him, Corbett unclipped a rurp (Realized Ultimate Reality Piton) from the carabiner that held it to his gear sling. The smallest piton in his arsenal, it could fit into a crack as narrow as a blade of grass. After deftly hammering it into the rock, he clipped a carabiner to the eye of the piton and his rope into the carabiner. To the carabiner; he attached a small sling ladder (etrier), then moved up its stirrups, gaining about three vertical feet. Three feet out of 3,600 – less than a tenth of 1 percent. No wonder it would take them more than a week.

Fifty pitons and 150 feet later, Corbett reached the end of his rope (marking completion of a pitch). He then anchored his climbing rope and a second loose rope, which he dropped down to Wellman. After rappelling down the loose rope, he helped rig Wellman for the three hundred pull-ups that would take him to the top of this pitch. While Wellman did his pull-ups – again, with bent elbows, so as not to stress his joints – Corbett jugged up the other rope and removed the pieces of protection. After Mark and Mike met at the top of the pitch, they began hauling up the first equipment bag. That accomplished, Corbett again rapped down and clipped on another bag. This was repeated until both climbers and all the equipment were at the top of the pitch. "At times I climbed a pitch four times," says Corbett, "and never less than twice."

They made it to Gray Ledge by midday. Though they were half a day behind schedule, they were confident they would make up the

Mike Corbett and Mark Wellman enjoyed a few upbeat moments during their climb of Half Dome. (Courtesy of Chris Falkenstein)

time later. While Corbett poured water down his parched throat, he estimated they were nearly halfway to the top. As one who tends to see the glass half full, he thought, "All we have to do is climb the other half of El Cap and we got this baby in the bag."

That night they learned via walkie-talkie that the world was watching. On the network news, their climb was the lead story. That was exciting—and mind-boggling. "The lead story is usually Gorbachev or a plane crash," said Corbett.

"We're getting a lot of attention, but what does it really mean?" Wellman wondered aloud.

"I'll be satisfied if NBC gives us a video clip of some of our climbing," said Corbett.

They agreed over beanie-weenies that it all sounded glamorous as hell, but that the bags were still heavy and the rock was still steep.

Day 4. It was unbelievable, Wellman thought, but almost two thousand feet above the Yosemite Valley floor they could still hear the P.A. system on the valley trams. He even thought he'd heard their own names mentioned, probably in the context of *"Folks, if you have binocu-*

lars or very good eyes, you might be able to make out two climbers, Mark Wellman and Mike Corbett, about halfway up El Capitan. What makes Mark Wellman unique. . . ."

Even more distracting than the audio was the visual, for they could still see whitewater splashes when swimmers jumped off bridges into the Merced River. "Being on El Cap with the sun beating down, and seeing those splashes, is a sort of Chinese water torture," Corbett says. "I want to be climbing, but I also want to be down there swimming. Why, if I had a long straw and could reach that river, I'd suck it dry."

They had enough water for a seven- or eight-day climb, but what if it took nine or ten? "There's nothing worse than running out of water on a big wall," says Corbett. "You can ruin the trip, end up being rescued. I ran out once for half a day. I can't imagine being without water longer than that. With all the exertion, you'd get so weak you'd become immobilized."

Why climb El Capitan in July when the likelihood of searing temperatures is so high? Why not a nice mellow month like May? For Mark and Mike, two reasons were paramount: First, both men feared and hated cold more than heat. The accident that paralyzed Wellman had also left him exposed at 13,000 feet for thirty hours, and he had nearly frozen to death. Corbett had flirted with death on Half Dome when a March snowstorm struck his party, freezing their ropes as hard as swizzle sticks and forcing a dramatic helicopter rescue. On that occasion, a hypothermic Mike Corbett went eye-to-eye with his maker. "I was so cold, I just wanted to go to sleep and forget about it," he says. "I was ready to die."

Secondly, their starting date had originally been April 19. But then Mark made two phone calls, the first of which was to his mother.

"I'm going to go up El Capitan," he told her.

"Up the backside, on the trail, right?" she said nervously. "I think that's marvelous."

"No, Mom, I'm planning to climb the vertical face."

The silence at the other end told him his mother was fighting back tears with incomplete success. Finally she said, "I think you're crazy. . . . Climbing took your legs and now you're going to go back up there? I don't want you to do it, Mark."

The second phone call was to Corbett, one month before their planned departure date. "Mike, I'm sorry," he said, "I can't climb El Cap with you. My parents are really bummed, especially my mom. My accident put her through hell, and I don't know if I can do it to her again. I'm going to have to bow out of this thing gracefully."

"Dude, you can bow out, but I don't think you can do it gracefully," said Corbett. "A lot of people know about this climb."

Wellman agreed to think about it. Corbett, who was devastated by the news, got Wellman to agree to talk to his parents when he went home for Easter. Although Mark never spoke to them again about El Cap, he announced to Corbett when he returned to Yosemite that he was committed to the climb, but not on April 19. "I need more time," he said. With Corbett continuing to pressure him to set a date, Wellman finally agreed to start on September 19. But then in the spring, Corbett set some fixed ropes on El Cap and he and Mark did a practice climb to Heart Ledge, eight hundred feet up the rock. Wellman has described the experience: "As I pulled myself up the rope, six inches at a time, it didn't take long before I could look out over the treetops and see the awesome panorama of Yosemite all around me. The exposure was incredible. Half Dome, Cathedral Rock, Glacier Point – there's nothing like seeing them from a bird's point of view."

For Wellman, the night they spent on Heart Ledge was positively liberating. "For the first time in eight years, I was separated from my wheelchair. . . . On the wall, Corbett and I had pretty much the same mobility. Up there he couldn't run away."

The next morning, as they prepared to rappel down, Wellman looked wistfully up the rock face and said, "Corbett, man, I wish we could just keep on going." Mike knew then they would do El Cap.

Too antsy to wait, they moved the climb up to July 19. Says Corbett, "The Mike and Mark Climb had a life of its own that just pulled us along. It included our friends and the reporters and the stories being written. Me and Mark were kinda swept into the rapids of the thing. We had no objections, though. It was cool."

Day 5. Since the first day, they had been staring up at an ominous granite overhang jutting out twenty-five feet from the wall. Called the Shield Roof, it was the crux of the climb and the point of no return. Once above the roof, their ropes would fall too far from the wall, precluding a safe rappel.

"Mike led the pitch perfectly, then rapped down to where I was," Wellman says. "I had to swing out away from the wall, and as I pendulumed out over endless space, a gust caught me and batted me around like a wind chime. I thought I heard my heart exploding."

Another sound reached Mark, but at first he could not identify it.

"It's people on the ground!" Mike shouted, his words echoing off the rock. "They're cheering for you!" Incredibly, nearly a half-mile below, friends and strangers were rooting with such vigor that the sound had wafted up to them. Mark was touched, then inspired. "That's cool," he shouted, smiling. With a fresh supply of adrenaline coursing through his system, he adjusted his elbow pad, gripped the bar with new resolve, and began cranking out pull-ups until he was up and over the lip of the overhang.

That evening, while lounging on their Portaledges, a peregrine falcon buzzed them like some hotshot pilot. Yellow talons tensed, the bird zeroed in on a hapless swift, making a deft dinner kill. Corbett would recall this scene whenever someone asked him why he climbed. It was true, you could get the same view from the top of El Cap by hiking up the backside. But unless you had wings, you had to climb to get a front-row seat.

For Wellman, the proliferation of wildlife on El Cap was amazing. Like most people, he had assumed it was a lifeless monolith. But it was actually a vertical ecosystem, housing a variety of flora and fauna. Over the years, Corbett had seen lichen, moss, wildflowers, ants, even ground squirrels. During the first ascent of El Capitan—by Warren Harding in 1958—Harding's sleeping bag was chewed by rats, which apparently live in the large vertical cracks. And on the first ascent of El Cap's North American Wall, in 1964, Royal Robbins was startled by tiny frogs cavorting on an anchor piton.

The sun finally slunk behind a western ridge, prompting Mark and Mike to issue a joint "Ahhh."

"Thank God," said Mark.

"See you tomorrow, sun," said Mike. Then after a pause, "It reminds me of the school bell ringing at three o'clock." He laughed. "School's out."

They liked to compare what they were doing to camping in space. Corbett had a friend who called climbers "the poor man's astronauts," which was right on. Climbers go where no one has ever gone before—on a shoestring budget. Unlike astronauts who escape gravity, however, climbers are at its mercy. Drop something on a big wall—say, a shoe or a pair of pants—and kiss it good-bye.

After a meager dinner (their appetites were stunted by the heat), Mike got on the walkie-talkie with Gwen, who had news. "I don't know if I should tell you this," she began, "but your brother Tony called. Your whole family has been watching you on TV—your mom, dad, and sister—and they want to come out and meet you at the top."

Though Corbett had not seen his dad in fifteen years, his mom in almost twenty, he was outwardly unruffled by the news. "That's great," he told Gwen. "I'll deal with it when I get down. We have a lot to talk about. But don't let them come to the top. That's too much. They're from the city—tell them what a tough hike it is. Make it sound like it's coming from someone else. I'll see them when I get down."

"Okay," Gwen said, adding, "Here's a funny story: your nieces and nephews will only eat cold bagels and cream cheese because that's what their Uncle Mike is eating on El Capitan."

After Mike signed off, Mark said, "Wow, that's a mind-blower. I thought *my* family was going to be the obstacle."

"It's no obstacle," Mike said evenly. "First of all, I don't see it as a negative. And even if it were, no way it would affect my climbing." Wellman had no trouble believing that.

That night, lying awake on his Portaledge, Corbett thought about his family for the first time in ages.

He had grown up urban. With dad in the army, the family was bounced from one city to another, with frequent return trips to Houston. He spent a lot of time at the Astrodome, which helped nurture his dream of becoming a major-league baseball player. "Football was cool, too, but I was a skinny, little kid," he says. "I thought I was going to be the next Joe Morgan."

His baseball career went up in smoke when he was sixteen and his parents divorced. His mother soon remarried, and while his three siblings stayed in Houston with Mom, Mike—who hated his stepfather ("a redneck, drunk plumber") and felt aloof from his mother—opted to join Dad in California. "That divorce turned out to be a good thing for me," he says. "If I had stayed in Houston, I'd probably be working for an oil company, like my brother. And I never would have come to Yosemite."

Ironically, he was living in San Francisco when he discovered the country. "At George Washington High School in 1969," he says, "it was *in* to have a Kelty backpack and a sleeping bag and to actually use them." Still sixteen, he accompanied a friend's family to Yellowstone and Glacier national parks and to Banff and Lake Louise in Canada. At Banff he met a guy from California who told him, "If you like Banff, you'll really like Yosemite."

Back home, he hitched two hundred miles to Yosemite to see for himself. On that first trip to the valley, he played Frisbee, rafted, and swam in the Merced River. He admired the big walls, of course, but gave no thought to whether anyone was climbing them. Four years later, when he was twenty, he stood in El Capitan meadow, looking through binoculars at two climbers on El Capitan's "Nose" route wondering, "How did they get up there?" and "*Why* did they get up there?" "My reaction was more negative than positive," he recalls. "Mostly I remember thinking they were crazy and that I would never do anything like that."

But a year later, when his friend Richard asked, for the hundredth time, if he wanted to go climbing, Mike decided to give it a try. "We did an easy five-one climb called Glacier Point Apron, and I loved it. Within a week I was leading five-sevens." A month later, he moved to Yosemite Valley, to Camp 4, the climbers' campground. It would be his year-round home for the next ten years.

When Richard was called away from Yosemite, he left his climbing gear with Corbett. "I was just a beginner," he says, "but here I had a rope and a whole rack of hexes, stoppers, and carabiners. I was in hog heaven. As for the danger, I had a little talent and enough sense to stay alive. Richard had pounded into me that climbing was an unforgiving sport and that if I made a mistake it could be permanent. I had a lot of fear—call it fear of splattering—but also this puppy-dog enthusiasm."

Richard eventually returned to claim his gear, but by then Corbett had acquired a modest rack of his own. Though he did it illegally, he doesn't shrink from the truth. "It was a plane crash that really got my El Cap career going," he says. "In the winter of 1977, word reached us in Camp 4 that a plane had gone down in Lower Merced Pass Lake. Overloaded with marijuana, it had been flying low to avoid radar. Four of us went up there and chopped through the frozen lake and fished out a fifty-pound bale of pot. I sold my part for forty-three hundred dollars, and with that I bought a whole rack of brand-new climbing equipment—Jumar ascenders, all kinds of stuff. Right after that I climbed El Cap for the first time."

Day 6. Corbett, stuck in a granite chimney, was sweating, swearing, and scraping his knuckles in a mad struggle to escape. He had tried something different—carrying a haul bag on his back—and now the straps had him in a death grip. "This is so stupid," he seethed.

Wellman, belaying Corbett from above, could offer no help. He could only wait for Mike to extricate himself, which would take more than half an hour. Of course, Wellman was used to waiting. "All the while Corbett was placing pro (protection), I was just hangdoggin' it," he says in the arcane climbers' lexicon. "I always had to be alert for a leader fall that might yard us both, but I still had plenty of time to think." He preferred to focus on the sensual pleasures of the climb itself – he knew he would never be on El Cap again – but his mind inevitably sneaked back into his past.

He had grown up in a suburban family, with a working dad and a housewife mom. He played Little League baseball and delivered the *Palo Alto Times* on his bicycle. He has described his childhood as something out of "Leave it to Beaver," and it seems clear that Dan Quayle would have approved.

Mark was six years old the first time he went backpacking. Despite the pain and suffering of hiking cross-country with weight on his back while trying to keep up with adults, he refused to quit. When he was eight, he bagged his first peak, Mount Lassen, a 10,457-foot volcano in Northern California, which he summitted with his uncle. At home in Palo Alto, trying to orienteer his way through school, his mind frequently wandered back to the mountains. "Except for wood shop and P.E., school didn't interest me much," Wellman admits. "While the teacher would be at the chalkboard working out math problems, I'd be counting the days until my next mountain adventure." Though he was not a good student, he avoided the adolescent pitfalls of drinking, drugs, and reckless driving. "Those things couldn't compare to the high I got every time I stepped onto a mountain," he says.

Wellman was into mountaineering, not technical rock climbing. He was, in the vernacular, a "peak bagger," who started small and worked up to the highest mountains in the Sierra Nevada and later the Swiss Alps. "My senior picture in the high-school yearbook pretty much captured who I was at that time: it showed me smiling on the summit of 13,715-foot Mount Abbot."

After high school, most of Wellman's friends went off to college, but Mark had neither the grades nor the academic drive for such a move. Instead, he stayed home and took a job at the Ski Hut, a local outdoor shop. "What I cared about at that stage of my life," he says, "was learning all there was to know about climbing and skiing."

When he was twenty-two, he and a partner, Peter Enzminger, summitted Seven Gables, a 13,075-foot mountain in the Sierra Nevada. Wellman added his name to the list of those who had climbed the craggy peak. He scribbled the date, August 19, 1982, followed by the message he always left in the registers: "Hey kids! It's the Wells again. Peak #48. See ya." Seven Gables was the forty-eighth he'd "bagged" in the Sierra Nevada. It was the last he would climb using his legs.

Moments later, in the lengthening purple shadows of twilight, Wellman and Enzminger were in full retreat down the mountain. Without flashlights, they picked their way through a rock-strewn gully, intent on reaching base camp before the curtain of darkness fell. The descent was not technically difficult – Class 3 – but it was chilly, and the ledges, chutes, and scree made the footing treacherous. To make better time, they were facing away from the mountain, not testing footholds, relying instead on balance and instinct. But Wellman's usually superior concentration was elsewhere. His mind was racing ahead to camp, imagining how good the freeze-dried dinner would taste, how snuggly his sleeping bag would feel.

Then it happened, "so quickly, I didn't have time to be scared," he has said. "One moment I was hopping onto a sloping ledge covered with loose rocks, the next I was thrown forward, tumbling head over heels into a somersault, landing on my back with an ugly crack, then continuing to bounce down the rocks."

"This is it," he said to himself. "This is what it's like to die."

Wellman wasn't dead, but for a long while he would wish he were. "I'm hurting, man," he groaned when Peter found him. "I'm hurting bad." Moving him was unthinkable; the slightest twitch sent high-voltage pain through his body. So Peter draped a pair of pants over his legs, a sweater over his torso, and reluctantly went for help. They were many miles from the trailhead, so Wellman knew he would be spending the night.

The night was hell – only much colder. Frigid air invaded his body, settled in his organs, ground his bones to dust. For thirty hours he lay wedged between rocks, unable to move, unwilling to sleep for fear of not waking. With so much time for contemplation, he reflected on his own mortality, edging closer to the Presbyterian faith he had all but abandoned.

Seventy-five miles away in Yosemite National Park, the call went out to the Yosemite Search and Rescue team. (In exchange for permission to stay in the park beyond the usual two-week limit, climbers made themselves available for search and rescue.) If the planned helicopter rescue were unsuccessful, the authorities would use climbers to snatch Wellman off the mountain. One of those put on alert that day was Mike Corbett.

Mike Corbett's three things to leave behind on a big-wall climb

1. Stove
2. Boom box
3. Beer

As it turned out, the helicopter rescue worked, and Wellman was flown to the Valley Medical Center in Fresno, where he was informed that he had a broken back. "The fracture involves the eleventh and twelfth thoracic vertebrae," someone said. So relieved was Wellman to be warm and safe and off the mountain that he was unable to read between the lines. "I figured that eventually my back would heal and the feeling would return to my legs," he says.

Two days after Wellman was admitted, Peter Enzminger tiptoed into the intensive care unit to see him. Flat on his back, with tubes emerging from nearly every orifice, he looked atypically weak and vulnerable. "How ya doing?" Peter whispered.

"Peter, at least we climbed the mountain," he croaked, ever the peak bagger.

The orthopedic surgeons who operated on Wellman, with their saws, drills, and chisels, resembled carpenters as much as doctors. They sawed off part of his pelvic bone and grafted it onto his spine. For stability they inserted two metal bars, called Harrington rods, on both sides of his spine. (They are still in his body. "Going through airport metal detectors," he says, "I have a lot of explaining to do.")

He was moved to the Kaiser Hospital Trauma Center in Redwood City. He had been in his room only a few minutes when the misnamed Dr. Smiley entered and said in curt, businesslike tones that Mark would never walk again. His words seemed to steal the air from the room. While Wellman's body struggled for breath, his mind fumbled with the notion that he would never climb another mountain, never walk on another trail. He was a paraplegic. A *paraplegic!* Before that moment, he had never doubted he would recover. Sure, it would take hard work, but he had never shrunk from that. Now they were saying that no matter how hard he worked, his body simply would not respond. Damaged spinal nerves were beyond the reach of the most ambitious workout program.

Thus began Wellman's black period. He would later describe it in countless motivational speeches: "I was on the sixth floor of the hospital, maybe seventy-five feet up, about the same distance as my fall. I thought, 'If I could crawl over to the window and jump out, I'd finish what the first fall didn't do.' But I was too weak to move more than a few inches. The only aspect of my life I had any control over was the remote-control button on the TV."

Despite frequent bouts of depression, Wellman simply wasn't wired for quitting. He took his inspiration not from able-bodied well-wishers but from other chair-people, guys like Bill Bowness and Mark Sutherland, the latter a quadriplegic in his late twenties. "There's nothing you can't do if you choose to do it," Sutherland would tell him during their late-night rap sessions. "If you choose to live, you get off your ass and you live. If you choose to die, lie down. Don't get out of bed."

"Meeting those guys," says Wellman, "it hit me that you could be in a wheelchair and still be cool." And still be active, too. Wellman was soon turned on to the expanding world of wheelchair sports, including basketball, tennis, marathon racing, skiing, and whitewater paddling. No one, though, ever mentioned climbing.

Six years after his accident, Mark Wellman met Mike Corbett in Yosemite Valley. Corbett was then a janitor at the health center (with his own studio apartment), and Wellman was a Yosemite Park ranger. Bored with many of the mundane duties foisted upon rangers – "Welcome to Yosemite. Toilets? Just to the right." – Wellman relied on sport for release. He was a workout fiend who could lift weights for hours. Mesomorphic from the waist up, an extreme ectomorph from the waist down, he could do more than a hundred pull-ups in a row.

Still, he couldn't help thinking there should be more to his athletic life than hitting tennis balls, swimming, lifting weights, and hand-pedaling his recumbent bike around the valley. He was badly in need of some extra jolt of adrenaline. "I love getting a wicked pump, getting aerobic," he says. "You can get to a place beyond pain where it's almost euphoric."

Corbett, on the other hand, was subsisting on a maintenance dose of adrenaline. Called "Mr. El Cap" by some, he was an elite big-wall climber with more than seventy-five multiday climbs on his résumé.

"I thought Mark was a pretty hip dude," Corbett says of their initial meeting. "But at first I wasn't that comfortable around him. I knew that he had hurt himself in a climbing accident. As a climber, why would I want to hang out with a guy who was in a wheelchair from a climbing accident?"

About a year later, they found themselves drinking beer together at a party. "You know this happened climbing?" Mark blurted out.

"I did know that, Mark."

End of conversation.

Then one day in January 1989, Wellman wheeled excitedly up to Corbett. "Look at this," he said, waving a magazine at him. It was a copy of *Wheels and Spokes,* a magazine for the disabled, and on the cover was a picture of a woman in a wheelchair being lowered over a cliff by rope.

"Incredible," said Corbett. "I've never seen anything like that." After a fertile silence, during which both men took the measure of the other, Mike said, "Would you ever want to do . . . something like that? Climb, I mean."

"Yeah. In fact I've already talked to two guys about it."

The two climbers to whom Wellman referred, Pat Teague and Kevin Brown, had both taken the idea of a paraplegic rock climber seriously, which pleased Wellman. But while Corbett knew them both as capable and honest, he believed neither would ever be able to devote the time necessary to get Mark up a serious chunk of rock. Mark had made it clear that he wanted to leave his wheelchair behind, that he wouldn't be hogtied and hauled up by ropes like the woman in the magazine. Corbett was convinced that success was possible but that it would not come easily. It would take dedication, analysis, engineering, and practice. Mostly, it would take time, which he just happened to have in abundance.

The next night they ran into each other in the Mountain Room Bar. Many of Yosemite's most famous climbs had first been drawn up on cocktail napkins in the Mountain Room. Amid a general discussion on how one might engineer a rock climb for a team having four arms and two legs, Mike's eyes brightened and he said, "Why not climb El Cap with me?"

"Sure," Mark said, without hesitation.

After last call at the Mountain Room Bar, they moved to Mark's cabin and stayed up until 4:00 A.M. making plans, discussing tactics, cementing their partnership. Before saying good-bye, they shook hands on a covert deal to climb two of the most recognized rock faces in the world: El Capitan and Half Dome. To avoid putting undue pressure on themselves, they kept Half Dome a secret from everyone but their closest friends.

Mike would later say, "I knew Mark was an athletic dude. I had seen him with his shirt off on his row cycle (recumbent bike) and knew he was strong. I mean, just look at his shoulders. Plus he had a climbing background. I figured if a paraplegic could climb El Cap, Mark could be the one to do it."

It was not immediately apparent that it could be done at all. A few days after their agreement, Wellman and Corbett met near Church Bowl, away from the prying eyes of tourists and other climbers. Mark was able to wheel his chair through the snow to the base of a black oak. Mike tossed one end of his climbing rope over a thick branch about fifteen feet off the ground. Then he clipped two yellow Jumars onto the rope and began jugging up, using only his arms. Like ratchets, Jumars slide up a rope but bite hard when pulled down. He stopped after a few feet and, in between breaths, called down, "Mark, it's strenuous, but I'm doing it."

When it was Mark's turn, he parked his wheelchair beneath the rope and grabbed the Jumars, one with each hand. Then, grunting, groaning, and red-faced, he moved up the rope, sliding first one Jumar, then the other, gaining about six inches with each thrust. Fifteen strenuous minutes later, he reached the branch. He had succeeded – or had he? Picturing himself using that technique on a 3,600-foot face of El Capitan, he could only conclude: "This is going to be horrendous."

The next day, they ran into a friend, a cave explorer, who gave them an ascending device called a Gibbs, a rival brand to the Jumar, and one favored by cavers. With one Gibbs and one Jumar, the amount of effort required of Mark was cut in half. Getting to the top of El Capitan began to seem possible.

One can readily see why Wellman would want to have a go at El Capitan. It was a great challenge, something no paraplegic had ever done before, as well as a chance to be temporarily independent of his wheelchair. But what was in it for Corbett? "I loved the problem of engineering a climb up El Cap with Mark," he explains. "And I knew the climb would be good for me, that I'd learn a lot. If nothing else, I'd be learning about a day in the life of a guy in a wheelchair."

More like six months in the life of a guy in a wheelchair. Except for Easter week, when Wellman went home to his parents, they met once or twice every day for half a year, talking, planning, practicing, talking, designing, rigging, testing equipment, and talking. "We lived and breathed that climb," Corbett says. "It was the last thing I thought of before I went to sleep, the first thing I thought of when I got up. 'What am I going to do toward the climb today?' I've never in my life been so devoted to anything. I loved baseball as a kid, but I don't think I lived and breathed it."

One of the behind-the-scenes problems to which Corbett devoted endless hours was the protection of Wellman's legs. Mark's legs would hang when he did a pull-up, then jackknife into an "L" when he pushed the Jumar up. This would cause his withered legs to scrape against the abrasive granite. Protecting his legs was Wellman's biggest worry, and to find a solution Corbett set up a one-man sweatshop in his basement apartment. After several failures, he eventually managed to hand-stitch a pair of rock chaps out of cotton canvas, nylon, and closed-cell foam.

Meanwhile, they continued to refine their climbing equipment. Usually on a Class 6 aid route like those on El Capitan, the lead climber ascends by inserting pitons, nuts, or camming devices into cracks, then attaching a little sling ladder. After one pitch, the lead climber stops and top-anchors the rope, which the second climber shinnys up with Jumars. Because Jumars are usually used with stirrups, the legs do about 80 percent of the work. But since Mark's legs were just along for the ride, other arrangements had to be made. The solution: a pull-up bar attached to the ascending device.

Eventually everything was in place – equipment, commitment, partner. Wellman was confident he had the right guy setting ropes for him. The first time he saw Corbett climb, he was struck by his catlike mix of grace and power. And not only was he an aid specialist, he was an El Capitan specialist. He had climbed the mother of all rock a record forty-one times by twenty-five different routes (favorite: the "Nose"). He had climbed it with thirty-five different partners, in every month of the year (favorites: April and October), taking anywhere from ten hours to ten days to reach the top. For every twenty starts, he had nineteen successful finishes, a .950 average that instilled in him an infectious confidence. Corbett had even led their portly, jovial friend Murray Barnett to the top of El Capitan. Barnett, who Corbett admits is probably the least qualified climber ever to top out on El Cap, says that he never would have considered doing it without the rock-steady guidance of Corbett. "Mike has absolutely no B.S. in him," says Barnett. "He strives for truth. I don't even question him on the wall."

Steve Bosque, who has been on more than twenty-five climbs with Corbett and is his close friend, says that Mike is unparalleled as an organizer, a rope manager. "Some of the worst times of my life have been with him," he says, "but he has this incredible ability to make the best of a bad situation." It would be tough to find a worse situation than the ice storm Bosque and Corbett faced on Half Dome in March 1986. "We had a real bad night," Bosque recalls. "Corbett, who was hypothermic, was drifting in and out. But the next morning, before we were rescued, he rose to the occasion, organizing gear, being his usual bossy self."

Day 7. It was afternoon when they reached Chickenhead Ledge, four hundred feet from the top of El Cap. "Prettiest damn ledge I've ever seen," Corbett mumbled, leaning exhaustedly against the rock. Bathed in gritty sweat, he felt as though he had been working on the pyramids. "Chickenhead Ledge, Mark," he called down. "Let me get clipped on."

"Right."

Corbett describes their mood that evening as "slightly less than euphoric," adding, "Even though it's not over till it's over, it was beginning to look like it was going to be over – and in our favor. We hadn't dropped anything, hadn't screwed up, hadn't hollered at each other. Things were going good."

That night, too excited to sleep, Corbett lay awake beneath a pointillistic canopy of stars until after 3:00 A.M., ruminating on his estranged family, on topping out the next day, on what he and Mark were accomplishing. "It's like making love with a beautiful girl," he thought, "and stopping while you're doing it and thinking, 'I'm really doing this!' Well, we're really doing this! As Mark says, 'The crip is doing the big stone.' But aahhh, tomorrow we demobilize. Get to see Gwen, take a hot shower and, most of all, not hammer any more pitons. Going to eat ice cream instead of beanie-weenies, drink soda, and just do whatever the hell I want."

Day 8. On what figured to be their last day, Mark and Mike were up by 5:30, ready to go by 7:00. "Still have to put in the protection," Corbett thought, hammering in a two-inch angle piton with that reverberating *ping, ping, ping* that told him all was right. "Still getting my three feet here, my three feet there. Checking every knot twice. Don't want to fuck up so near the end. Going to be a lot of hoopla on top—gotta go suck it up. We deserve to wallow in a little glory."

Waiting for them on top of El Capitan were maybe seventy-five reporters, friends, acquaintances, and interested strangers, possibly more people on the rock than ever before. Certainly more hoopla. All available pack animals in the park had been rented. An NBC helicopter darted and dived noisily overhead, defying a federal law that required aircraft to stay higher than two thousand feet above the rim.

On the rock, Wellman called up to his partner: "Corbett, man, I can smell the summit." Only a hundred feet from the top, a grimy, exhausted Mike Corbett was working as fast as he dared. "We hauled ass the last day," he would say, "though we still weren't setting any speed records. People may laugh at this, but I'm not a daredevil. We did three pitches and finished just after noon. We were inspired. Also, I was in desperate need of a cigarette." (He smoked a carton on the climb, but has since quit.)

At last the rock lost its verticality. They reached a ledge near the top, still separated from the masses by a low-angled granitic slab. Since Mark could not pull himself up rock that deviated so far from vertical, Corbett would have to carry him the rest of the way.

As they removed their gear, they hooted and hollered like merry pranksters. Corbett chuckled and said, "We definitely came up El Cap the hard way." Wellman shook his fist at the valley and said, "It feels really good to be here."

Mike bent down and Mark scrambled onto his back, lacing his arms loosely around his neck. As they started up the final rise, Mike stumbled, sending loose rocks clattering down the slope. A lightning bolt of terror ripped through Wellman. "Whoa, Corbett, man, this is the scariest part of the whole climb. You fall here and we roll all the way to the valley."

"Sorry, I guess I haven't walked in a while."

As they crested the last hump, human heads came into view. People began clapping and cheering and pointing cameras at them. *Click, click, click* went the shutters.

"Wow, it's like the World Series," said Mike.

Still on Corbett's back, Wellman raised his fist in victory, and the crowd let out a thunderous cheer that sent shivers down their spines. The camera clicks continued, like automatic gunfire, only friendlier.

As Corbett (left) *and Wellman finished their ascent of El Capitan, they were met by a small crowd of reporters and well-wishers. (Courtesy of Gwen Schneider)*

One picture appearing the next day in newspapers all across the country best captured the emotional moment. Corbett has on his trademark headband. Wellman, still on Corbett's back, is cheek to jowl with him. Both men are gritty and stubbly and bonded in manhood. Both men wear triumphant smiles, with Corbett's threatening to split his face. With his head thrown back, his eyes closed, his teeth bared, he is the very embodiment of ecstasy.

After being led to an area cordoned off from the masses, they sat on sleeping bags and fielded questions.

"How do you feel now?"

"Exhausted."

"Filthy."

"Good."

"Did you ever think you weren't going to make it?"

"No."

"No."

"Why did you do it?"

"Challenge."

"Fun."

"What's next?"

All four of their eyes darted toward Half Dome, but Wellman simply said, "Hot shower and hot meal," then looked at his partner.

"We just want to enjoy the moment," said Corbett, flashing him a look in return.

This was the first time they could see Half Dome since they had started up El Cap, but it had never left their minds. If anything, Half Dome had the stronger magnetic appeal. In 1863, Josiah Whitney, the first head of the California Geological Survey, had pronounced Half Dome "perfectly inaccessible, being probably the only one of all the prominent points about the Yosemite which never has been, and never will be, trodden by human foot." Although Whitney was proven wrong twelve years later, and although Half Dome has been climbed many times since, both Wellman and Corbett were lured by the challenge of scaling something once declared "inaccessible."

It was now accessible – to scramblers relying on a pair of steel cables connected to the rock, and to technical climbers via several routes. Two years after their El Cap climb, Corbett and Wellman would do the Half Dome route called "Tis-a-ack." It had first been climbed by Royal Robbins thirty-five years earlier, and only about twenty times since. "The rock on 'Tis-a-ack' is crumbly, piton placements are insecure, and retreat is just about impossible," Corbett says. "Unlike the El Cap routes, 'Tis-a-ack' stays in shadows until late afternoon, and those frosty mornings make it hard to get out of your sleeping bag.

"I like to compare El Cap and Half Dome to people," adds Corbett, a man uniquely qualified to employ such a metaphor. "I see El Cap as this jovial, bright, sunny person bouncing up to you, shaking your hand, saying 'What's happening, brother?' But Half Dome is dark, foreboding, someone you wouldn't want to meet in an alley. El Cap is a cliff," he adds, "while Half Dome is a mountain, with a summit that was once thought inaccessible. El Cap's summit is not at all remote. You could easily build a road to the top."

Corbett and Half Dome have had, well, a rocky affair. Prior to the Mark and Mike Climb, he had scaled El Capitan forty-one times, Half Dome only six. His closest brush with death – and his only rescue – happened on the south face of Half Dome. On another occasion, he and a partner were in position to do a route on the southwest face of

Half Dome when Corbett discovered a badly mutilated body. End of climb. "Apparently he had gone up the cables, then tried to go down the face," says Corbett. "He had taken the ultimate winger. I was so shaken I didn't go up there again for about six years."

He got over it. In September 1991, Corbett and Wellman did unto Half Dome as they had done unto El Capitan. Their dramatic thirteen-day (five days over budget) rain-soaked, flu-ridden ascent stands as a testimonial to teamwork, endurance, and rock engineering.

On top of El Capitan, Corbett and Wellman moved to another spot and, with Half Dome framed appropriately in the background, did a live interview with Tom Brokaw, himself a climber.

"Mike, was this climb harder than you expected?" Brokaw asked.

"Yeah. It's the hardest thing I've ever done in my life," Mike said matter-of-factly.

"Mark, any advice for other disabled people?"

"Focus your abilities and go for it," Mark said.

Following a brief lead by Brokaw, NBC News suddenly had Mark and Mike on one half of the screen, Corbett's family in Houston on the other half. To Corbett's mother, Brokaw was saying, "Jean, what do you say to a son who hasn't been in touch all these years?"

"We certainly enjoyed watching him every night," she replied with a heavy Houston twang.

With that, Mike Corbett, heretofore the most private, anonymous of athletes, was having his family laundry aired before millions of viewers. When Brokaw queried him, he looked more uncomfortable than he'd ever been on El Cap. "Yeah, I hope they can come to Yosemite," he said haltingly. "They'd really like it here. Uh, we got a lot to talk about."

After nearly four hours of relentless attention, the two climbers left the top, Wellman on horseback, Corbett by foot. When Corbett reached Tamarack Campground, some kids recognized him and began following him as if he were Rocky Balboa. Caught up in the adulation, Corbett responded by bestowing gifts. He gave away his harness, hardware, clothes—everything but his pants. "You don't know how happy this will make them," gushed one kid's mother. As he was leaving the campground, a man gave him a fried trout. "Wow, hot food!" Corbett exclaimed, eating while he walked.

When Mark and Mike returned to the valley, they had to stop and look up at their big stone. Mark, head tilted back, eyes misting over, smiled and said, "Wow, that's where we were this morning. It's nice to be here looking up, with it done."

Corbett smiled and said, "Dude, doesn't it look smaller now?"

Epilogue I. A year after the Half Dome climb, I met Wellman and Corbett in Yosemite Valley. For them it was a reunion of sorts, as Wellman no longer lives in Yosemite. Having quit his ranger job and hit the lecture circuit (one thousand dollars per), he now shares a house near Lake Tahoe with his girlfriend, Paulette Irving. He was in Yosemite to sign his new autobiography, *Climbing Back.*

Though not the climbing bum he once was, Mike Corbett still does a lot of hanging out in Yosemite. He and his wife, Nikyra, and their ten-month-old daughter, Ellie, are shoehorned into a tiny trailer in El Portal, gateway to Yosemite National Park. The El Portal Trailer Park, perched on the banks of the Merced River, is more aesthetically pleasing than most of its ilk, but only slightly. On this 101-degree August day, the heat claws at the trailer's metal roof as though it has talons. It is like living in a box of matches.

Visit Mike Corbett and you can't help thinking that maybe he too should be cashing in on the Mark and Mike Climbs. After all, it was a partnership, and he did his share of the work. Of course, that's an outsider's view, for there is no evidence that Mike feels slighted. From his perspective, he has plenty: a workable marriage, a daughter he adores, and the opportunity to live twenty minutes from a climbing mecca that just might be the most beautiful place on Earth. On the days Nikyra goes off to work as a park ranger, Corbett plays dad and househusband; on her off-days, he often climbs. He had just scaled El Capitan for the forty-eighth time. Life could be a whole lot worse.

On the twenty-minute drive into Yosemite Valley to attend Wellman's book signing, he says, "I have no resentment toward Mark and what he's been able to make off the climb. He was the hook. I'm just glad I could be part of something that inspired so many people, that is still inspiring so many people.

"I may be in the shadows, but that's okay. I don't need to be patted on the back anymore. I had my fill of that. Resentment toward Mark— nah! Besides, it's not his fault that people would rather shake his hand than mine."

The book signing is a case in point. For two hours, wide-eyed devotees line up, some in wheelchairs, all clutching copies of *Climbing Back*. Wellman greets everyone with a warm smile. In a tank top, his weight-lifter's shoulders are evident. Like his friends say: "After a few minutes you forget Mark is in a wheelchair."

While waiting for Wellman to finish, Corbett says, "One of the high points of my life was doing El Cap and Half Dome with Mark. Things happened—like Senator Dole's bill of commendation [passed unanimously in the U.S. Senate "for their extraordinary feat of bravery"], like going to the White House—that wouldn't have been in my wildest dreams. I have some pretty vivid dreams, but going to the White House wouldn't have been one of them."

Their friend Murray Barnett points out that the Half Dome climb almost didn't happen. For weeks prior to that climb, Wellman and Corbett didn't speak to one another. "It was the promoters and agents that threw a wedge between them," he says. "Mike, especially, couldn't stand the hype." Though the climb and even their friendship were threatened, they eventually got past it. On this day they are friends.

Corbett says he intends to do El Capitan twice more—"fifty is a nice round number"—then retire from big-wall climbing. "I still love climbing and I'll never quit, but now that I have a baby and a marriage, those things are more important. After several thousand pitches, I guess I've lost some enthusiasm. You spend some cold nights out, have some gear stolen, it's disillusioning. Kinda like finding out Elvis is fat."

Although Corbett is hanging up his rurps, bongs, and ascenders, he has no intention of becoming a flatlander. Instead, he will become a peak bagger. "About 98 percent of my climbing has been big-wall aid climbing in Yosemite," he says. "I've lived in Yosemite for twenty years and I've never even climbed the highest peak in the park (Mount Lyell, elevation 13,131 feet). I want to do Mount Hood and Mount Shasta. It's embarrassing to say I haven't done Mount Shasta."

Though Corbett's words suggest that he cares what others think, his character suggests otherwise. He is heavily inner-directed, though he still pays attention to those he respects. "John Dossi, head of Yosemite Search and Rescue, instilled in me that being a good climber doesn't make you a good person. That's so true. At this stage of my life, it's more important to me to be a good person. And more of a challenge, too, because being good is so hard. Doing the right thing is the hardest thing in life."

Back at his trailer, he says, "I used to think if I was afraid up on the rock, I didn't belong there. But now I know that fear is healthy. It's not

In recognition of their accomplishment, Wellman, with Corbett by his side, throws out the first ball at an Oakland Athletics game. (Courtesy of Mike Corbett)

shameful to be afraid, it's intelligent. With fear comes respect. I'm still afraid of heights, but I know if I tie that rope around my waist and onto the rock that nothing is going to happen to me unless I make a foolish mistake – and I'm not the kind to make foolish mistakes. I don't drive fast; I don't ride my bike with my hands off the handlebars; I do what I know I can do, without pushing the envelope."

He acknowledges that some climbers "might be critical of that, might say I'm not fulfilling myself. But. . . . " – here he gazes with fatherly affection upon his daughter, who smiles and gurgles at him in return – ". . . I feel very fulfilled."

Epilogue II. In April 1993, Mark Wellman and Jeff Pagels, teammates on the United States Disabled Cross-Country Ski Team, became the first paraplegics to ski across the Sierra Nevada mountains. The two began their fifty-mile journey near Lee Vining, pushing their sit-skis up over 10,000-foot Tioga Pass, finishing four days later at Crane Flat. While Pagels required the assistance of two able-bodied skiers to get over some difficult terrain, Wellman completed the trip under his own power. "I like to test myself to the limit," he said, grinning.

Mike Corbett, a collector of climbing antiques – gear, articles, books – is working toward opening a climbing museum around Yosemite. In May 1993 he climbed El Capitan for the fiftieth time.

SHARON WOOD

On Top of the World

Reaching the summit is not the significant thing, because you learn nothing on the top. It is during the journey that the learning takes place.

—John Amatt

Sharon Wood, alone, in the dark, and 28,000 feet above sea level, felt panic well up in her throat like bile. Fighting demons, she sucked hard through her oxygen mask but couldn't get her fill. A not-too-distant rumbling filled her with dread. She was in what the Europeans call the "death zone," and far out of her own comfort zone. Swallowing, she tried to remember . . . what? It was so laborious, thinking at high altitude. More than five vertical miles above sea level, buffeted by ferocious winds that had plunged the chill factor to minus fifty degrees, ideas trudged through her brain like soldiers through molasses. She had to sort out each thought, arrange it, impose order.

She'd been to the top of Mount Everest—that was certain—and now she was heading down—equally certain. She'd had a partner—Dwayne Conglin, er, Congdon—but where was he now? He'd been right behind her—and then suddenly he wasn't. . . .

Now she was questioning everything: "Is he behind me? Or ahead of me? Did I take the right route? Of course, I did—these are our fixed ropes. . . ."

Ah, the dreamlike lunacy of it all. Leaning against a wall of ice, she dozed off for a moment, then jerked herself awake. "It's getting harder and harder to rouse myself from sleep," she thought. "Better get going." She guessed she had waited thirty minutes for Dwayne, but who could know for sure? Her watch was hanging on a string around her neck, protected from the severe cold by six layers of clothes.

It was a clear, windy night ornamented by a full moon, but little light reached her in the Hornbein Couloir, a steep, rocky gully, a wicked gash up the side of the mountain. She relied instead on her headlamp, which illuminated an area no more than three feet in front of her. Picking her way down the steep ice, her mind churned out another ragged series of ideas. "I'm doing the right thing," she thought, with only partial conviction. "I'll get to the tent, light the stove, get some water happening. We've had nothing to drink or eat since . . . well, a long time ago."

But when she got to where she thought Camp VI should be, nothing looked familiar. "I've gone past our camp," she thought. "I can't possibly find it. I'm finished." Then, just as she began to feel panic's cold clutches, she spotted the ghostly glint of an oxygen bottle in the snow. Camp!

The tent was cold and empty—just like she felt. Lying in her sleeping bag, she was struck by how quiet it was. Even her mind, previously so cluttered, was temporarily silenced. The mental focus she had maintained for seventeen hours—get to the top and back to the tent—had dissolved, leaving, briefly, a vacuum. Then the question, terrifying in its isolation: "*What have I done?*"

"*I'll tell you what you've done,*" *said another voice.* "*You deserted your partner, that's what.*"

"*But Dwayne kept telling me to go ahead, said he was fine. Besides, I had to go ahead when we got to the fixed ropes.*"

"*Not that far ahead!*"

"*How could I know?*"

She thought of John Laughlin, a climber and close friend who was a big reason she was on Everest. John, an artist and writer, a fit and robust man, was killed by an avalanche while climbing a frozen waterfall. The kind of guy who was always pushing the envelope, he had been a huge inspiration to her. His death made her think, "What if I died now? Would I feel fulfilled? Would I feel I had done what I needed to do in this life?" It made her get off the fence, made her start pursuing her guiding certificate, made her start doing serious climbs and preparing for Everest. With the sudden realization that she was living far below her potential came the thought: "Oh my God, I better start doing everything I've always wanted to do. I better start living."

Ninety difficult minutes after her arrival at the tent, Sharon heard the crunch of crampons on snow. It was 3:30 A.M. Dwayne was home.

There was no time for celebration. As with every other victory that day, this one was immediately followed by a life-threatening challenge. Dwayne had fallen behind when he ran out of oxygen; he'd had to stop and rip off his mask, which instead of nourishing him was suffocating him. Without the elixir of oxygen, his extremities had become frostnipped. His feet were numb and his fingers lacked dexterity. Sharon took off his crampons and boots for him and rubbed his feet.

Next she began to heat ice for water. Suffering from a lack of sleep and oxygen, she was moving slowly. After struggling briefly with a new gas canister, she decided she had a proper seal and struck a match. *Fumph!* The tent was a fireball with the two climbers at the center. Frantically, they heaved the stove and some burning clothes out of the tent. In the oxygen-scarce atmosphere, the flames died quickly, but not before they had melted Wood's goggles, singed off every hair on her face, and burned a basketball-size hole in the roof of the tent.

At the moment of conflagration, when death seemed near, Wood's mind lost its sluggishness, and became hyperactivated. In her mind's eye, she saw a newspaper headline: "First North American Woman to Summit Everest Dies on Descent." She saw her own epitaph: "A cruel twist of fate – reached the top of Everest and died in a fiery tent."

Conceived in Ireland, Sharon Wood was born in Halifax, Nova Scotia, on May 18, 1957. The youngest of four kids, Sharon credits her parents with introducing her to the outdoors and encouraging her to pursue the things that make her happy. Heading the list of things that didn't make her happy was school. "I was the kind of kid who had trouble staying inside the margins," she says. "I hated doing things that didn't make sense to me and was always looking for different ways of doing routine jobs."

Her father was a pilot in the Canadian Navy and Air Force. Later he flew small planes, excelling as a crop duster, fire bomber, and bush pilot. He often took Sharon hiking in the woods of Eastern Canada. "My father gave me adventure," she says. "He had a passion for the outdoors. I lived for the days he would take us skiing, hiking, or canoeing."

When she was seven, the family loaded up a trailer, drove across Canada, and took up residence in Burnaby, British Columbia, a suburb of Vancouver. Sharon's troubles with school intensified; she found it crowded, impersonal, restrictive. "It was like we were two thousand kids being squeezed through a small hole," she says.

Like so many other disenchanted students, she found physical outlets. She climbed rocks competitively with her brother and rode

Sharon Wood's eight reasons to climb

1. For the opportunity to find the best in myself
2. For the adventure
3. For the intense relationships and camaraderie
4. For the confidence it gives me
5. For the spiritual benefits
6. For the natural beauty
7. For the endorphins I get from really exerting myself
8. For the challenge of channeling fear

her bike long distances around Vancouver. Her roaming spirit was given a long leash by her parents. "My father really encouraged me to think for myself," she says. "He recognized that I was a free thinker, or at least a different kind of thinker. My mother encouraged me no matter what I did, whether I was cutting out scraps of paper or scribbling on the walls."

With so many choices, she was bound to make some mistakes. One road she temporarily trod was the one posted Drugs and Delinquency. "I was good at pushing the limits with anything I did," she says. "There was a time when that meant staying out late, taking the most drugs, even stealing." She became an accomplished shoplifter because "there was good adventure in it." A skinny kid, her signature snatch was wearing several pairs of pants out of a store.

At fifteen she hit bottom, which was not rock but rubber. First she overdosed on LSD, wandering the mean streets of Vancouver in a hallucinative haze. "It was a terrifying experience that affects my life even today," she says, "I never want to get that low again. It makes me strive for high-quality, positive experiences, and to make life as good as I can because I've seen how ugly it can get."

Apparently her epiphany was not immediate, because soon after that bad trip she was arrested for shoplifting. She can still remember the sound of the cell door slamming behind her, the sinking feeling of her spirit being smothered. Although she spent only a few hours in jail, it seemed like days. "The bars really brought home the fact that I could affect my experiences. I came to realize that I had to take responsibility for my own life. It was like being the writer, the director, and the actor in my own play."

At age sixteen she dropped out of school and took a job, first as an A&W carhop, then as a waitress in a pancake house. Open the diction- ary to *adventure* and neither of those places are pictured, so Sharon left home and went to Jasper, Alberta, in the Canadian Rockies. "My sister, whom I had always looked up to, first told me of this magical place with mountains surrounding it in all directions." In Jasper she fell in with some like-minded friends, and together they hired a mountain guide and took a rock-climbing course. Sharon was fascinated by the mix of mental and physical gymnastics required to be a good rock climber.

At seventeen, she took a three-week Outward Bound course, which further stirred her passions. One of the instructors was Laurie Skreslet, who would become the first Canadian to summit Mount Everest. "He made me feel special," she says. "Seeing people working as mountain guides, instructors, I wanted to be an instructor at Outward Bound so badly it hurt."

After the course, she applied for a job. She can still remember the director's condescending retort. "You know," he said, "everybody here has been to the Himalaya or done something outstanding," leaving the taunting question – "What have *you* done?" – hanging in the air.

"That man drove me deeper into the mountain world," she says. "I decided the next time I came back I was going to be so overqualified, they wouldn't be able to say no."

With a talented but inexperienced group of friends, she started the Yamnuska Mountain School to teach adults and kids how to rock climb. "Our skills were just a notch ahead of most of the people we were teaching," she remembers.

Not for long, for she quickly improved. Willing to try most any- thing, she even dabbled in ice climbing, a daunting sport that con- vinced her that psychological strength is more important that physical strength. "I'm probably not even as strong as most women. I couldn't win most arm-wrestling contests. But then most people couldn't go up Everest. I do have good cardiovascular strength, but the real contest is here (points to head) not here (points to body). It's trying to penetrate those mind-made limitations and tap our potential. Ninety percent of our potential we rarely use."

She had a chance early to explore her mountaineering potential when she joined an all-woman expedition on Mount Logan in the

Yukon, Canada's highest mountain, (19,850 feet). "The goal wasn't so much to climb the mountain as to prove that women could do it on their own," she says. "Now that's not really my cup of tea, but then I was young and impressionable and had read all the feminist literature.

"It's amazing that we made it to the top of the mountain," she adds, shaking her head. "Especially when you consider that I was the most experienced on the team, with only two big mountains to my credit – Mount Robson and Mount Athabaska."

Although Wood is a high-school dropout, she has remained a student all her life. Besides reading voluminously to compensate for her limited schooling, she has gleaned lessons from every major event in her life. "On the Mount Logan climb, I discovered that it's important for me to climb with people I like to be with. And that you should climb a mountain because you want to climb a mountain, not to try to prove some point. Others on the expedition had a more feminist viewpoint."

In 1979 she journeyed to Yosemite and climbed the "Nose" on El Capitan with Albi Sole. The lesson? She discovered that big-wall climbing was not her forte. "I was terrified," she says. "Overwhelmed by the exposure. It wasn't my element. Big walls didn't come naturally to me like alpine did. With climbing you have to love it to be good at it."

In 1982, a Canadian expedition succeeded in putting the first two Canadians, Laurie Skreslet and Pat Morrow, on the summit of Mount Everest. "I entertained fantasies of applying for that team," says Wood. "I'm glad I didn't. It was a huge production, and they had a lot of problems [three Sherpas were killed]. I wasn't ready anyway. I wasn't sure yet if I loved the sport or just loved what it stood for."

Her test piece would be Mount McKinley, at 20,320 feet the highest mountain in North America and one of the most dangerous in the world (eleven people were killed on McKinley in 1992). "When Greg Cronn and I went to McKinley, we considered ourselves novices. But we had a lot of experience with ice and frozen waterfalls and eventually decided the Canadian Rockies must be the best training ground in the world."

They attempted the classic Cassin route (Ricardo Cassin was a pioneer in difficult, high-altitude alpine routes). Reportedly, a dozen expedition parties were starting about the same time, but when Wood and Cronn got to the base of the route, they had it to themselves. "Climbers had turned around because of the black ice or the bergschrund, but that was just everyday stuff for us."

The climb was no romp in the snow. Caught in a storm at 19,000 feet without food, they had to burrow under a boulder for a day and a half, but Sharon never felt out of control. "We aced McKinley," she chirps in her charming English accent. "And I found out I loved that kind of climbing. High-altitude alpine work is the most involved climbing you can possibly do. It takes so much from you in every area. It demands physical strength, yes, but mental strength too. It's about eighty-twenty mental. What I love about this sport is it's a fantastic way to explore your potential, to find out what you've really got in there. On McKinley I found out that I thrived in that environment and that I could do so much more than I thought I could."

Meanwhile, Everest was still on the back burner.

Soon after her success on McKinley, Wood began a four-year partnership with a man named Carlos Buhler. It was Buhler who would supply the necessary push elevating her to the next level of mountaineering. "Carlos had a passion for mountains and pursuing women, and that was about it," she says with a chuckle. "He needed a partner and liked having a protégé – for a while – and I liked being a protégé."

In 1984, Buhler and Wood joined an expedition to Makalu, the fifth-highest mountain in the world (27,824 feet). With an ultra-light expedition – four climbers, one doctor, no Sherpas – they climbed within three hundred feet of the summit. It was, in strict summit thinking, a failure. But Wood was incapable of seeing it that way. "Very few light expeditions had ever succeeded on such a high mountain," she says. "We spent three months above 18,000 feet, and almost made it."

On Makalu she saw Everest almost every day. Ten miles away, it was nearly in focus now. "Makalu reconfirmed my commitment to the sport," she says. "I discovered that I did well above 24,000 feet, relatively speaking. I felt at home there. I could eat, drink, and sleep – if I took the right combination of drugs (favorite: Halcion). I began to see Everest as a real possibility."

There was another important Makalu lesson. "Missing the top on Makalu made me want an eight-thousand-meter summit [there are just fourteen in the world] that much more," she says. "I knew I'd be willing to step further out of my comfort zone the next time."

Wood applied to the 1986 Canadian Light Everest Expedition. Even though most of the climbers on that team were her friends and peers, and her climbing career was an open book, they added her only reluctantly to the expedition. "They feared the dynamics of having one

From her childhood in Canada to her expeditions in the Himalaya, Sharon Wood has always been at home in the mountains. (Courtesy of Bruno Engler)

woman and twelve men," she explains. "I was shocked. I love men — they've been my peers, my partners, all my life — but not necessarily in a romantic way. It was really disappointing that they were worried about that."

She countered in the only way she knew how: by adding something bold to her résumé. She and Buhler traveled to South America, where they did an alpine ascent of the south face of Aconcagua (22,834), the highest peak in the Americas. "It is a 14,000-foot face, very difficult, bad conditions, bad weather, one of the seven great climbs of the world, according to Messner. And we made it!"

From there they went on to Peru. "Carlos was guiding a lot while we were down there," says Wood, "which left me on my own. So I soloed a couple of alpine faces that required a bivouac on the way. It was another big test. Being there alone, a hundred percent committed, it really sealed it for me. I remember standing on the summit, looking out at the Andes, thinking, 'Whoa, I really did it!'"

There was one final South American test of Wood's mettle — a six-thousand-foot unclimbed face on Huascaran (22,205 feet), the highest mountain in Peru. They reached the base of the face at noon, when rockfall was most likely, but they were too excited to wait till morning. In the funnel of a steep, narrow ice gully below a five-thousand-foot mixed face, Wood had just finished putting in an ice screw when baseball-size rocks began cascading by her. Before she could look up, she was struck in the left shoulder, a blow hard enough to rip her off her stance. It felt like her arm had been torn from its socket. She shrieked in pain, then stayed very still for several minutes.

They spent the night on the mountain, assuming that they would turn around at first light. All night long, Wood kept testing her shoulder. Next morning her arm was so stiff and painful, she couldn't lift an ice ax above her waist. But the weather was good, and she discovered she was more committed to the climb than ever. Reaching deep within, she persevered all the way to the top – six more days of climbing, the last two without food.

Two weeks later, back in Canada, she learned that she had a broken scapula. The lesson: "On Huascaran I learned about my threshold," she says. "If I could do that climb under those conditions, I could do anything. As long as I kept it together mentally, I could do it. I had significant pain, but it was the kind of pain I could transcend. I could override the alarm bells going off saying 'Stop.' It was fascinating to me. I could survive. I took that experience and applied it to Everest."

In preparation for Everest, Wood ran hills and did mountain guiding, burnishing her already highly developed cardiovascular system. "After months of some wild trail runs and hauling people up mountains, I was in pretty good shape," she says modestly. "But I could never get very scientific about it. I hated the weight room, and if I measured my resting heart rate, it was just out of curiosity." Her resting heart rate, about thirty-eight, is indeed a curiosity; normal is about seventy.

Attack Everest from the less-traveled Tibetan side, as the 1986 Canadian Light Expedition did, and you can drive to 17,000 feet. Instead of the twenty-day trek into base camp that climbers face on the Nepalese side, the Canadians faced only seventeen miles by foot to base camp.

That was, however, seventeen miles with three tons of gear. Sure-footed yaks hauled their equipment the first nine miles of the bouldery morraine that was more rock than ice, until the glacier forced them to turn back. Philosophically opposed to using porters or Sherpas, the climbers themselves lugged multiple loads the rest of the way from the glacier to base camp.

At the foot of the Rongbuk Glacier, 16,800 feet above sea level, base camp was set in a bowl formed by mountains rising above 20,000 feet. There were a few tufts of grass here and there, but mostly the landscape was barren, rocky moraine. The only apparent wildlife: a few fat birds scurrying about. "They looked like they might be good eating," Wood says. "They were slow, but not slow enough."

The next day, an American team arrived at base camp, intent on climbing Everest's Great Couloir. This team, too, included one woman: Annie Whitehouse, of Albuquerque, New Mexico. A week later a Spanish team arrived to climb the North Ridge, adding some color to the huge, rubble-strewn, monochromatic wash plain.

The deleterious effects of a rapid ascent to 17,000 feet soon became apparent. People moped around as though suffering from a hangover of Himalayan proportions. More than 12,000 feet below Everest's foreboding summit, they were already bitterly cold. "I put on every layer I had and was still freezing," says Wood. "It was ridiculous. We had driven to an altitude that we should have been physically working through. I also think that's what led to so much sickness on our team."

Wood visited the nearby Rongbuk Monastery, one of the highest places of worship in the world. She lingered over the memorial cairns honoring those who had died on the mountain. Supposedly one climber had died on Everest for every three who had made it to the top. Especially sobering was the cairn for Marty Hoey, an American woman who died in 1983 trying for the summit by the same route the Canadians would be attempting.

Despite the acclimatization problems, the bitter cold, the barren, lifeless surroundings, the reminders of death, Wood felt strangely at home at base camp. "I had a feeling I belonged," she says. "I felt like I was going to do it."

In the next forty-five days, the team anchored three miles of rope linking five camps. By the end of March, Camp II was established at 19,500 feet at the base of a spur. Camp III was then carved out halfway up the spur. After a succession of storms buried Camp III in snow, it had to be reclaimed several times and was finally occupied in mid-April. Benefiting from a spate of good weather, they established Camps IV and V by the third week of April. But with the monsoon season fast approaching, they were running out of time. The first summit team would have to install Camp VI at 27,000 feet en route to the top.

The load-by-load labor of slogging tons of equipment to supply camps on a big mountain is anything but glamorous. Carrying heavy packs day after day over the same terrain requires a vision of a greater good and an ability to work with a team—an ability alien to many climbers. It is a special challenge for those with no realistic chance of going to the top. By the time Camp V was stocked, Sharon estimated she had gained vertical distance equivalent to climbing the mountain seven times.

The sustained stress of doing hard physical labor at high altitude took its inevitable toll. A respiratory virus ravaged the team, eventually crippling everyone except Sharon, who points out, "Everyone on the American team got the same virus except Annie Whitehouse. Coincidence? I doubt it. I mean, look what we're designed to do — have babies, for God's sake. That's the ultimate."

Even if climbers escape illness, they are destined to experience a marked physical deterioration above 24,000 feet. "It's a paradox of expedition-style ascents," says Sharon. "All the incremental steps — the hauling of loads, the establishment of camps — tend to block the attainment of the ultimate objective. Long exposure to altitude burns you out by the time you're in position to make a summit bid."

Like most expeditions, they fell behind schedule. At best they had another two weeks before bad weather shut them down; at worst it was already upon them. Expedition leader Jim Elzinga suggested a time-saving detour. Instead of climbing the West Ridge Direct, they could traverse out onto the north face and ascend the Hornbein Couloir. Some of the climbers thought this a cop-out. They preferred to fail on the original route than succeed on a less technical one. Wood, and all the others who had a chance for the summit, argued that with bad weather on the way, success demanded an adjustment to reality. For a while the dispute divided the team, but eventually the revisionists carried the vote and the dissenters came around.

When it was time to decide the summit teams, only four of the thirteen climbers were still able to function above 24,000 feet. Only Sharon Wood, Dwayne Congdon, Barry Blanchard, and Kevin Doyle were fit enough to be considered for the summit. The others, beaten down by sickness or fatigue, lay around base camp like torture victims. Even the Big Four were mentally and physically exhausted after enduring weeks of rampaging winds, subzero temperatures, and severe oxygen debt.

"I think Sharon and Dwayne should be the first summit team, and Laurie agrees," said Elzinga. "Barry and Kevin would be on the second team."

"No way," put in Wood. "That's not fair. Barry and Dwayne have been climbing together. They deserve a shot. I'll wait till Albi is

Sharon Wood's two best places to climb

1. Near my home in Alberta
2. The Peruvian Andes – a high-altitude Alpine mecca with thirty peaks over 6,000 meters, most within a day's reach

healthy and go with him the second time around." After a pause, she added, none too convincingly, "The routes will be established, Camp Six will be established, the possibility is there."

The meeting broke up with nothing decided. Laurie Skreslet immediately began lobbying for Sharon to be on that first summit team. He thought it would be good for her, yes, but also for Canada. National pride was at stake, he said. The Americans, farther out on the face, had reached the same elevation, with Annie Whitehouse targeted for the summit. (Beset with dissension, the Americans would eventually drop out at about 25,000 feet.) Would the first North American woman to summit Everest be Canadian or American?

Elzinga, in a private conversation with Wood, asked her, "Sharon, what's the difference between a Canadian and an American?"

"What do you mean?"

"Canadians too often seem content with second place. Do you want it or not?"

"Sure I want it."

Later, alone, she thought, "If I wait around much longer I'm going to lose this edge I'm riding on. And if I spend very long at altitude, I'll get weaker, not stronger."

It was something to consider. At 25,000 feet, the alveolar pressure forcing oxygen into a climber's blood stream is one third of normal. Muscle mass gets metabolized for energy, causing a precipitous loss of weight. But it's the brain that suffers most at high altitude. Ideas come slowly, sluggishly; judgment falters. And the higher one climbs, the more faculties deteriorate. Sleep becomes all but impossible. "It is so discouraging," Wood says. "You're dead-dog tired and can't sleep. Without enough oxygen, you wake up gasping for air."

What it all adds up to is a marked decrease in the amount of work a climber can do in a day. Says Elzinga: "To put it in layman's terms, if you were to go to your local health club and take an exercise test, then go to Nepal and do the same, you'd find your work capacity at 20,000 feet is one third what it was at sea level."

Next morning she told Elzinga she had changed her mind. He suggested she discuss it with the others, particularly Barry Blanchard, who would have to switch places with her. Blanchard's response nailed it down for her: "Woody, I'm going to climb this sucker if I have to stay till August. Go for it!"

On May 15, when Dwayne and Sharon were set to leave Camp I to begin their summit bid, Elzinga took them aside for a pep talk. He counseled them to treat Everest like any other mountain. "Don't lose your caution over the glory of this mountain," he said. "Don't die for it!"

Barry and Kevin went along as backup. They would carry in support, help establish Camp VI, then retreat to Camp V. As Camp VI did not yet exist, it would take four people carrying heavy loads to support two people for one night.

At Camp II they waited out two days of storms before starting up for Camp IV in unsettled weather. Midway through that five-thousand-foot carry, they ran into a vicious storm. A frigid wind lashed them, spitting snow between its teeth. Spindrift avalanches were everywhere. Suffering under the worst conditions yet, they might have measured their progress in inches per minute.

Sharon tried out the Elzinga philosophy on Kevin. "I think we should turn around," she screamed over the bawling wind.

"Why?" Kevin shouted back.

"Look at the conditions. They're the worst yet. Jim said . . . ."

"To hell with that! This is not like any other mountain. It's fucking Mount Everest! We can't come back tomorrow."

And so up they climbed, a team in the truest sense of the word; for when one member flagged, another was always there to provide the needed boost.

The higher they went, the more conditions deteriorated. In the war between time and their wasting bodies, supplementary oxygen was their only weapon. The downside of using oxygen was that each tank weighed twenty pounds, which upped their packs to seventy pounds.

Above Camp V, they followed the last stretches of anchored rope out across the face. The pace was excruciatingly slow. So powerful was the wind that at times they were driven to their knees. Six hours into the brunt of a howling storm netted them barely half a mile.

Prepared for the conditions, Wood takes a quick break on Mount Everest. (Courtesy of Dwayne Congdon)

At 26,500 feet, they reached the end of the fixed ropes. Their umbilical cord severed, they were now staring up at the ominous Hornbein Couloir. Varying in width from three to thirty feet, this trough was regularly flushed with rocks and snow torn from lofty perches by the relentless wind. To imagine the Hornbein Couloir, picture an asymmetrical bowling alley tilted to forty-five degrees; picture the climbers as bowling pins.

Peering up the chasm, Sharon and Barry could make out the ghostly remains of past expeditions: shredded tents and scraps of climbing rope dangling high up on the walls like cobwebs in a haunted house. Rather than dwell on the tangible remains of others' broken dreams, Wood returned to her own problems: sorting out her own tangled rope. It took all the mental acuity she could muster.

Suddenly from behind his oxygen mask, Barry let out a muffled cry. He pointed up the chute then dropped to the ice. Sharon, trapped in a hypoxia-induced lethargy, could only stand and stare in helpless horror as rocky detritus ricocheted off the walls of the gully and bulleted past her, missing her head by inches.

A few minutes later, Dwayne reached the still-shaken climbers. Knowing nothing of their near-miss, he demanded, with uncharacteristic gruffness, "Well, what are we waiting for?"

That night they realized they had forgotten a shovel. So they used their hands to scratch out an icy perch for Camp VI in the Hornbein Couloir. Sharon did not like groping around on her hands and knees in that ice. It was spooky, she thought, like digging in a graveyard. And laborious: doing the simplest chores took forever. By the time Sharon and Dwayne said good-bye to their backup team, tied everything down, and rehydrated themselves, it was 2:00 A.M. They had no chance of getting the early start they needed for a summit bid.

They awoke at 5:00 A.M., groggy and full of foreboding. A thin sheet of snow covered their sleeping bags, having osmotically seeped through the single-walled tent. Outside, the wind howled mercilessly. They called base camp on the radio and were told there was a lenticular cloud blanketing the summit, a sure sign of strong winds that could make a summit bid impossible.

Despite this dispiriting news, they prepared to go. What else was there to do? Sharon put on everything she had: thick longjohns from neck to ankle, a synthetic fur suit, a down suit, a double-layered wind suit with hood, a balaclava, goggles, two pairs of mittens, two pairs of socks (including a battery-powered pair), inner and outer boots, and crampons. At 9:00 A.M. – eight hours behind schedule – she finally stepped out of the tent into a bone-numbing wind, and knew she wasn't overdressed.

They climbed unroped, a calculated risk. They knew if they wanted a chance at the summit, they couldn't carry lots of rope. Moreover, being roped doubled their chances of being yanked off the mountain, since they had no anchors.

To protect the radio from the severe cold, Sharon had it nestled beneath several layers of clothes. Broadcasting meant baring her fingers to the cold and risking frostbite, so for hours they did not speak to base camp. But by keeping the receiver on high, they could occasionally hear their teammates, and at one point, while cowering against some cliffs, they heard Elzinga's hoarse scream above the wind: "Ya gotta want it!" Those words took Sharon back to a gray day in Toronto, when she and Jim were doing his favorite workout, running the 1,375 feet of stairs to the top of the CN Tower – not once but three times without stopping. Always several turns above her, his words would echo down the cold metallic stairwell: "Ya gotta want it!" He was the trainer from hell, but she had finished that stair climb, and now on

Everest he was exhorting her to do the same. Pushed to her feet by a new resolve, she thought, "No one else has the power to inspire me so."

Sharon and Dwayne had been on Makalu together and knew each other's habits, strengths, and weaknesses. "Normally, Dwayne is cautious, methodical, while I am impatient, impetuous," she says. "On Everest we had a real compatibility, almost a synchronicity. We could trust each other's strengths without having to talk. That's good when you have to scream to be heard."

Their sync was more spiritual than physical, for their pace differed. At first Dwayne was the stronger climber. When an exhausted Sharon caught up with him at the bottom of the Yellow Band, a 5.7 section of yellow intrusive rock that engirds Everest (from about 27,000 to 28,000 feet), she was prepared to turn around. If he had been of like mind, they would have done just that, but instead he looked at her and said, with no preamble, "Your lead," and handed her the rope. She thought about it, but only for a moment. As she would later say, "That turned my whole day around. I realized the only thing that was going to help me was to go out ahead and commit. The state of ultimate commitment is the most exhilarating for me. When I'm hesitant, I'm not effective. When commitment appears, doubt, hesitation, and fear disappear. Things begin to click."

Around seven in the evening, they stood just below what appeared to be the summit. Wood radioed base camp the good news. "Doing well. Twenty feet from the top," she said, surprised by the sound of her own voice.

Cheers of congratulations crackled through the receiver.

But they were not twenty feet from the top. What they thought would take minutes took two more hours. It was the most frustrating phase of the whole climb, as they surmounted one false summit after another. What's more, when Sharon had stopped to radio, she had left her ice ax. "I had been carrying that frigging ice ax all day and I was tired of wrestling with it. But leaving it was bad, bad judgment—a sure sign that I was on the edge." She had also lost the radio's aerial, precluding further contact with base camp.

At last the up ran out. At nine o'clock, twelve hours after leaving Camp VI, Sharon Wood and Dwayne Congdon struggled the last few feet to the top of Mount Everest. Had they been videotaped, one would have thought the tape was running in slow motion.

Sharing a commitment to set foot on the summit at the same time, they wordlessly walked the last twenty feet side by side – step, breathe, breathe, breathe, breathe, step, breathe, breathe, breathe, breathe . . . Atop the wind-scoured, table-size summit they embraced with the awkwardness of two astronauts in space suits. It was an emotional time but not an exultant one. Ironically, in this their moment of ultimate triumph, their lives had never been in greater danger. Instead of happiness, they felt disbelief that they were actually there, relief that there was no more up, apprehension about the chasm separating them from security.

They found but one clue that any human had ever preceded them (though about 220 people had, over the years): a raised footprint sculpted like bas-relief in the ice. The wind had blown away the loose snow around it, preserving the compressed footprint like a fossil.

They felt a desperation bordering on panic to get their photographs taken and get off the summit. "It was awful late to be up there," Sharon would say. "Everything was running out on us."

When Sharon posed with the Canadian flag, Dwayne had to shout through his mask that she had it upside down. Fighting the unobstructed wind, Sharon unfurled the various sponsors' flags while Dwayne took snapshots. A sudden blast ripped one of the banners from her gloved hands and blew it into oblivion.

After thinking about Everest for decades, planning it for years, climbing it for months, Sharon and Dwayne would spend but twenty minutes on its summit. Before starting down, they took one last look around at the world arcing away from them. The sun seemed to linger near the horizon, but already the valleys below were plunged into deep shadow. Ten miles to the southeast, Sharon noted, Makalu's craggy cone pierced the penumbra.

Picking her way down through the icy rubble, Sharon entered what she calls the "survival state," an incredibly efficient mind-set in which "you become tuned into how much energy it takes to do even simple tasks. You get rid of all the peripheral stuff that doesn't directly contribute to the task at hand. You can't afford the fear, can't afford the hesitation, can't think of the past or future. You can afford to concentrate only on this little sphere of light that is illuminating the next step down."

She regularly pulled ahead of Dwayne. At first she waited for him, but he kept telling her to go ahead. "I'm fine," he assured her. She had taken him at his word, and now she was playing out her worst night-mare: a freezing, fatigued, nighttime solo descent.

Standing outside the garish Mirage Hotel in Las Vegas, dressed in Lycra tights and fleece jacket, a knapsack on her back, Sharon Wood looks as incongruous as a marshmallow in a martini. At five-ten and 135 pounds, she has a lean, athletic build with well-defined thighs and calves. She has bottle-green eyes and a strong nose, straight brown hair in a pony tail, and a lightly freckled, intelligent-looking face.

Unlike the flour-faced multitudes shuffling by, she is not there to gamble—at least not with money. She and her husband, Chris Stethem, an avalanche expert, are on a climbing vacation.

Before I can say "Blackjack!" the valet has brought their rental car around and the three of us are cruising toward a group of mottled sandstone outcroppings called the Red Rocks, twenty miles out of town. The transition between the urban congestion of Las Vegas and the wild beauty of the surrounding desert is abrupt, suggestive of a Wild West town. In minutes we are on a straight road, no other cars in sight, under a preternaturally blue sky. It is autumn, and the intense summer heat has given way to cool breezes. Apart from the ruby-red bark of madrone, the desert foliage tends toward a dusty green. But the hues of the rock are as though from a box of crayons: burnt umber, sienna. . . .

While we hike trails that skirt the Red Rocks, Stethem moves ahead, pausing periodically to consult his guidebook. While he searches for a particular climb, Wood talks about her life. This puts her solidly in her comfort zone. Since Everest, she has earned most of her income as an inspirational speaker. "Mostly I talk about what motivates ordinary people to do extraordinary things," she says.

"What motivated you to climb Everest?"

"Well, we're all by nature explorers, curious about what's around the corner. Climbers are just an extreme example of that."

"But not every climber does Everest."

"I wouldn't have felt like I lived if I hadn't done Everest. I guess I'd rather be defined by my possibilities than by my limitations."

As might be expected, the expedition that put the first North American woman atop Everest received a lot of media attention. Wood has openly expressed disappointment that the focus has been on her and, to a lesser extent, Dwayne Congdon, at the expense of the other expedition members. Climbing Everest is, she reminds us, a team game. All thirteen climbers played a vital part, and certainly a summit bid would have been impossible without the backup team of Kevin Doyle and Barry Blanchard. "Some people are the drivers and some are the driven," says Wood. "Climbers are goal-oriented, selfish, strong-willed, egocentric, used to making their own decisions. Getting them to work for a team is difficult. In spite of that, we had a pretty compatible group."

Some reporters wanted to know what it was like to have a woman "shacking up" with a dozen men. The reality was not the stuff of romance novels. Jim Elzinga stated, "The goals of the expedition are clear and focused. It's incidental that Sharon is a woman."

"I don't try to hide my femininity," Wood says. "On the other hand, we *were* always wearing six layers of clothes. At first on expeditions I tried to be like the men. But then I realized that I bring some unique strengths to a climb; after that I just tried to be myself. On Everest, I don't feel people treated me like a man; they just treated me like a person, with respect. After Everest, when Jim Elzinga was asked what having a woman on the team meant, he said, 'It helped us behave. Helped us treat one another with a little more respect, to be a little more civilized.'"

I remind her of something Laurie Skreslet once said: "Everest can be cold and brutal and just take you, or it can be kind to you and make you feel very, very lucky." Does she feel lucky?

"Definitely," she says. Her soft-spoken manner masks her extraordinary intensity. "Not only am I alive but so are most of my friends."

In the wake of her success on Everest, her attitude toward high-altitude risk went through a metamorphosis. "Even before I had two children, I'd become more cautious," Wood says. "Fear began to edge in and replace passion. I went back to the Peruvian Alps after Everest, but spent a lot of time there being scared. I realized how lucky I'd been to get down from Everest alive. How far did I want to push that luck?

"But I'm not sitting back on my laurels. I'm still a recreational climber [and a devoted one: she went climbing on her wedding day]. It's just that now I'm having other adventures, too. Having children is an underrated adventure."

"I don't have the need to work hard enough to look over the edge. I have different priorities now." She pauses, allowing a beatific smile to wash over her; it is a look of nearly pure contentment. "But I did get a good look over the edge."

JOHN BACHAR
Rock Star

On a soon-to-be-hot September morning in Yosemite Valley, free-solo-ist John Bachar, age thirty, laces on his climbing shoes and stares intently at the sheer granite wall that towers before him. He closes his eyes and pictures himself climbing one of its 250-foot vertical routes, the one called "Crack-A-Go-Go." Its polished surface is marred by only a few tiny irregularities and two dime-thin vertical cracks.

The difference between Bachar and countless souls who have preceded him is that after Bachar is finished picturing himself climbing "Crack-A-Go-Go," he'll do it. He's done it before, maybe a hundred times. Alone. Without ropes or hardware or the old- fashioned camaraderie of a partner. What he does is called free soloing, and he's the best in the world at it.

He straps on his equipment: a bag of grip-enhancing gymnastic chalk and his tight-fitting rock-climbing boots. That's all. That and a lot of courage, talent, and determination.

He stands and stretches, not stiffly but slowly, carefully. Wearing only baggy white shorts and no shirt, he has a body worthy of one of the world's best rock climbers. Tanned from countless hours on the rock, it ripples with definition. Although listed as five-foot-eleven and 160 pounds, he appears smaller, almost thin. He carries no excess weight, for, as everyone agrees, John Bachar travels light.

Slowly, with the grace of a lynx, he moves to the rock. Reaching into his bag, he dusts his hands, turning them as white as a mime's. He places one hand, then the other, on the rock, his finger joints tensing, swelling to fill the crack. "Finger jam" in place, he lifts his right leg to hip-level, fitting his toe-tip onto a postage-stamp-size depression in the rock. With less effort than most people expend getting out of bed, he lifts himself off the ground and onto the granite, moving from the horizontal world to the vertical – equally at home in both.

Rock climbing predates man's use of tools, but it wasn't until the nineteenth century that climbing became a sport. Before that, people climbed rocks only when they couldn't go around them, and then without relish. As equipment improved, making virtually every mountain in the world climbable, many mountaineers sought new challenges in rock climbing. The focus shifted from the destination to the dance.

The revolutionary changes in climbing have occurred about once a decade:

In the 1940s came the nylon rope.

In the 1950s came the steel piton.

In the 1960s came the artificial chockstone.

In the 1970s came John Bachar.

In the conventional sport of rock climbing, a two-member team is joined by a 150-foot lifeline. One partner climbs, placing the protective hardware, while the other, anchored to the rock, belays the first with nylon ropes. If a climber rests on – or pulls himself up by – his safety equipment, he is said to have climbed "aided." If he uses his equipment only as a safety net, he is said to have climbed "free." If he leaves behind his rope, hardware, and partner, he is said to have "free-soloed." And if he free-solos an extremely difficult climb – say, a 5.11c, like "Crack-A-Go-Go" – he is said, in some circles, to be crazy or to have a death wish.

Bachar, who has heard it all, is not amused. "I don't even listen anymore," he says. "If they were saying something intelligent, I might worry. Actually, I'm a conservative climber. Yeah; chicken. I'm always operating way below my level of ability. That's what I call the cushion. I hate feeling like I'm thrashing around up there. If I can't do it with control, I'll back off. In my own mind, I'm really a chicken."

No one privy to what Bachar does on a rock will buy that, but the man climbs with such self-possession, in such harmony with the rock, that one is temporarily persuaded that he doesn't take risks. Like all great performers, he makes it look easy. It is, in fact, impossible to gauge the difficulty of a route merely by watching Bachar solo it.

But no risks?

John Bachar's five tips for free soloists

1. If you quit free soloing now, you greatly reduce serious risks to your health.
2. He who downclimbs and runs away lives to free-solo another day. Climb one move at a time, and always be prepared to down-climb if you feel the next move is too hard for you.
3. Never bite off more than you can chew; always solo climb well beneath your roped free-climbing capabilities.
4. You can fool your friends into thinking you're in control; never fool yourself. If you feel scared, the route is too hard for you to solo.
5. Style and control are the hallmarks of a great free soloist. No summit, however prestigious or desirable, is worth the sacrifice of these qualities.

"Look at the things I don't do," he says. "I don't climb frozen waterfalls. Or crumbly rock. In Yosemite, it's solid rock, good weather. And the more I do it, the better I get. The odds are always with me."

According to Bachar, free soloing is the most popular participant sport in the world. "Everybody free-solos. When you walk to the store, you're free-soloing. It's just a matter of the difficulty of the route."

In the American (Yosemite) decimal system, routes are classified in difficulty from class 1 to 5.

Class 1: A walk.

Class 2: A hike or easy scramble; proper footwear required. ("Of course, that's ridiculous," says Bachar, "because the Nepalese go barefoot everywhere.")

Class 3: Ropes sometimes advised, not because the climb is so difficult but because a fall could be injurious or fatal.

Class 4: Most climbers – except free soloists – use ropes.

Class 5.0 to 5.14: The heart of the matter for most climbers. (Bachar, though, won't look at anything less than 5.10.) Ropes required, except by free soloists. The most difficult climbs are further delineated with a,b,c, and d, as in 5.11a, 5.11b, 5.11c, and 5.11d.

Bachar, already a hundred feet up "Crack-A-Go-Go," is spread-eagled on the rock like a spider. His toes are jammed into such tiny holds that, from the base of the rock, the entire outline of the sole of his boot is visible.

Forty feet away, on a different route on the same rock, a German couple is climbing in the more conventional manner. Although they are "free climbing," they are heavily attired and laden with ropes and loops of hardware. Next to the half-naked Bachar, they appear otherworldly; next to them, Bachar's approach to climbing seems absurdly clean and simple.

When the German man spots Bachar, he stares, transfixed. He calls down to his partner, who is still on the ground, belaying him: "Solo?"

"Ja. Solo."

The woman, also intrigued, snaps several pictures of Bachar. When two American climbers arrive at the base of the rock, she calls to them in a heavy accent: "Excuse me. Do you know the name of this climber?"

"That's John Bachar."

Eyes light up in recognition. "Oh. Ja. Okay then."

Meanwhile, 150 feet above the valley floor, with a straight drop to his starting point, Bachar ponders his next move. After studying the problem for a moment, he dusts his right hand with chalk and forces it into a crack in the rock. Called a "hand-jam," the hold would be brutally painful to the ordinary mortal. But Bachar has extraordinary strength in his palm and finger muscles, the product of countless hours of exercising; by flexing those muscles, his hand expands to fill the crack, creating a pivot-point so secure that it allows him to lean away from the rock while he dusts his free hand. That accomplished, he lifts his foot to hip-level, setting it in a small depression in the granite. Then, with a gentle lift, a fluid ease, he moves farther up the rock.

Mr. and Mrs. Bachar didn't raise their son to be a rock climber. It was assumed that John would follow his father and become a math whiz. It sounded all right to John, who played along with straight A's in high-school math. Meanwhile, he was also an athlete, playing baseball, then giving that up for pole vaulting. "I tied the school record in practice," he remembers. "I dug vaulting. But by then I had discovered climbing. I started going to a climbing spot north of L.A., called Stony Point. I'd ride my bike thirty-five miles each way for an hour and a half of climbing. By the time I was sixteen, I could do all the bouldering problems there, something no one else could claim."

By his senior year, he was cutting track practice to go climbing. "I started out cutting Wednesdays, which, with the weekend, gave me three days to climb. But it wasn't enough, so I started cutting Tuesdays and Thursdays, too."

Because few could climb with John Bachar, he learned to climb alone. "I didn't have any friends in high school," he says with a trace of sadness. "I met a few people climbing – including Ron Kauk."

Kauk and Bachar were compatible on and off the rock. They were several levels better than anyone else, as though they played in a league all their own. When summer ended, Kauk urged Bachar to join him in Yosemite, regaling him with stories of the valley, "home of the best rock climbing in the world." But Bachar, not yet able to see the light, enrolled in math at UCLA. Kauk dropped out of high school, moved to Yosemite, and began free-climbing new routes, making a name for himself.

During his freshman year, a distracted Bachar got a C in math. He was depressed and realized he had to get out of L.A. Most of the rock he'd seen in the last few months was in Japanese tea gardens, and Kauk's letters from Yosemite created a yearning he'd never felt before. "It is the best in the world!" Kauk wrote. "Granite spires reaching for a blue sky, all waiting to be climbed by you and me. When you do a new route in Yosemite you get to name it. I've got thirteen already."

John, anguished, sought advice. His mother, with whom he had lived since his parents split up ten years before, had learned a thing or two about life. "Do what you love to do," she counseled, and the next day he quit UCLA and went to study in Yosemite. "It was a very big decision," he recalls. "My father was a research mathematician, a respected professor, and it was chiseled in the family rock that I should follow that route. He understood athletics all right – he'd played pro baseball – but he didn't understand giving up college for climbing. Now he digs it – seeing my name in all the magazines."

Bachar moved to Yosemite and set up permanent residence in

Camp 4, the climbers' campground. Quickly he and Kauk rose to the highest rung on the rock-climbing ladder. Bachar studied kinesiology and set up an outdoor gym in the middle of Camp 4 to work on certain muscle groups. They worked out together, climbed together, and partied together, competing in all three. Comparing their progress, Kauk was forced to conclude that Bachar had it all: physical talent, discipline, fine analytical powers. Kauk was physically talented, and he was willing to work hard, but he lacked Bachar's ability to tear a problem apart and look at all its parts. Like a grand-master chess player, Bachar could see many moves ahead, a skill he figured he inherited from his analytical father. "He gave me a logical way of thinking," says Bachar. "It's made me a more thorough thinker."

When he was nineteen, Bachar became the first person to free-solo a 5.11 climb – Yosemite's 400-foot "New Dimensions." It was a climb that had severely tested the mettle of the world's best two-man teams, and when word reached Camp 4 that Bachar had free-soloed it, the other climbers were stunned. The following day, a message appeared on the camp bulletin board: "Tell Webster's to change the meaning of insanity to 'John Bachar free-soloing New Dimensions!'"

Bachar remembers the furor. "I didn't tell anybody. Word just spread, but it was weird – nobody would talk to me about it. I could hear them whispering behind my back: 'There goes John Bachar. He soloed New Dimensions.' Nobody understood it."

It didn't get any easier for Bachar. He further ostracized himself when he became the first person to solo a 5.11c route, "Nabisco Wall," which had been listed in the *Guinness Book of World Records* as the world's most difficult roped climb. Then he did an "on-sight" (unrehearsed) free solo of "Moratorium," a 5.11b and, as such, the hardest on-sight free solo ever. "On-sight is really the big leagues," says Bachar. "Not knowing what's up there makes all the difference in the world. Climbing "Moratorium," I got too close to my limits and it didn't feel good. I didn't have that extra padding of security. I've only had a bad feeling on a couple of solos, but that was one of them."

Competitive tension between Kauk and Bachar intensified when Bachar was asked to do a TV commercial for 7-Up. It escalated when Bachar discovered that an obscure Spanish climbing boot, the Fire (pronounced FEE-ray), was far superior on Yosemite rock and started the Sole Survivor Corporation to import the boot. The last straw was Bachar installing himself as vice president in charge of testing the

Routes like "The Gift," 5.12c, in the Red Rocks of Nevada, allow John Bachar to do what he does best—free solo. (Courtesy of John McDonald)

boots (that is, climbing in them), for which he was paid a salary of $60,000.

Says Bachar: "The jealousy among climbers is intense. I wasn't living in Camp 4 and eating beans anymore. I wasn't one of the boys. For the first time in my life I had to file a 1040 form. A lot of climbers were asking, 'If he can do it, why can't I?' It got so bad between Kauk and me that one day he took offense at something he thought I said and began to slap me around. He was daring me to fight him. There was a time when I would have taken him up on it, but I guess I'd matured. I could see Ron had problems. Our relationship has gone downhill since then.

"Sometimes I wonder why I ever wanted any notoriety. In climbing everybody is watching every little thing you do; then it gets reported and blown out of proportion. At times I feel like I don't have any friends. A lot of guys want to be number one so bad, they'll sacrifice any friendship for it. It's sad. I'm competitive, sure, but it doesn't drive me nuts.

"There are only two guys in the world who have impressed me

with their climbing ability – Jerry Moffatt and Ron Kauk – and on certain days they can do things with their bodies that I can't do – and vice versa. That's all right; I learn from that. So many guys burn out and quit; they can't love the sport very much if they quit so easily, can they?"

Bachar certainly loves it, and he intends to climb until he dies. The force raging within him is much more a life wish than a death wish, but he willingly accepts the possibility of the end coming while he is climbing in what he calls Zone 3, which means quite simply, "If you fall, you die."

"Better there than in some dumb car accident," he says.

Saying free soloing is John Bachar's specialty is like saying ballet was Rudolf Nureyev's speciality. It does not go nearly far enough, for it is not just what the man does, but what he is. And no climber does it – or is it – better than Bachar. Without ropes, he climbs routes that 99 percent of the world's climbers wouldn't tackle *with* them. He is to most of the Camp 4 climbers as they are to a stone-cold novice.

Despite such domination, Bachar receives no income directly from climbing. He disdains sport-climbing competitions. And the sport, relatively staid for today's television market, generates few endorsements (though Bachar, with his beach-blond good looks, did garner an "Essence of Shaving" ad, which earned him in excess of $10,000).

"I didn't have to do anything really stupid," Bachar says, "like climb through a mountain of shaving cream. But they wanted me to wear a helmet." He grimaces at their naivete. "Nobody in Yosemite wears a helmet. Then they didn't like my voice and dubbed in someone else. At least they let me free solo."

Bachar has also appeared on TV on "That's Incredible," "Real People," and "Evening Magazine." He finished third in a "Survival of the Fittest" contest, earning $5,000 and wiping out the competition in the stick-fighting event. "It took place on a swinging bridge," he remembers. "Most of the other guys couldn't even walk across it. I could jog across it. I do well in the balance tests."

Sometimes the movies call him for stunt work. "They come to me," he says. "I give them my price and tell them to take it or leave it. They pay well, but I don't need money. I need rock."

One is inclined to believe him, for Bachar appears not to have a materialistic bone in his body. After six years of living in a tent or a van, he moved into an unpretentious cabin in Yosemite with his wife, Brenda. The couple owned little. John's one concession to a five-figure income was his black Toyota 4-Runner, into the back of which he piled the tools of his trade: boots, weights, ropes, chalk, bicycle. He could often be seen driving around the valley, moving from one climb to another, less circumspect behind the wheel than on the rock, a Peter Tosh tape blaring from the car stereo.

Less than fifteen minutes after he began, Bachar is 250 feet up "Crack-A-Go-Go," poised to go over the top. Nearby, the German woman struggles on the rock, fifteen feet off the ground. Although the Germans are accomplished climbers, they are tortoises to Bachar's hare. He will require one-tenth the time they will. Yet Bachar does not give the impression of racing up the rock; his moves are dutifully deliberate. Moreover, he claims that speed is not his main concern, but rather a by-product of his perfect solo technique. "The summit is definitely secondary to me. I don't know about other people, but for me it's the dance that's important. The quality of the movements, like in Tai Chi. Or diving off a ten-meter board. Lots of people can dive from that high, but how many can do it with grace and control?"

Nevertheless, there is ample evidence that Bachar is proud of his quickness. "Some mornings I'll do "Crack-A-Go-Go" and "Hardd" [another 5.11], then go down to Arch Rock and do "New Dimensions." When I come back, the roped climbers are still on their first climb. It saves a lot of time not having to put in and take out hardware."

One particular Yosemite climb offers proof of just how segregated Bachar is from the climbing masses. The guidebooks say that Fairview Dome, a 1200-foot vertical ascent at Tuolumne Meadows, is a five-to-eight-hour round-trip for a roped party of two. Bachar, who uses it as a workout, has done it base to summit in seventeen minutes.

Incredibly, he has also climbed El Capitan and Half Dome in the same day. Bachar explains: "Peter Croft and I started at the base of El Capitan at midnight. Using no fixed ropes, we arrived at the top at ten-o-five A.M., passing four parties who were spending two or three nights each. We ran down and arrived at the car at eleven-ten A.M. Then we started hiking up to the base of Half Dome, arriving there at one-twenty P.M. We started climbing Half Dome at exactly two P.M., passed seven parties, all of whom were going to spend the night on the wall, and topped out at six-o-three P.M., with two hours of light left.

Total time from the base of El Cap to the top of Half Dome: eighteen-oh-three. A killer day!"

The way some keep score in climbing is to count first ascents, but Bachar isn't even sure how many he has. "About a hundred in Yosemite, I guess. That's not all that many, but they've all been fairly difficult."

The willingness of climbers to flout gravity has led them into inevitable conflict with the National Park Service, which is responsible for retrieving the battered bodies of the fallen. Of the hundred or so search-and-rescue missions in Yosemite each year, at least twenty involve climbers. To the park rangers, free soloists like John Bachar are the lunatic fringe of an already ticky sport. To the freewheeling climbers, rangers are wilderness cops; as such, they are viewed with the same disdain shown, say, a climber who tackles a boulder with ropes.

Bachar's relationship with rangers is more aloof than tense. "They think I'm crazy, but they can't stop me from doing what I'm doing," he says, with rising inflection. "They've stopped people from hang gliding and parachuting off El Cap, from kayaking the Merced River – but they can't stop me."

One pictures John Bachar in tights and cape, leaping from rock to rock, laughing in the face of the law. Except that laughing doesn't come that easily to Bachar. Still, he has had a giggle or two at the expense of the rangers. He recalls the time he had to convince one at Big Rock, in Southern California, that he was adequately equipped to climb in the park. Showing him a spatula, he told him it was a "crack-jack," an important climbing tool. He was waved through before he could produce his "inverted storm detector," a garden fork.

Yosemite's former chief ranger, Bill Wendt, found little humor in the park's relations with climbers. It was difficult not to think of them as, well, riffraff. After all, they caused more than their share of problems, from shoplifting in the Village Store to falling off mountains. But Wendt was concerned with more than the welfare of a few climbers who were a burr in the side of the Park Service. He worried about the dangerous example they set for others. He once halted a television shoot of Bachar and Kauk until assurances were given that the program would carry a safety message. "It's too easy to copy someone on TV," he said. "Anyone attempting to free-solo should realize that Bachar and Kauk are at the Olympic level."

Does Bachar worry about leading, by example, novice climbers to their doom? "No way. Free soloing has a built-in safety device. Someone who doesn't know what he's doing isn't going to get very far up a five-eleven climb. It's not going to happen. The novice will drop out long before Zone 3."

Climbing statistics support such a contention. Of the approximately 850 mountaineering and rock-climbing fatalities in the United States from 1951 to 1984, only one was the result of a free-solo rock-climbing fall.

Others have come close. Bachar's pal Rick Cashner has twice fallen more than thirty feet. "The average climber will die if he falls more than forty-seven feet," Bachar explains. "But thirty feet can do a lot of damage. Rick's a tough guy. He's broken a few bones, lost a few teeth, but he's still a climber. That's the way it is—real climbers do it for life. The second time Rick fell, he knocked out his front teeth and gashed his eyebrow pretty bad. A ranger scrambled up to him and found blood spurting from his brow. He thought it was coming from his eye and fainted, hitting his head on a rock and knocking himself out. So Rick had to hike out to get help for the ranger. Like I said, he's a tough guy."

Bachar himself has taken only one serious fall. On a difficult solo in Colorado's Eldorado Springs Canyon, he tumbled twenty feet. His amazing balance allowed him to land right-side up, but a dislodged rock knocked him down, badly bruising his back. After standing up, he fainted, then revived and drove himself home. He, too, is a tough guy.

But even tough guys possess a realistic fear of falling. For climbers—particularly free soloists—it comes with the territory. The irony is that the fear itself—a supposedly self-protective emotion-can disrupt concentration and short-circuit skill. A climber can die as a direct result of being afraid to die.

How does Bachar deal with the fear?

"It forces me to concentrate. I zoom right in. But it's a relaxed sort of concentration. I get so into doing each movement—with grace and control— that it makes no difference whether I'm fifty feet up or five. If I think about falling, I can't put all my energy into doing the moves.

"You hear people say you shouldn't look down, but I look down all the time. I dig it. It's beautiful up there." Bachar reflects a moment. "People are obsessed with the dangers of soloing, but what they don't realize is that just about every move is reversible. If it's too hard, I can undo it. That's not the case with, say, speed skiing or hang gliding. In those sports, once you've started, you're committed.

"I accept the consequences of all that I do," he adds. "No matter what we do with our lives, our bodies are temporary. We're all going to die, and I'd rather die climbing than doing anything else."

For Bachar, a shy smile is usually maximum evidence of amusement. He displays that smile, and his remarkable attitude toward falling, whenever he is asked for a climbing anecdote. "A guy was doing "Reed's Direct," a five-nine climb in Yosemite, he relates. "Not only was he tied in, but he had a drag line for hauling up equipment. From a hundred and fifty feet up, he fell. But he had tied into his harness wrong and the rope ripped apart the harness, and now he's doing the death fall. He's history, except that his drag line wrapped around a tree on the wall, caught, and stopped him five feet from the ground." That shy smile resurfaces. "He was doing the death fall and he lucked out. Most people don't even have a drag line on that climb. After that, he sold all his equipment and quit climbing. That one is pretty funny."

One of climbing's main attractions is the exhilarating freedom it offers its participants. In the absence of a rule book, a climber is allowed to ascend a route employing any or all of the available hardware – unless, of course, he wants the respect of John Bachar.

"Someone says they did this five-eleven-a or that five-eleven-c but how do you know? They write into an editor of some climbing magazine, what does that prove? Besides, with artificial aid, anybody can climb anything. It's about as challenging, as meaningful, as a repairman going up a telephone pole."

It's impossible to talk climbing with Bachar without talking ethics. For him, the two are inseparable. "Only in the last fifteen years have climbers quit a route because it couldn't be done unaided. In the past, if that happened, the party would just bolt up and go for the summit. Now the real purists figure if it can't be done right, it shouldn't be done at all."

Count Bachar among the real purists. A few years back he was invited to a climbing conference in Germany, one purpose of which was to discuss the ethics of climbing. "I thought it was going to be great," he says, shaking his head in disgust. "They paid my way there, which is unheard of. They had over five thousand people in attendance, which is also unheard of. Here we'd have maybe five hundred. In Europe, climbers are revered as stars. In America, I never get asked

Bachar brings all his skills — strength, discipline, problem solving — to bear on "Father Figure," 5.13a. (Courtesy of John Bachar)

for my autograph, but the first day in Germany, I signed about three hundred.

"Unfortunately, the discussions on ethics turned out to be bogus bullshit. They're just missing the point. They see nothing wrong with starting out at the top and putting in protection so you can climb safely from the bottom. Seems to me that's like getting a copy of the final exam before the exam."

Bachar's standards, as high as the walls he climbs, force him to question even his own methods. "I'm not as free as I could be," he says shamefully. "I use boots and chalk. If I was truly one with the rock, I'd use neither. But the chalk is organic, and climbing barefoot thrashes your feet." Again a smile is hinted at. "And I'm not into pain."

Returning from the top of "Crack-A-Go-Go," Bachar scampers down a dirt trail next to the rock, displaying his characteristic grace and coordination. He removes his climbing shoes and puts on his beat-up Nike tennis shoes. Carrying his boots in one hand and his pouch of chalk in the other, he takes a route dominated by huge, slippery granite boulders. In love with the world he inhabits, he prances over the rocks with the surefootedness of a goat.

Thirty minutes later, after a short lunch break of grapes and an apple, he is in Camp 4, staring at quite a different boulder. Thirty feet high, it has a name – "Midnight Lightning" – a problem (bouldering, a rock-climbing subsport, calls its challenges "problems"), and a history. For years, climbers passed beneath its overhang, dismissing it as un-climbable; but in the mid-seventies, a denizen of Camp 4, his acuity sharpened by LSD, declared that he could see a solution. His vision was interpreted as divine revelation in Camp 4, and some of the world's best climbers came to try to solve the problem of "Midnight Lightning." Although that was more than a decade ago, only seven have succeeded. Ron Kauk was the first, John Bachar the second. Bachar has continued to do it as a regular part of his workout. "I've probably done 'Midnight Lightning' three hundred times."

Not today, however. This time the "steel hooks" weaken, the hand slips, and he drops ten feet, landing on the ground with a surprisingly heavy thud. Surprising because, up to then, he had seemed lighter than air. He sits for a minute, collecting his breath, contemplating his mistake. Finally, he gets to his feet, saying, "First time I've fallen on this one in over a month. That's enough for today. I'll finish the work-out at the gym."

Bachar's workout, which he does four days a week, is so strenuous that most people can't bear to watch him go through it. First, two to three hours soloing 5.11 climbs; then bouldering behind Camp 4 for a couple of hours, usually finishing with an assault on "Midnight Light-ning"; then exercising in his outdoor gymnasium until dark.

"I built the gym myself in my friend Rick Cashner's backyard when the one in Camp 4 became too much of a tourist trap. It got to the point that crowds were gathering just to watch me work out. Guys smoking cigarettes – it drove me crazy. Most people would rather watch someone else work out than work out themselves."

Among the gear Bachar has rigged there is a two-by-eight board nailed between two pine trees. Attached to the board are tiny blocks of wood that provide holds for one-armed fingertip pull-ups. The *Guin-ness Book of World Records* says that only one person in 100,000 can do a one-armed pull-up. Bachar regularly does one-armed *fingertip* pull-ups – with barbell weights dangling from a harness around his waist!

"I do more than is necessary," he says, in between breaths. "That's my cushion. I want to be stronger than I'll ever need up on the rock.

It's not just making it to the top; it's making it with control. There's no satisfaction in thrashing around and just barely making it. You can fool other people, but you can't fool yourself."

Bachar wants to be stronger and better-balanced. After several sets of pull-ups, he moves over to his "slack chain," which is strung between two trees. He hops up on the chain and, like a tightrope walker, tiptoes from one end to the other. "Besides balance, the chain tests concentration and relaxation," he says. "You gotta relax or it will throw you around."

Next he moves to the "crack machine," a long board with a built-in slot, for practicing hand jams. Then back for more pull-ups. "The only people who really do one-armed pull-ups are climbers," he says. "They aren't very good pushers, but they're usually great pullers. There are plenty of climbers who are stronger than me in the gym, but they can't always do it on the rock. Strength isn't everything. There's a woman here in Yosemite, one of the five best female climbers in the world. Not particularly strong, but great at solving climbing problems."

Working from power to endurance, Bachar moves to another piece of equipment, a personal invention of his called the Bachar Ladder. Tied to the top of a tree, it is a seventy-foot modified rope ladder, which he climbs without the use of his feet. "I call it a rope ladder, but elsewhere they call it a Bachar Ladder," he says. "It's funny. Where you live, they're jealous and don't want to call anything after you. In other places, they idolize you and name everything after you."

With a soft but determined hand-over-hand pull, Bachar glides to the top of the ladder. Without the use of his feet, he must utilize his superior upper-body strength. Though he never thrashes about or appears to struggle, his bulging back and shoulder muscles indicate maximum exertion.

Back on the ground, in the lengthening shadows of the forest, Bachar puts on a T-shirt that reads "Damn the rules, It's the Feeling that Counts," beneath a picture of a man playing the saxophone. "John Coltrane," he explains, identifying the man on the sax. "One of my heroes. He was so dedicated, he used to practice eight hours a day, then go play gigs at night. He once lived in a place where he couldn't make noise, so he'd blow silent scales for two hours at a time. Dedication, I admire that."

Bachar recalls an article in which the writer described him as "the Babe Ruth of climbing." "I didn't like that very much," he says. "Ruth had talent, but he wasn't very dedicated. I would have preferred the

Marvin Hagler of climbing. Or maybe the Bruce Lee. Yeah, or John Coltrane."

Bachar has played the saxophone for years, and it is rumored that he plays it while driving. "Only on the straightaways," he says, smiling uninhibitedly now. "When I go to L.A. on business, I'll put on a jazz tape, steer with my knees, and jam to the music."

In his gym, he straps a watch around a conventional pull-up bar. Then he clips a twenty-pound weight to the harness belt that he wears. It dangles in front of him, suggestive of some medieval torture. For the next twenty minutes, he does sets of three one-armed pull-ups, resting one minute between sets.

"You hear a lot now about the 'Type T' personalities of the people doing risk sports," he says, in between exercises. "Supposedly these Type T's get off on danger. I don't buy it. They may start climbing because of the danger, but real climbers won't stay with it for that reason. We have a saying: 'There are old climbers and there are bold climbers, but there are no old bold climbers.' I think people do the so-called risk sports because they find their jobs aren't physically demanding. So they get out and climb a rock."

In preparation for his next set of pull-ups, Bachar closes his eyes and steadies his breathing. "I practice mental imagery while I'm working out," he says. "That way I can use it on the rock, when it really matters. I might pretend that a light switch has suddenly been turned on and that electricity is surging through me and there's nothing anybody can do to stop it. It works great for a two-second move."

At other times, Bachar imagines that his fingers are steel hooks, and given his prodigious displays of strength, he must have an excellent imagination. *People* magazine ran a picture of Bachar that produced a collective gasp from its readers. He is doing a one-armed hang from a rock ledge, high over oblivion. "That was a pretty ledge," he says. "I can hang from something like that for over a minute anyway."

His sport, he insists, is as much mental as physical. "Take that slack chain. Lots of people could walk back and forth on it when it's only two feet off the ground. But put it a hundred feet up and see what happens. It's the same physical event, but it tweaks you mentally to be that high without protection."

Unquestionably, Bachar has great physical ability – strength and balance – and he works like a demon to stay in shape. But he feels his real advantage over others is from the neck up. Mental toughness.

"You have to be able to look at a climbing problem logically, dispassionately. Up on the rock, you don't get textbook situations. You need to be able to stay cool and improvise. Previsualization. I can look ahead and see that certain moves aren't going to work. A knowledge of the body is helpful, but even more important is an intuitive feeling for what it can do in tough situations."

It makes sense that John Bachar is a great rock climber, because he loves it so much. When he talks about it, he is uncharacteristically animated. You get the feeling that hardly anyone has ever loved a thing as much as Bachar loves climbing. "It's goddamn great," he effuses. "I can't understand why people play baseball when they could be climbing. It's so many things, not just one. Outdoors . . . beautiful, with unbelievable exposures . . . mentally challenging . . . gives you the chance to face fear and overcome it. . . . And it's so natural. . . . Little boys are always climbing trees, aren't they? But the real reward is being able to look within, to learn about myself. It's a transient thing – that's why I keep going back up the rock – to relearn it.

"I don't have a list of goals. I'm like a dancer working on his dance. It may seem like I'm doing the same thing over and over, but each time it's a new experience. Each time I'll be more in control, more efficient, more artistic."

But what about the approval of the fans? What about the cheers of the crowd that greet other sports stars when they finish their events? Doesn't Bachar miss the sound of applause?

As he removes the harness from his waist, his lips widen to a smile. Then a laugh. "Ha!" he cries. "I'd rather hear the wind."

1993 Update.   One day before finalization of the sale of Bachar's Yosemite home, a forest fire raged through the little mountain community of Foresta and transformed John's residence and lot into a flattened wasteland of sooty gray ash. For the two years since that fire, he has been living at Mammoth Lakes, on the east side of the Sierra, and fighting a string of battles with lawyers, government bureaucrats, and insurance company hacks. On mornings when he would rather be off climbing or snowboarding, he often finds himself on the phone to someone who doesn't know the difference between a rappel bolt and a lightning bolt.

It's ironic that Bachar, the apostle of freedom, is caught in such a tangled web. "Yeah, I ended up getting sucked into the whole stupid system," he says, with a touch of fatalism. "I was better off in a sleeping bag with no money."

Mammoth is not quite the climbing mecca that Yosemite is, but it still offers plenty of high-class rock, and most days Bachar is still able to extricate himself from his business hassles and do his solo circuit in the nearby Owens River Gorge. Typically, he will rip off seven to ten 5.12 walls, with time left over to practice his saxophone (he plays in a band). As always, the blonde, sleek-muscled man who climbs without ropes draws the unabashed stares of any roped climbers who happen to be in the gorge.

More than ever, Bachar feels the ethical chasm separating him from the climbing masses. "Now I have nobody to relate to," he says, matter-of-factly. "With the takeover of rap (rappel) bolting, I'm even more isolated than before," he says. "I climb even less with people. My specialty has always been free soloing and first ascents, but first ascents to me means walk-up-to-the-face-and-just-do-it. No one does it that way anymore. Everyone starts at the top, ropes down, scopes it out. If they can't put a bolt every eight feet, they'll go home. It's even wimpier than before. That last year I was in Yosemite, I even found glue on holds. . . . It's so screwed up."

Bachar has even lost touch with his erstwhile climbing buddy, Ron Kauk, who has gone into sport climbing. Even though Kauk once intoned that "John Wayne didn't wear Lycra," that's exactly what he does while competing for prize money. Bachar can only shake his head over Kauk. "Deep down, I'm sure he's unhappy," he says. "He knows he sold his soul."

The words suggest a bitter old man, but his tone belies that, and Bachar is neither old nor bitter. He only mentions these matters because someone asked. True, he's not happy with the climbing scene, but then he's never really been part of that anyway. True, he is divorced, but he accepts that as his fate: "Brenda just didn't realize how fanatical about climbing I am." Meanwhile, throughout it all, he continues to do his own thing, which pleases him no end. Now in his midthirties, he believes he is a more capable climber than ever. All in all, the guy seems to be a terribly healthy specimen.

He must be getting his exercise.

DAVID BROWER

Mountain Guardian

Lord, grant that I may always desire more than I can accomplish.
———Michelangelo

It was David Ross Brower's eightieth birthday party, a public celebration hosted by actor/environmentalist Dennis Weaver. For two hours, speakers marched to the podium and sang the praises of America's most respected radical environmentalist. Brower himself got up and spoke at length about the state of the world in 1992 and what his Earth Island Institute was doing about it. (The institute was founded by Brower in 1982 after he had been ousted as executive director of the Sierra Club, and later, Friends of the Earth.)

I was struck by the imposing physical presence of this man. Many eighty-year-olds are drooped and decrepit, falling into themselves like a dilapidated shack, but not Brower. He stood tall, as erect as one of the redwood trees he'd spent the last fifty years defending. He appeared every bit the six-foot-one-and-a-half he was said to be. His visage had not escaped the ravages of time, but the delicate facial features and wispy white hair, thinning but not balding, suggested a much younger man. That portrait was completed when he spoke in a voice that was – if not exactly mellifluous – clear and resonant, with none of the wavering or croaking often associated with the aged.

Phrases like "direct action" and "bold vision" floated through the auditorium all evening. Brower's accomplishments were cited, the consensus being that his record for sustained environmental boldness is second to none.

Over the next few months I would discover how much of that boldness was honed in the wilderness.

David Brower was born in 1912 into a passionate camping family, the third of four children. He grew up with a love of nature and a fear of heights. Perhaps the latter grew out of an incident in which he scrambled out of his baby carriage and fell to the sidewalk, damaging his gums and baby teeth.

As a little boy, he could often be found hanging around the University of California at Berkeley, where his dad taught mechanical drawing. He liked to dam up Strawberry Creek, then destroy the dam and watch the water rush to freedom. As a first-grader, he made his first ascent of the west face of Founder's Rock, a ten-foot-high stone on the Cal campus.

Despite such boyish antics, David Brower was a rather timid, unathletic kid, more at home with a butterfly net than a baseball bat. When he was six, the family went car camping in the Sierra in their 1916 Maxwell. Traveling one-lane dirt roads, which Brower likens to some Sierra trails today, they took four days to drive from Berkeley to the south end of Lake Tahoe. (Today it is a four-hour trip.) On the western slopes of the Sierra, they watched with horrified fascination as hydraulic miners with huge eight-inch water hoses blasted the hillsides with such force that it seemed they would soon level them.

They camped where Harrah's Club is today, but in 1918 they were surrounded only by pine and fir trees. The urban blight that would eventually infect that end of the lake — Jimboy's Tacos, Shakey's Pizza Parlor, Harrah's Thrifty Gambler, Shell, Texaco, and Standard — could not even be imagined. "Our hotel room was a ground sheet with blankets laid out on top," says Brower. "Our parents slept on the outer edges of a three-children sandwich. That was security."

They traveled south along the eastern edge of the Sierra, then up and over Tioga Pass and into Yosemite. At Tioga Pass, the family stopped and climbed Gaylor Peak. Though Brower today knows it as a "minor, pleasant summit," back then he opted to stay behind.

In Yosemite Valley, he made the same decision on the Vernal Falls trail. "I rebelled at the bridge over the Merced River. That's where you can first see Vernal Falls. It wasn't today's sturdy bridge, but a log flattened on top with a rail on one side. I wanted no part of it." His sister Edith stayed behind to babysit her younger brother. Later, the rest of the Brower family climbed Sentinel Dome, but the only climbing David did was into the back of the Maxwell to sleep.

When Brower was eight, his mother developed a brain tumor, eventually losing her sight, her sense of smell, and half her hearing. But she still loved to hike, and David often took her on walks, the longest of which were to the summit of Grizzly Peak, above the UC campus. He would describe in detail to her the flora and fauna. "You don't take eyes for granted when you grow up with a mother who has lost her sight," he says.

Year after year the Browers returned to the mountains. One summer David's father did a solo ascent of Echo Peak, overlooking Lake Tahoe. Darkness fell, and no dad. To the kids, the peak was a world-class climb, and they worried themselves sick. "It had been a tougher scramble down than he'd expected," says David. "He finally got back all right, but that didn't exactly hasten my own mountain confidence."

When David was fourteen, he still possessed a seemingly pathological fear of heights. "We hiked the Eleven-Mile Trail from Glacier Point down to the valley. There is no rail at the edge of Panorama Cliff, which this trail passes right by. Well, not right by—more like three hundred feet back from it. But I still felt nervous even about that distant exposure." Ironically, thirteen years later, in 1939, Brower made the first ascent of the Glacier Point East Face. And only a few years after that, he could stand at Glacier Point and look out at a majestic sampling of High Sierra peaks—Cloud's Rest, Mount Clark, Mount Maclure, Half Dome, Grizzly Peak, Mount Lyell, North Dome, Mount Hoffmann, Mount Watkins, Mount Broderick, Liberty Cap—and know that he had reached the summit of every one of them.

Brower's father insisted that he enter Cal right out of high school. He wanted to major in entomology, or perhaps agricultural economics, but dropped out before it became much of an issue. (Despite his glibness today on the subject—"I am a graduate of the University of the Colorado River"; "I'm still working on my education"—and his nine honorary college degrees, being a college dropout still gnaws at Brower. For sixty years, he has been haunted by the same dream, in which he is back in class at Cal. "They all end the same," he says. "After a brave start, I seem to forget to go to class and go off on a guilt trip instead.")

At age eighteen, Brower was, in his own words, "not quite a mountaineer, willing to climb Gaylor Peak, butterfly net in hand, but unwilling to cross a small snowfield, for fear there might be hidden crevasses there. I was reading about mountaineering, glaciers and all, but was not yet ready for the real thing."

He could type, so he took a summer job as a clerk at the Berkeley-run Echo Lake Camp, near Tahoe. He became infatuated with a woman who was the camp's hiking leader; ergo, David became a hiker. On their first trek to Desolation Valley, they got lost. Brower, who was able to read the topographic map, stepped forward and became de facto leader. "I was trail guide for that summer and the next two, leading many, many trips, including six up Pyramid Peak and thirteen up Mount Ralston." In a single day, Brower led an intrepid bunch on a forty-two-miler to Mounts Tallac, Dick, Jack, and Pyramid, with a midnight return.

In the summer of 1931, David, his father, and two brothers climbed Mount Lyell, Yosemite's highest peak. The following summer, they tackled Mount Whitney (14,495 feet), highest peak in the continental United States. At 12,500 feet, David remembers being "in the highest of spirits," singing "I Love You, California," and meaning it. At 12,600 feet he was sprawled on a rock, vomiting with mountain sickness. None of the Browers made the summit that day – Dad went the farthest – and all suffered from severe sunburn. "Faces swollen, blistered, peeling," recalls David. "We were learning."

Around that time, he and two friends tested their camping skills against a Sierra winter. "It was difficult, because we had no skills," Brower says. "Wrong footgear, inadequate camping equipment, no parkas, tents, or ropes – and just as well because we knew nothing about using ropes." With no shortage of youthful enthusiasm, however, they hiked up the Yosemite Falls trail, across to North Dome, down through Indian Canyon, slogging through not-too-deep snow, "enjoying the days well enough, if not the nights." One of those nights they made camp directly beneath the Cascade Creek Bridge. They were comfortable, but their illegal campfire was detected by rangers who made them leave. "That happened two winters in a row," says Brower. "We all agreed on one thing and that was that rangers are no damned good. And my partners agreed that he who follows a Brower never follows a trail."

One of the guests at the Echo Lake Camp had told Brower that since he liked mountains so much, he should contact the Sierra Club. Following that advice, he visited the club's San Francisco office, soon becoming known as the young man who kept returning to buy back issues of the *Sierra Club Bulletin*. He read each issue cover to cover, paying particular attention to the accounts of explorations and climbs. Inspired by those old bulletins, he and George Rockwood set off in 1933 on a seven-week backpack trip in the High Sierra.

Early in the trip, Brower decided to climb a peak in the Palisades, the one called The Thumb. Rockwood wanted no part of it, so Brower did a solo scramble up a couloir, then over to the peak's east wall. One rock jutting from the wall seemed to offer a perfect hold. "I grabbed the top of it with both hands, and it seemed secure. But when I brought my knee up onto it, it came loose." While the 150-pound rock let gravity decide its fate, Brower put up a fight. With a last-second lunge, he was able to latch onto a tiny ledge with two fingers. "It was the only thing I could reach," he says. "That rock went the way I would have gone – a sheer seventy-five-foot fall and subsequent roll that I doubt I would have survived."

Two nights later, they met mountain-man Norman Clyde, who, after listening to Brower's story, told him about "three-point suspension." When in doubt, he said, move only one limb at a time after making sure the other three are secure.

Armed with this new strategy, Brower climbed the North Palisade from the glacier, wearing Keds and using a sharp granite rock for an ice ax. "I should have had nailed boots and a rope," he says today, "but back then I climbed it solo with nothing for protection but Norman Clyde's advice about three-point suspension."

Brower met two more men on that trip who would influence his development. The first was Hervey Voge who was tramping alone through the Sierra. "We traded information about routes," Brower says, "and I told him of my climbs. Hervey told me I should join the Sierra Club and take advantage of their rock-climbing classes." That would turn out to be pivotal advice.

Next day, en route to Hutchinson Meadow, they came upon a bearded man carrying a camera and tripod on his shoulder. "You must be Ansel Adams," Brower said, to which the man nodded. They chatted for a while, before saying good-bye. They would meet many times again, eventually becoming close friends, and Adams's photographs would quicken Brower's aesthetic development.

Near the end of the seven weeks, Brower and Rockwood raced each other over Mount Gibbs and Mount Dana and down into Tuolumne Meadows. There they climbed Cathedral Peak, John Muir's favorite mountain. Brower felt on top of the world, as reflected in the following paean to his youth. "I would probably never again be in as good shape. I was twenty-one, tan, lean, able to shame a horse at mealtime, and ready to take the three-thousand-foot ascent to Glacier Point via the Ledge Trail in just over an hour. This would not make the *Guinness Book of World Records,* but it suited me just fine."

Brower took Hervey Voge's advice and joined the Sierra Club. He came under the tutelage of climbing instructor Dick Leonard, who would later become a friend and climbing partner.

In the summer of 1934, Brower again chose to escape the madding crowd, this time on a ten-week Sierra trek with Hervey Voge. Brower, now twenty-two and brimming with confidence, decided to up the pace. He describes a single day in the Kern Basin: "A moonlight ascent of Mount Tyndall, breakfast after sunrise on Mount Williamson, lunch on Mount Barnard, a second lunch at Wales Lake, and a ten-mile walk back to camp." Two days later it began to snow, continuing for twenty-

David Brower (right) joins (left to right) Oliver Kehrlein, William E. Colby, and Richard Leonard for a 1939 meeting at a dunnage pile at Hutchinson Meadow in the High Sierra. (By Cedric Wright, courtesy of Colby Memorial Library, Sierra Club)

four of the next forty-eight hours. "Already our trip had enlightened us. We'd learned that we could leave the beaten path, and that snow-storms could be enjoyed for their own sake, or rendered innocuous by song."

One June evening, Norman Clyde wandered into their camp beneath an enormous pack. It was a vaguely prearranged meeting, as they intended to climb together in the Palisades. Clyde, a legendary mountain personality, was a man of many surprises, the first of which occurred when he pulled from his pack several dozen unbroken eggs.

Two weeks and several first ascents later, it was time to say good-bye to Clyde. "In his company we had learned much about safety precautions, about using an ice ax, about geology and botany, and we had heard his stories and anecdotes about the Sierra."

By July 24, Brower and Voge had scaled sixty-two peaks in sixty-four days. On only a couple of summits had others preceded them that year, and now they were to scale Matterhorn Peak. Around the camp-fire that evening, they recalled having read of a lunar eclipse that was to begin at two the next morning. They decided their *chef d'oeuvre* would be the first ascent of Matterhorn Peak by the light of a partially eclipsed moon.

They started at midnight, after only three hours of sleep. Despite the limited light, they stumbled very little on the way up. Dave recalls, "We were only a few feet below the summit when the sun rose, allowing us to see the earth's shadow on the moon."

After ten weeks in the backcountry, Brower and Voge returned to Tuolumne Meadows, where they split up to head home. Alone, Brower was consumed by the question "Could the mountains offer more than a transitory escape?" He worried that the Sierra had lost some of its allure for him. But as he rode out of the mountains and into the superheated Central Valley, the highlighted answer came to him as if from God Himself: "You are not going home; you have just left home."

"Although I would not leave it for long, I would never again be so self-reliant in the wild for so long, or see so few people there, or be so totally absorbed in exploring and enjoying, and so unconcerned with protecting the wildness that had made the experience possible."

Brower's account of how he spent his summer vacation was published in the *Sierra Club Bulletin*. That led to an invitation to climb Mount Waddington, British Columbia's most notorious unclimbed summit, as well as K2, in Pakistan's Karakoram, the second-highest mountain in the world. He couldn't afford to go to K2, but did join an eight-man expedition to Waddington, "the most challenging and defiant of North American peaks that remained unclimbed in 1935." In all, twenty-five climbers had failed in thirteen attempts to reach its summit.

Why the string of failures? At 13,260 feet, Waddington is not as high as many peaks in the United States. Less than two hundred miles northwest of downtown Vancouver, it is not as remote as others. It must be the weather. In the heart of a range that parallels the Pacific shores of Canada for five hundred miles, the mountain is host to tremendous snowfall and glaciation. Just reaching base camp required a daunting backpack through dense virgin forests and glacier-choked canyons.

The eight-man crew was composed of seven Sierra Club members and one from the Harvard Mountaineering Club. After months of preparation, they drove three packed cars twelve hundred miles to Vancouver, where they boarded two seaplanes to Knight Inlet.

After being dropped off, they watched the planes rise, pontoons dripping, and turn southward. The loud growl of the motors became a drone, then silence. It was literally the calm before the storm. They immediately had to strip from the waist down to wade the thirty-three-degree Franklin River, prompting team member Dick Leonard to remark that their climb was beginning two feet below sea level.

That night their sleep was tortured by no-see-ums, biting insects smaller than mosquitoes. Early next morning they started tramping upriver. Lugging sixty- to ninety-pound packs (Brower's weighed ninety), they struggled through rain-forest underbrush, over and around countless fallen trees in various stages of decay. After thirteen hours, they had traveled six miles and gained only five hundred feet of elevation. "And that was the easiest approach to Waddington," says Brower.

They navigated the rock-littered terminus of the Franklin Glacier, then up onto the glacier itself. Brower found the thirty-mile river of ice fascinating. They paused often to examine its many features: moraines, sand cones, glacier tables, crevasses, and surface streams. Occasionally someone would sink through a snow bridge to his hip or knee, but as they were roped it was little more than an amusement.

At quitting time, they climbed over a lateral moraine and found a lake and grassy campsite. They cooked over open fires and gazed at the stars from heather beds. "We knew the stars wouldn't be out for long," says Brower. "We had all read about the Waddington weather."

The third day, comparatively easy, brought them to the main ice-fall, where the Franklin Glacier cascades nearly a thousand feet in a chaotic jumble of ice blocks, towers, and crevasses. There they left the glacier, finding a detour over a nearby ridge.

That evening it began to rain and snow. Everything was shrouded in a dreary gray that was soon swallowed by the black of night. They spent a miserable night in their saturated shelters, waking the next morning to more of the same. Since their plans called for relaying the rest of their gear in bad weather, they returned to their dropoff point, a twenty-mile trudge in a driving rain.

Three days later they were again back at Icefall Point, ready for a ten-day attack of the peak. But then another, colder storm blew in, this time bringing heavy snow. While it continued, the team moved gear farther up the mountain. "We entered an arctic realm of rock and ice," says Brower, "where winter and Waddington rule undisputed."

On July 3 they made their first serious attempt at the mountain. Having reached the highest crevasse – the bergschrund – on the Dais Glacier, they broke into two roped teams. The first was to attack the steep two-thousand-foot face leading directly to the summit; the second was to try a nearby couloir, then traverse Waddington's south arête.

Another storm hit: freezing winds, heavy mists, monster snowfall, and zero visibility drove them back down the mountain. Snow fell for fifty-four straight hours, dumping several feet at higher elevations. The Fourth of July came and went, with their only celebration the unfurling of a small American flag lashed to a tent pole.

To conserve heat during the freezing nights, they slept two or three to a sleeping bag. To pass the time while they lay on their beds of ice waiting for merciful sleep to take them, they would hum songs or recite poetry. Bestor Robinson knew several of the poems of Robert W. Service, and he would sometimes recite one of those tales of the far north with suitably dramatic inflection.

Four days after their first attempt on Waddington, they attacked again. The recent snow had not packed, and with each step the crust would collapse and the climbers would break through to their knees. Farther up, on a forty-degree snow slope, they began to sink in to their hips. "Our troubles had just started," says Brower. "As we crossed the bergschrund, an almost continuous avalanche poured from a couloir to our right. The angle of the slope increased to fifty degrees. The recent loose snow lay over old snow that was packed to the consistency of ice. This demanded the slow, tedious work of cutting steps deep enough to reach the safe snow."

The sun, now overhead, melted and released huge sheets of ice, causing a shower of icicles to descend upon them. To escape the line of fire, they had three choices. They could move left, where the route hit a hopelessly sheer face; or right, where all the ledges, heavily covered with new snow, sloped steeply downward. They opted for the third alternative – a dangerous but manageable retreat. "The mountain had beaten back two of our attempts," Brower says in summary. "And we had barely touched the rock."

That night, back at their Dais Glacier Camp, another storm bounded in on tiger claws. By morning, eight inches of new snow covered the old, and still nature's assault continued. By now, enormous masses of snow and ice lay piled up on the mountain, needing only the slightest urging to come tumbling down upon them. Loud thunderings from high up on the slopes were proof of just how likely that was.

Still, they went back up, battling to a point well above twelve thousand feet, before reaching a narrow knife edge of rock leading to the summit that was truly Himalayan in character. It was 6:00 P.M. when four of the climbers, including Brower, set out for the summit on snowshoes. For two more hours they plodded upward through the wintry powder snow. Now the summit was just above them, its slope so steep and windswept that they put aside the snowshoes and took up their ice axes.

A few moments later, they reached what from below had appeared to be the top. Indeed, the tenuous snowpack fell away on all sides, revealing startling glimpses through the mist of glacier-filled cirques thousands of feet below. "My God, look at that!" someone said. Towering above the evening alpenglow was the true summit, separated from them by a yawning notch and rising another five hundred feet into the clouds.

It was late, with lengthening shadows and a rising wind, the temperature well below freezing. They had no choice but to descend to camp, but did so believing that they would return the next day, place some fixed ropes into the notch, and ascend the arête, which was heavily guarded by overhangs and ice.

That night another blizzard struck, whiting out the dream.

After each of Brower's mountaineering adventures, he again had to face the necessity of financing his life. In the summer of 1938, with the Great Depression still in full chill, Brower lived with his parents and bounced between jobs, working in a photographic darkroom, making candy, editing 16mm film.

In early 1939, Brower's Sierra Club friends found part-time work for him in the club's San Francisco office. His job was to help map, describe, and catalog climbing spots in the San Francisco Bay Area. He also edited the local chapter's first newsletter, *The Yodeler.*

He was thrust into the campaign then raging to establish Kings Canyon National Park. In the summer of 1939, he became assistant manager of a Sierra Club High Trip, trekking in backcountry that would eventually be included in the park. With a borrowed Bell & Howell 16mm camera, Brower made the first Sierra Club film, *Sky-Land Trails of the Kings,* which played a role in the eventual park victory. With that film, Brower began a speaking career that has lasted more than fifty years.

After the arduous battle with the arctic conditions on Waddington, Brower set his sights on bare rock, specifically on unclimbed Shiprock, a dramatic formation rising like a huge pipe organ from the flat New Mexico desert. By 1939, Shiprock had turned back a dozen attempts. Its weird shape had long made the mountain a famous landmark; now, some said, it was the number-one climbing problem on the continent.

Brower has described his first jarring look at Shiprock's rhyolitic breccia (with basaltic intrusions): "When Bestor's yodel announced the break of day, I made the mistake of drawing back a tent flap for a peek to the west. Awful vertical cliffs, a cluster of needles thrust through the early-morning velvet of the desert plain, met my startled eyes, and I recoiled into my bag, hoping the whole thing was a nightmare."

Of course, that feeling quickly passed. Standing at the foot of the great rock, scanning the two-thousand-foot walls, Brower found the problem tantalizing. "There were plenty of climbable pitches – up gullies, across ledges, along sharp ridges – but the problem was, they didn't connect into a route to the top."

The upper ramparts of Shiprock split into three distinct pinnacles: the north tower, the south tower and, in between, the much-sought summit tower. The latter could only be approached from the east, from a bowl at the top of a deep gully riddled with overhangs. No one had ever entered the gully, much less the bowl.

They managed the gully all right, but then came face to face with a thirty-foot double overhang. As a balance climber with only average arm strength, Brower had never wasted any affection on overhangs.

The team met on a sloping, scree-covered ledge to decide strategy. They voted unanimously that there should be reliable anchorage to the ledge before anyone could risk the overhang. But there were no good cracks on the ledge. "Had we been equipped only with pitons," says Brower, "we would have had to retreat."

But unlike expeditions in the past, they were not dependent only on pitons; they had brought expansion bolts, equipment never before used on a climb. They made their holes by pounding a star drill into the breccia with a piton hammer, an exhausting, arm-aching process that took half an hour for one hole. Into the two-inch-deep hole, they inserted a special half-inch eyebolt and skirt. As the bolt was tightened, the skirt expanded, holding the bolt in the rock. A carabiner was snapped into the eye of the bolt and a rope was run through the carabiner. Then and only then could a belayer be sure of holding a serious fall.

The other overhang reared up, calling for another expansion bolt. By the time the hole was drilled and the bolt set, it was four o'clock and time to descend to their camp on the desert flatland. Four experienced climbers, each working a full day, had advanced the team twelve feet.

They were spending too much time commuting between their camp and the double overhang. "It was nice having home-cooked meals every night," says Brower, "but it was slowing our progress. So the third morning we arrived at our ledge prepared to spend the night. We each had food, three pints of water, clothing, cameras, and other knickknacks a rock engineer considers standard equipment. I even wore my pajamas under my jeans and parka."

They fought like invading soldiers, pounding in pitons, snapping and unsnapping carabiners, tying foot slings, until they were able to inch their way over the top of the overhangs.

That night they camped in the opening of a cave high up on the rock. Over a frugal supper, they gazed out onto the desert that stretched illimitably to the horizon. Far out across the curving expanse, tiny fires flickered in the night. Navajos on a campout? The desert had appeared lifeless by day, except for scattered groups of grazing cattle. The climbers wondered what the Indians must have

Brower in 1976 with a pair of Sherpas. (Courtesy of Earth Island Institute)

thought of their own campfire, just beneath the supposedly impregnable summit of Shiprock.

On the fourth day, they placed their fourth and last expansion bolt. A small overhang remained. Two pitons helped Brower over that. Then past a slanting, grass-covered ledge, through a tunnel burrowing beneath a jumble of blocks, up a simple friction slab, and through a little alcove with a rocky floor. Brower, who was leading at this point, espied blue sky filling a notch in the ridge just above him. He clamored up to peer through the notch. "Never mind the hardware," he called down to his team. "Bring the register."

At the top, the weather was fine, the view unobstructed. "There was room on the topmost crag for all of us, and a cairn besides," Brower has written. "We were not at all worried about the route back. So why didn't I experience that elation that had previously marked an arrival on an untrodden summit? This had been a far better climb than any of us had ever made."

Brower finally came to realize that each victory along the way, each solution to a problem, had been climactic in and of itself. "The lure of the top had been magnetic, but somehow four days of concentration on a single, lofty objective had stolen the surprise at its attainment." So disoriented was Brower by this response that he recorded the wrong date in the Sierra Club register that they placed just below the summit block. "Someday I must go back and change it," he says.

In November 1941, a month before the Japanese attacked Pearl Harbor, the first U.S. mountain troops began training on Mount Rainier. When Brower enlisted, rather than be drafted, in October of 1942, he was concerned that neither his mind nor his body would hold up to the rigors of Army life. After all, he was thirty, a long way from school, and a fairly heavy smoker. He was also in love, to the point of distraction, with Anne Hus.

Some of his climbing friends were already working with the Quartermaster Corps, designing new climbing equipment. It came to the attention of the right brass that Brower was not only a climber, but also an editor who had worked on the *Manual of Ski Mountaineering.* A captain, who happened to be a friend of some of Brower's skiing pals, brought him to headquarters to put together a mountain-training manual for the Army.

It was a good job, but all that time working on the manual cut into his formal basic training. This was glaringly apparent when he appeared before the board that would decide his qualifications for Officer Candidate School and was unable to answer many of the questions put to him. The president of the board was a major who happened to have been snow camping with Brower. "Uh, Private Brower has been assisting us at headquarters with a mountain-training manual," he explained to the board, before answering the next several questions for Brower.

Brower wrote almost daily letters to Anne Hus, and she was an equally prolific writer to him. He proposed to her by mail and she accepted. In April 1943, as a new second lieutenant assigned to the mountain troops in Colorado, he detoured to Berkeley and married Anne. If she didn't fully realize what she was in for, she soon found out. David's best man was a close climbing buddy; David and Anne spent the third night of their honeymoon in a tent in the rain alongside Shiprock. "And the rest is best forgotten," laughs Brower.

After a stint in Colorado with the 86th Mountain Regiment, David moved with Anne to the West Virginia Mountain Maneuver Area, where he taught mountaineering at the Seneca Rock Assault Climbing School.

But the war would be more than a training exercise for Brower. From February to May 1945, the 10th Mountain Infantry Division saw plenty of action, fighting its way across the North Apennines, the Po Valley, and into the Alps. Their rock-climbing background and training paid off for the soldiers in the Apennines with a successful surprise night attack on Riva Ridge, a key German observation point. They gained a commendation, but lost a lot of troops.

In the Alps, they were loaded down with weapons and ammunition, but had no mountain equipment. "We didn't have so much as a change of underwear for six weeks," says Brower. "Not to mention ropes, mountain boots, sleeping bags."

Just as the 10th Mountain Division was poised for another high-altitude assault, the war in Europe came to an end. The Tenth stayed on in Europe for three more months, "with nothing particularly important to do." On weekends and rest leave, they went climbing and skiing and taught others how to do the same, happy to direct their mountain training to nonmilitary use. In August 1945, Brower signed out for rest leave, with a declared destination of Rome, but instead went off to climb the Matterhorn (his party was stopped eight hundred feet from the top when a teammate got altitude sickness). While he was away, his unit was ordered to Japan (via the United States). Unable to find

Climber, environmental-ist, educator, David Brower is always looking for adventure. (Courtesy of Earth Island Institute)

Brower in Rome, the 10th left without him. He caught up with them in Florence, but his punishment for not being where he was supposed to be was mess duty aboard the ship that took them across the Atlantic.

In Europe, Brower had witnessed up close what he would call "the shattered remains of what must have once been beautiful wildernesses. They had lost their immunity and felt the ravages of a conqueror. Now they were dead, although their death wasn't irrevocable, as is that of man."

Brower and his mates were crossing the Atlantic, one day from the States, when they got word of the ultimate human and environmental devastation: the dropping of the atomic bomb on Hiroshima. Within months, Brower was back at his editorial desk at the University of California Press, deep into volunteer work with the Sierra Club, "with wilderness at the top of my agenda."

Brower has not climbed a significant mountain in almost forty years, yet he is still reaping the benefits of an intrepid youth. He believes that the boldness engendered by climbing toughened him for his later environmental battles. "Sometimes luck is with you, and sometimes not, but the important thing is to take the dare," he likes to say. "Those who climb mountains understand this. Variety is not the spice of life, risk is. You have to take chances. You might get banged up a bit, but you give yourself the opportunity to fall more than once, and you learn about your abilities. I think we need to do that more in life."

It's no accident, says Brower, that the early Sierra Club leaders, starting with John Muir, were climbers. "The early leaders of the club gained daring from their exploration of Sierra summits," he says. "Of the club's first thirty-eight presidents, only two were All-Americans in football, but at least thirty were All-Sierrans as mountaineers. Seven have had Sierra summits named after them. They learned things like judgment from those mountains. In order to get to the top of a mountain, you have to select the best possible route and overcome obstacles along the way. Climbers with poor judgment are weeded out early."

Although he's no eco-terrorist, Brower believes the environmental movement can always use an infusion of right-thinking boldness. "I wish that every person who seeks to lead the environmental movement could experience the peak moments of a climb," he wrote in an article for *Sierra* magazine. "Unfortunately, mountaineers no longer venture forth under the Sierra Club banner."

He blames himself, and others, for shameful timidity when the

Sierra Club voted to withdraw from club-sponsored mountain training and technical climbing lessons. As a board member in 1988, he voted with several colleagues to disband their climbing sections when the insurance companies announced an enormous increase in premiums for "risky" outings involving the use of ropes or ice axes. Although only about four thousand of the Sierra Club's then half-million members were participating in outings where technical climbing skills were required, and although there were "many wonderful ways to spend the premium money," Brower still views that decision as an inexcusable cop-out. He now says, "We should have put the half-million dollars in the club's budget, sought financial help and battle support from our allies, and fought the insurance companies. We should have kept the Sierra Club tradition of teaching people to be safe in the mountains." Success in such an effort, he feels, would have assured continuity in the molding of bold environmental leaders, something the world needs now more than ever.

Brower, for his part, has been a bold environmental leader for almost fifty years, albeit with a handful of different organizations. After seventeen years with the Sierra Club, he was asked to resign as Executive Director after a dispute over who should decide how to spend club money. Many accused Brower of being too bold; no one doubted his commitment to the cause. After the Sierra Club schism, he immediately founded another environmental organization called Friends of the Earth. Years later, when the board voted to relocate to Washington, D.C., Brower had another showdown. "He was vehemently against Friends of the Earth moving to Washington, says Anne Brower. "He thought the Beltway people were out of touch with the grass roots." Brower stood firm and once again stood alone. Friends of the Earth moved east, and Brower stayed in California to found yet another environmental advocacy group, Earth Island Institute.

For Brower, one senses, life is a little like climbing Mount Humphries, a mountain west of Bishop, California. "There's a place on that climb called Married Man's Point," he says, "where all the married men are supposed to turn around. Although I would accept different standards for married men, with their extra responsibilities, I think it's important for people to push on past the point where it's easy."

David and Anne are still married. In fact, 1993 brought Anne's eightieth birthday and the couple's fiftieth wedding anniversary. She has been hobbled by a bad fall she took over her dog, but her mind is as sharp as ever. She reads a lot, is highly political ("a congenital Democrat"), and is full of spunky fun. That came out when she spoke of plans for their golden wedding anniversary. "David is going to the Sierra Club annual meeting that night," she said. "I'm inviting my children to dinner. I refuse to go and be bored. But he'll go, I'm sure. That's the way he is. He's still very loyal to the club, even after what they did to him. I think ladies take these things much harder than their spouses. The night they voted him out, I vowed I wouldn't cry in front of the bastards."

When they were first married, Anne Brower didn't much care for mountains. She likes to point out her accordance back then with Edna Ferber's sentiment that "mountains were beautiful but dumb." "They didn't do anything," Anne says. "I preferred the sea, which I saw as the beginning of life. David saw it as the end."

Then she reluctantly agreed to go on a Sierra Club High Trip. "I was talked into it by a girlfriend," she says. "To get through it, I took occasional nips from a flask of bourbon. But then things changed; I began to love it. Such incredible country!"

Oddly, the man who has sixty-nine first ascents to his credit, who fought mountain battles in World War II, who has broken seven skis in falls but never a bone, and who regards balance as his greatest physical asset suffered his worst injury in a twenty-nine-inch fall. He had climbed up on his desk at the Friends of the Earth office to put up a sign that read 'David Brower has been fired as Executive Director of the Sierra Club – Protest Here.' Lowering himself down, he was protecting his trick knee (injured in a skiing fall) when he slipped and broke his wrist.

Brower's son-in-law is a rock climber and guide in the Tetons, and David likes to talk climbing with him. He can't help but reflect with bemusement upon all the pitons he once drove into glorious rock formations. "I used to find beautiful little rock gardens growing in climbing cracks," he says. "I would rip them out so I could use the crack more easily. I wouldn't think of doing that now. I would turn around and not do the climb rather than disturb one of those gardens."

More than one person has suggested that if Brower were truly faithful to his philosophy, he would be wearing a skin and living in a cave. Brower actually lives in a modest redwood-sided house in the Berkeley hills. He is the father of four children, yet he has supported a tax on people with more than two. He is a conservationist who owns, among other things, two cars, four color television sets, three video recorders, two video cameras, four still cameras, three record players, three pianos, one accordion, two telephone lines, four speaker phones, and three computers.

"I can explain away everything when pressed," he explains. "I need most of those things in my work – or will, just as soon as I get them fixed."

Brower, who talks to groups all over the country about conservation, has estimated that he was away from home an aggregate twenty-four years out of his first forty-six years of marriage. Even when the Browers were united, they were often on the road or trail, backpacking in the mountains, exploring the deserts of the Southwest, traveling to Europe. As soon as each Brower kid turned six, the child was baptized with a Sierra Club High Trip, a huge wilderness hiking/camping maneuver for up to two hundred people. "We hurried John by taking him before he was four," says Brower. "Near Bishop Pass his pulse climbed too high, and I had to carry him on my shoulders. We were about twelve thousand feet above sea level, which did *my* pulse no good."

Brower led his last High Trip and his last major climb at age forty-four. He hung up his skis before he was fifty. His weight ballooned to 217 pounds. But he still loved the mountains and could still walk, and so at age sixty-four, when the opportunity arose to join a trek in Nepal, he didn't hesitate.

The trek was originally supposed to peak at Everest Base Camp, but they were told that the 1976 American expedition had left the place so cluttered they wouldn't want to see it. Instead they went to Kala Pattar, a bump on the Everest ridge, eighteen thousand feet above sea level, that afforded spectacular views of the north and west bastions of Mount Everest.

During the planning stages of the trip, Brower was hopelessly out of shape. His doctor worried openly about the potentially fatal combination of high-altitude exertion, thin air, and poor conditioning. What he failed to factor in was the Brower resolve. "I had made a commitment," he says. "If I were ever to see the Himalaya, I couldn't put it off any longer. There was no way I was going to get two- hundred-seventeen pounds up where I wanted to be. So I put away the car keys, put away far less food, pushed away Tanqueray martinis, walked down to mass transit every day and walked the vertical eight hundred feet back up, put five hundred miles on my boots, five thousand fewer on the Volvo, discarded twenty-five unnecessary pounds, saved travel and parking expense of three thousand dollars in ten months, went with a group of twenty on a five-week trek, left another twenty-two pounds behind in Nepal, and arrived home weighing what I did when Anne agreed to marry me."

So cheered was Brower by the trek that he decided he wouldn't retire at age sixty-four after all; instead he has opted to wait until he is one hundred and twenty-eight.

In 1992, at the age of eighty, Brower was inspired by the example of legendary mountaineer Fritz Wiessner, who had still been climbing rock when he was eighty-six. Brower again resolved to "lose weight, get the right shoes, and get back on the rock." He lost the weight – for a while he was down to 184 pounds, then went up to 192 – but didn't obtain the right shoes. "I don't think I have the right knees," he says by way of explanation.

In March 1993, Brower was scheduled to return to Nepal for the fourth time to lead a trek into Chitwah National Park. The trek was canceled due to poor attendance. Brower was disappointed, but undaunted. Merely rerouted. He went to India and New Guinea instead.

RESOURCES

Tips to Improve Your Climbing

BASIC CLIMBING EQUIPMENT

Rock-Climbing Boots. A pair of lightweight, soft-soled, high-friction climbing boots is probably the most important item in the rock-climber's arsenal. Start with something comfortable and durable, rather than the latest in high-tech fashion. The latter is quite expensive, and unnecessary until you sort out how serious you are about the sport.

Whatever rock-climbing boots you buy, you will have paid good money for them, so take care of them. Some suggestions:

• When buying boots, don't forget to try them on with the thickness of sock you plan to use. You want them snug, but not too.
• Keep the soles of your boots wiped clean with a damp cloth, as gritty particles will quickly wear away the soft rubber.
• Don't wear your rock boots when walking to the crag. They are not designed for this and will only wear out more quickly.
• Avoid cramming your boots in a backpack, deforming them.
• If boots become wet from rain or sweat, don't dry them in direct heat, as this may cause the sole to peel. Allow them to air-dry slowly.

Rope. A single nylon rope 45 or 50 meters (about 150 or 165 feet) long and 11 millimeters (about half-an-inch) in diameter is easiest to handle. Today's climbing ropes are universally kernmantel, the term for nylon ropes constructed with an inner, usually braided, core that is protected by an outer woven sheath.

Most of a rope's strength (an 11 millimeter rope has a breaking strain of about 4,400 pounds) derives from its elasticity. Lose that elasticity and it's time to buy a new rope. If so, make sure you get one that carries a UIAA (Union Internationale des Associations d'Alpinisme) sticker.

Some suggestions for rope care:

• When traveling with gear in your car, keep your rope away from battery acid, oil, and other caustic substances.
• Never stand on a climbing rope. There may be a sharp edge underneath, or you may press small bits of grit into it. Gritty ropes can be

washed in fresh water with mild detergents, and dried by hanging out of the sun in airy, naturally heated places.

• Ultraviolet radiation damages ropes, and glass is no protection, so don't leave ropes in direct sunlight or in windows. (Don't buy the demo model hanging in the shop window.)

• Normal use will eventually fray the fibers of any rope, and abrasive rock like granite will do it more quickly than smooth rock like limestone. Falling rocks can nick, occasionally even cut, ropes. Check yours often by running your hand and eye along its length.

• Know your rope's history, especially how many falls it has endured. Modern ropes are tough, but a fall *can* damage a rope: **1.** A rope may be stretched taut over a sharp piece of rock that cuts into, or even through, its fibers. **2.** A moving, weighted rope, rubbing quickly against another rope for longer than a few seconds, can generate enough heat to melt the nylon; make sure any rope likely to be used in a fall will not run across another rope. **3.** A very hard fall can stretch the filaments beyond the point of complete recovery; most manufacturers recommend replacing your rope after a serious fall.

• Coil your rope properly, eliminating tangles, then store it in a clean, dark, dry, well-ventilated place. The trunk of a car does not qualify.

• Some suggest that a rope used for regular weekend climbing should be retired after two years – even if there is no apparent damage.

Harness. Once upon a time, climbers tied their climbing rope directly to their waist. An arrested fall with a rope tied to your waist can yank your spleen up into your throat. Fortunately, those days are past, and spleens can breathe easy. Today most climbers use a sit-harness, made from wide nylon tape sewn together. The advantages of a harness over tying directly to the waist:

• It's a more convenient way to join rope and torso.

• In the event of an arrested fall, a harness distributes the impact force over a wider area of the body.

• It offers convenient loops for clipping on runners and other gear.

Choose a comfortable harness; you may wear it for hours, with several pounds of hardware dangling from it. Try several on in the shop before deciding which one to buy.

Tips for taking care of your harness:

• Read all instructions carefully.

• Keep your harness away from caustic substances like battery acid.

• Inspect it regularly for signs of damage.

Carabiners. Modern carabiners have spring-loaded gates and are made of aluminum alloy and forged into D or oval shapes. These "snaplinks" are an integral part of a climber's gear collection, serving many purposes: clipping the rope to runners, attaching different equipment to a harness, or as part of the belaying system.

For loving care of your carabiners:

• Keep them away from alkali, which will attack the alloy.
• Rinse them in freshwater if they get near saltwater; even sea spray will rapidly corrode aluminum alloy.
• Lubricate the gates with a silicone-based spray if the action becomes rough.
• Don't drop or throw carabiners long distances; the impact can cause fractures.
• Don't put a three-way pull on carabiners; they are designed for a two-way pull only.

Runners. The runner is a loop of webbing or rope used to connect anchors to the climbing rope. Along with the carabiner and the rope, it is at the heart of the climber's protection system. Standard runners are one-inch-wide tubular nylon webbing, usually six feet long, that can be made into a loop with a water knot or a double fisherman's knot. Check the knots periodically to make sure they haven't worked loose.

Friends (camming devices). A Friend is an active (spring-loaded) cam device that is inserted into a crack as an anchor point. It includes four independently operating cams, enabling it to grip irregularly shaped cracks. (Other brands use either three or four cams.)

The Friend – on the market since the seventies – has revolutionized climbing protection. Almost any crack of any shape, from less than half an inch to five inches, can be easily protected. Tests by a German alpine club found Friends to be "bombproof." The downside is weight and cost: They are weighty and very expensive.

Because they are complex, Friends can jam or malfunction. They also have a tendency to work their way farther into a crack. Some suggestions for minimizing problems:

• Do not place the Friend too deep in a crack. When it's time to extract it, the cam release trigger may be out of reach.
• Realign the Friend if one or more of the cams does not bite into the crack walls.
• Don't let the cams invert, thereby losing their holding power.

- Avoid placements where the cams are open too wide. Try a larger Friend.
- Don't force the Friend into too tight a crack. Use a smaller Friend.
- For best performance, the size of the Friend should be such that the cam release trigger is in the middle third of its total length of travel in the retaining slot.
- Always close the cams completely and allow them to expand inside the crack.
- Minimize movement of the Friend by making sure it is connected properly to the rest of the climbing system.
- Keep Friends off the ground and away from dirt particles.
- If the movement becomes stiff, spray the moving parts with a lubricant like WD40 (not oil).
- If you have trouble with extraction, carry a special retrieving tool.

BASIC CLIMBING RULES

- Make sure you bring enough clothing, food, and drink.
- Read the right guidebook and any other pertinent information.
- If climbing in a remote area, leave details of your plans, including time of return.
- Find the right partner. Explore each other's capabilities on easy climbs first.
- Select the right route – one that matches your skill level and interest.
- Stay with easy climbs when starting to lead.
- If route-finding looks tricky, carry the local guidebook with you.
- Make sure you and your partner understand each other's calls.
- Devise an equipment and safety checklist and use it. Make it a pre-climb ritual to go through that checklist.
- Tie into your harness with care, and don't interrupt someone else tying into theirs. It is possible to leave the job unfinished, (see the chapter on Lynn Hill).
- Don't stand or walk on ropes or gear.
- Always clean your feet well before climbing, especially on wet rock.
- Don't stand directly beneath a climber, lest a rock or the climber's body fall on you.
- While climbing, don't be afraid to put in lots of protection. In other words, don't be macho. Take care to put the pieces in correctly.
- Never be afraid to turn back if a climb gets too difficult. Once again, don't be macho. The route will be there another day.
- Don't ever throw rocks. If one should dislodge, immediately yell

"Rock!" or "Below!" as though you mean it. Call "Rope!" or "Below!" when dropping ropes for rappelling.

- If someone else yells a warning, look to locate the danger. If it's headed your way, crouch into the rock and protect your head.
- Check the screw-gates on locking carabiners each time you use them.
- Concentrate. Accidents often occur when climbers relax, say at the top of a climb. Pay special attention to wet or muddy rock.
- Take as much care with the descent as with the ascent. Too many accidents occur on rappel.
- Know what to do in case of emergency, such as where the nearest phone and hospital are. Check the guidebook for that information.
- Cultivate self-awareness. Monitor fatigue and concentration levels.
- Don't get overconfident. That won't happen at first, but is a definite risk after you complete a few routes, a phenomenon known as Intermediate Syndrome or Sophomore Slump.

BEHAVIOR ON THE ROCK

- Respect other people's right to use the outdoors—even if they aren't climbers.
- Follow the ethics and traditions of whatever country you're in.
- Don't leave litter, such as chalk wrappings or old slings.
- Don't use offensive language if you're in areas visited by the public.
- Don't be loud and raucous; others might like a quiet day in nature.
- Show restraint with chalk; it gums up holds and looks ugly.
- Wait your turn. Climbing is done on a first-come-first-served basis.
- Don't rappel down where others are climbing. It's best to ask first.
- Don't wipe mud off boots onto the rock; your blank rock may be someone else's hold.
- Respect local regulations: routes may be closed due to nesting birds, rare plants, or the danger of falling rock.
- Warn other climbers of imminent danger, such as poor belay or rappel anchors.
- Defecate and urinate away from the rock.

BELAYING

When a climber falls, it is up to the second person—the belayer—to hold the rope and prevent the climber from hitting the ground. The belayer is able to do this with the help of friction on the rope, usually from a special belay device. Some tips for the belayer:

- Face the climber, and stay alert to the possibility of a fall. Anchor yourself well using two anchors if possible.

- Select the belay device that works well for you. A common belay device is the Figure-8 descender, which is just about idiot-proof. You slide a bight of rope through the large hole and over the shaft, then clip in. Voila – friction.
- In the absence of a belay device, you can use a waist (hip) belay. It is not as efficient as a belay device, and things can go wrong. There can be extreme friction at the back, hands, and forearms. You should wear gloves, long sleeves, and some kind of padding around the back. (Make sure the live rope comes around on the same side as the rope to the anchor.)
- Leave in only as much slack in the rope as your partner needs; not so much that you get into a tug-of-war, not so little that a fall will be dangerous.
- Always pay the rope out smoothly, without jerking. It is easy to pull a leader off balance.
- When belaying from a ground stance, don't stand too far from the crag, because that can put an angle in the rope that increases the chances that pieces of protection will pull out during a fall.
- Stay roughly beneath your partner, lest you be pulled sideways by a fall (but not directly beneath, in the path of rockfall).
- Move the foot opposite your brake hand forward and plant it securely.

COMMUNICATION

Clear, concise communication between climber and belayer is vital. Some common terms:

Climber: "On belay?" (Have you got me secured?)

Belayer: "Belay on" (I've got you; I'm managing the rope and am prepared to catch a fall.)

Climber: "Climbing." (I'm done fooling around; this is for real.)

Climber: "Slack." (Let out more rope.)

Climber: "Up rope." (Take in rope.)

Climber: "Tension." (Take in rope till you feel tension, and hold it firmly at that point.)

Climber: "Off belay." (I've anchored myself at the next belay stance; you can relax.)

Belayer: "Belay off." (I've released the rope; you're no longer on belay.)

Climber: "Rock!" (Something hard is falling fast in your direction.)

DESCENDING. Contrary to popular belief, climbing down is frequently harder than climbing up. It's nice if you can face out from the rock. Besides being faster, it will allow you to assess the problems that lie ahead. If it gets steeper, you can turn sideways or traverse. On real steep terrain, however, you must face the rock. Such down-climbing is more of a challenge than climbing up because it's harder to see your footholds. It is a skill that must be practiced, preferably while you're top-roped.

As a last resort, you can rappel (French for "to recall"; in German, the word is *abseil*). This is the most dangerous maneuver in climbing because you are totally committed to the rope and the anchor.

Some suggestions for safe rappelling:

• When learning to rappel, use a top rope.
• As in skydiving, the hardest part of a rappel is getting over the edge. Knowing that may make it easier to start; then again, it may not.
• The most important element of a rappel is a safe, reliable anchor. Suitable ones include pinnacles, chockstones, pitons, bolts, trees, or flakes.
• When starting a rappel, avoid dragging the ropes across sharp rock, such as the edge of the ledge you are leaving. Avoid side-to-side movement, which can saw the rope back and forth across that edge. When a rope is weighted, it is more susceptible to cutting.
• Stay even and consistent in movement, to stress anchor points as little as possible. Avoid the bounding Hollywood-style rappel, which can stress anchor points, heat up the rope, and dislodge rocks.
• The speed of descent is ultimately controlled by allowing the trailing rope to run slowly through your gloved hand. If you go too fast, it's possible to burn your hand.
• You'll hate it if you rappel off the end of your rope. You can avoid that pitfall by tying the ends of the rope together (and also by attaching a safety line from your harness to the rappel rope with a prusik knot).

MENTAL PREPARATION. Some suggestions for gaining climbing confidence:

• Practice on easier climbs to gain competence in the physical techniques.
• Develop good equipment management—and take no more gear than you need.
• Learn as much about a climb beforehand as possible. Read guide-

books, ask other climbers.
• Warm up on an easy climb that practically guarantees success.
• Do bouldering or stretching exercises to loosen muscles. Tight muscles use up more energy and are more prone to tears and strains.
• Set goals for the day's climbing.
• Do climbs that are fun. If you hate chimneys, avoid them.
• Don't be afraid to retreat. There is much to be learned from tactical retreats. When a so-called defeat later becomes a victory, the feeling of accomplishment is that much sweeter. As the old saw goes: "He who turns and walks away lives to climb another day."
• Develop climbing skills at your own pace. Nobody can do everything all at once; enjoy your apprenticeship.
• Don't go climbing with a hangover or after an all-night party. Celebrate *after* the climb.
• Put in pieces of protection as often as you need them. If a protection placed six feet off the ground boosts your confidence, so be it.
• On the other hand, be aware of the big picture. It won't help your confidence one bit if you run out of protection hardware before you reach the end of the pitch.

BOULDERING

The subsport of bouldering offers a good way to begin climbing. It requires minimal equipment, and falls are seldom fatal.

Suggestions for what to take bouldering:
• Boots. The high-friction boots are the best.
• Drying cloth. Important for drying and wiping dirt from boots.
• Chalk bag. A small bag that ties to the waist.
• Chalk. Grip-enhancing material that can be bought in either block or powder form.
• Toothbrush. For cleaning rocks or old chalk from holds.
• Wire brush. Used the same way as a toothbrush, but more effective. The holds on busy routes may become burnished from overuse, and a wire brush will promote better friction by removing the shine.
• Renzine. A brown liquid used on the fingers to help chalk stick longer. It also helps heal cuts.
• Tape. For protecting fingers.
• Mat. If the ground is damp or muddy, a mat at the foot of the problem provides a clean, dry starting point, as well as a target when jumping off.

Safety

Humans are the most adaptable of all animals. This ability to adjust to a wide range of meteorological and topographical conditions has enabled members of this species to travel to any place on earth, though not without problems. We'll take a look here at the main health and safety hazards faced by climbers, and offer solutions for beating them.

General Sickness. There are few things worse than being sick away from home. Yet leaving home vastly increases your chances of getting sick.

Solution. If you are traveling to another country, get the requisite shots: typhoid, paratyphoid, tetanus, polio, cholera, or any others recommended by health officials for the countries you plan to visit.

- One gammaglobulin shot reduces the chances of getting hepatitis and is probably worthwhile, especially in the Andes.

- In malarial areas, including the Indian subcontinent, you should take weekly malaria pills, called maloprim, starting a few weeks before entering and ending a few weeks after leaving a malarial area.

- Check with the embassies of the countries you will visit to determine if you need a formal certificate of inoculation in order to enter the country.

- Once you are abroad, be careful of bad water, which does not necessarily look bad. Carry water-purification tablets and/or water filters (the best of which are lightweight and effective against giardia, bacteria, and viruses as small as .005 microns). Use them whenever the water is of questionable origin, which may be all the time until you are well above both human and animal habitation.

- Most dysentery clears up on its own, but if symptoms persist for more than two days, you may need drugs. Amoebic dysentery and giardia are both common, and once you have them the only effective treatment is a powerful drug called Flagyl. Bacilliary dysentery can be alleviated with Lomotil.

Dehydration. This is a big problem at high altitude, where the air is thin, cold, and extremely dry. Hard work, heavy breathing, and sweating in the bright sunlight can lead to rapid dehydration. This causes muscle cramps, loss of energy, and thickening of the blood, which can mean greater susceptibility to frostbite and possibly even to blood clots.

Solution. Drink lots of water, tea, etc. Drink often – more than you think you need – even if you do not feel thirsty. A daily liquid intake of four quarts may not be enough to replace moisture lost during twelve hours of climbing.

Cold Weather. Mountains tend to be cold, windy places – which means cold climbers, unless they take the right precautions.

Solution. Be informed. When you climb a mountain, the higher you go, the colder it gets. The average temperature declines by three to five degrees Fahrenheit for every thousand feet of altitude. The air gets thinner, and usually drier, and thus absorbs less heat from the sun.

• Temperature differences at various elevations create wild mountain winds. That means a windchill, which can play havoc with your comfort level. For example, a temperature of 10 degrees Fahrenheit combined with a modest 20 mile-per-hour wind will cool the body as rapidly as 25 below zero with no wind! Windchill is a prime cause of frostbite.

• Wear or bring clothes for the top of the mountain, not just the bottom. Sometimes the difference can be dramatic. I once started out for the top of New Hampshire's Mount Washington wearing shorts and a tank top, only to encounter near-blizzard conditions higher up.

• In cold conditions, wear layers. Lots and lots of layers. As a starter, long underwear helps trap heat against the skin. Wear a hat to keep the head warm. A lot of warmth is lost through the head.

• Keep your feet warm and dry. In extreme cold, plastic boots are de rigueur, because they are warmer and they don't freeze. Tips from the experts: put plastic bags between two layers of socks; consider battery-powered socks.

Hypothermia. Hypothermia results when the body's metabolism is unable to produce enough heat to cope with heat being lost. It can be deadly because it means a lowered body core temperature, not just cold fingers and toes. Symptoms include uncontrollable shivering, irrational thought, and apathy, making the victim incapable of self-help. Hypothermia is insidious because it can strike even when air temperatures are above freezing; moderate temperatures combined with wet and wind can be deadly.

Solution. Snack frequently. Trail foods like gorp provide sugar for use by the muscles and for conversion into heat energy.

- Keep warm and dry. A hat is essential, because as much as 40 percent of our heat is lost through our head.
- Members of a party should watch each other closely for developing signs. The time from initial symptoms to death can be as little as two hours, so treatment must be immediate.
- If you are alone, allow a wide margin of safety by building a good shelter and utilizing adequate clothing in any threatening conditions. Never ignore shivering or fatigue.
- In a case where a climber's body temperature has dropped so far that normal metabolic processes cannot reverse a continually declining temperature, additional outside warmth must be applied. Get the victim out of wet clothes, out of the elements. Build a fire. Put the victim in a sleeping bag and have a second person lie in the bag with him. The more skin contact, the more warmth.
- Hot liquids can be given but not before external heat sources, because the cold blood from the extremities can surge into the core region of the body, chilling it to the point of death.

Frostbite. Frostbite occurs when tissue, usually at the extremities, is frozen.

Solution. Frostbite is not as common as it once was, thanks to better clothing, such as Gore-Tex gloves and plastic boots.

- Always carry a spare pair of gloves.
- If superficial frostbite occurs, you can warm the affected areas by putting them against warm skin. Take care not to break the damaged skin, as that increases the chances of infection.
- As tissue thaws out, it is more susceptible to infection, and antibiotics need to be taken.

Snow blindness. A temporary condition caused by excessive glare from ice and snow, it can occur even on cloudy days.

Solution. Sunglasses with both front and side protection should be worn all day. Also, a wide-brimmed hat will help shield you from some of the glare.

Sunburn. At higher elevations, the thin atmosphere filters out fewer ultraviolet rays, which puts you at greater risk for sunburn. It may seem minor compared to, say, pulmonary edema, but the incidence of malignant melanoma, a deadly skin cancer, has risen nearly 100 percent in the past ten years.

Solution. Use a good sunscreen (one that works through perspiration) with a skin protection factor (SPF) of at least fifteen. Cover exposed skin whenever possible.

Altitude Sickness. Most of us live near the bottom of a ten-mile-deep ocean of air. This air, having weight and being compressible, becomes denser as it gets deeper. At sea level, we are adapted to this density, or pressure, which is fifteen pounds per square inch. When we gulp in air, the fifteen pounds of pressure forces sufficient oxygen through the thin linings of our lungs to give our blood what it needs to sustain us.

As one goes higher, the pressure diminishes. At 10,000 feet, it is down to ten pounds, and much less oxygen is forced through the linings of the lungs. As a result, the blood may carry as much as 15 percent less than its normal load of oxygen, a shortage that can cause headaches, fatigue, and shortness of breath. At 18,000 feet, the air pressure is only half what it is at sea level, and almost no one escapes unpleasant symptoms. For most, mental processes are dulled, decision-making suffers, and vision weakens. The simplest exertion takes a terrible physical toll. The risk of life-threatening edema skyrockets. Above 25,000 feet, a climber's heart races and his blood becomes thick and sluggish, increasing the peril of frostbite in the severe cold.

Solution. Acclimatize. Move up a slope incrementally. Not everyone will be affected by altitude sickness at the same rate, but everyone will experience some symptoms if they go high enough fast enough.
- If symptoms are severe, the victim should descend in case pulmonary or cerebral edema has begun to set in. Once edema has started, it will be fatal unless the person descends.
- Everybody must go through the acclimatization process no matter how many times they have been to high altitude. There is evidence that climbers adapt a little better if they have regularly been to altitude. Nevertheless, even accomplished climbers of Himalayan peaks will be off their game, perhaps severely, if they go from sea level to 12,000 feet without acclimatizing. And anyone whisked from sea level to the top of an "eight-thousander" would quickly die. As a general rule, do not gain more than about 2,000 feet per day in altitude.
- Climb high, then return low to sleep.

- Avoid unnecessary exercise until fully acclimatized.
- Drink plenty of fluids at all times.
- If you descend, remember that your hard-won acclimatization is lost in a few days. Do not reascend rapidly to altitude.
- Beware of pills that mask the symptoms of altitude sickness, allowing you to carry on, ignorant of physiological deterioration.
- Conditioning seems to help a little, but the main criterion for successful adaptation to high altitude is what is called the hypoxic drive to breathe. Simplified, it is a measure of how much compensatory breathing you do when your tissues get underoxygenated, as they do at altitude.

Accidents. Accidents can occur for a variety of reasons, such as bad or wrong equipment, rapid change in weather, or "operator errors" like getting lost, overstepping one's ability, inexperience, incompetence.

Solution. If you help an accident victim:

- Note the state of consciousness of the victim.
- If the person is unconscious, make sure the air passage is not blocked by the tongue or vomit. Keep the patient on his side or front.
- Safeguard the unconscious or thrashing patient from any further fall.
- Stop any bleeding by using pressure with a handkerchief or first-aid dressing. Cover open wounds with a clean, light dressing.
- Make the person as comfortable as possible, keeping him dry, insulated from the ground, with no more movement than is necessary.
- Use a temporary splint, or some other means of immobilization, in the case of a broken limb.
- Keep the victim warm, using extra clothing, survival bag, whatever. Unless internal injuries are suspected, hot drinks can be given; but in cases of exposure, warming a person too quickly can be dangerous.
- Try to attract attention by shouting, whistle blasts, use of flashlight or distress flares, mirror to the sun, smoke signals. The Alpine Distress Signal is six long blasts, or six flashes of light, repeated at one-minute intervals.
- If the wait for rescue is likely to be long, try to construct some type of shelter.
- If it is impossible to fetch help, continue trying to attract attention.
- If the injured person has to be left alone while you get help, you should do two things before you leave: 1. Take note of the exact location of the injured person, paying particular attention to any

landmarks. **2.** Use a fixed object to put a belay on the injured person to prevent him staggering off semiconscious.

OVERNIGHTERS

If you spend a night out, you have three basic choices of accommodations: tent, snow cave, bivouac. It's important to make your accommodations as safe as possible. Know the advantages, the disadvantages, and the dangers of the types of shelter available to you.

• Tent. Huddling in a tent high on a windswept mountain is not exactly the way they described camping in *Boy's Life*.

The first consideration is finding a place where it is physically possible to pitch a tent; the second is safety. In choosing a site, be prepared for the worst. Consider wind, avalanche potential, rockfall. If fierce winds are tearing at your tent during the night, sleep will be nigh impossible. If an avalanche buries you in snow, you may have forever to sleep.

Tent pegs are of no use once grass line is left below. When camping on snow, ice axes, and snow stakes, are potential anchors for the guys. Here's a creative, lightweight idea: wrap a guy rope around a plastic bag filled with snow and bury it.

Watch for and avoid spindrift snow building up between the tent and the slope behind. That can force the tent off its platform.

• Snow cave. A snow cave offers the best chances of survival in bad conditions. Sheltered from the elements, a snow cave makes an ideal home for a mountaineer. Winds will not affect you, and with luck, avalanches should roll right over you as well. A snow cave is far warmer than a tent at night, but pleasantly cooler in the heat of the midday sun.

The disadvantages of a snow cave are that you have to dig the damn thing (it is tiring, time-consuming work), and it's not always easy to find the soft, deep snow you need.

• Bivouac. This is the least comfortable and potentially most dangerous option, though there is a big difference between one bivouac and a series of them. Each night will likely be damper and colder than the one before. Time will drag, and sleep will be intermittent, at best, in bad weather.

The danger of bivouacking can be mitigated by any or all of the following: a bivouac tent (though there may be no suitable ledge on which to put it); a good Gore-Tex sleeping bag; a good jacket with a large hood.

In the absence of all of these items, hug the person you're with in order to share body heat.

Lightning. Contrary to the cliche, lightning *will* strike twice in the same place.

Solution. During electrical storms, avoid exposed ridges, summits, and the mouths of shallow caves.

• Avoid precarious stances, where you can be knocked off.

• Find a safe refuge well below exposed positions. The best place is supposed to be a ravine formed by the intersection of two slopes.

• Get an early start, setting out early in the morning to complete the climb and be off the mountain before the afternoon storm builds up.

Avalanches. Snow avalanches are of two main types: (1) loose snow avalanches, which start at a point and gather mass into a fan shape as they fall, and (2) cohesive slab avalanches that start sliding over a large area all at once, creating a well-defined fracture line.

Both types require a "trigger," which may be a falling rock or cornice, the collapse of a weak layer in the snowpack, a sudden change in temperature or barometric pressure, wind, new snowfall, a nearby jet breaking the sound barrier, or the weight of a climber.

Of the two types, slab avalanches are more likely to be started by the weight of a climber on a stressed slab that is weakly bonded to the ground or to other layers within the snowpack. An avalanche of either type need only travel a short distance to gain deadly force and mass. People have been buried at the bottom of a thirty-foot slope.

Solution. The following information can improve your chances of avoiding, and if necessary surviving, an avalanche.

• Avalanches most often occur on slopes between thirty and forty-five degrees, low-angle enough to allow poorly bonded snow to accumulate to significant depths.

• Slab avalanches most often occur on convex-shaped slopes, though they may occur on concave-shaped slopes if other factors overcome the natural compression on such slopes.

• Snow on north-facing slopes in the Northern Hemisphere (and south-facing slopes in the Southern Hemisphere) receive less sun, so such slopes are often slower to stabilize than other slopes.

• Snow tends to be blown from windward slopes and deposited as slabs on leeward slopes, which are often unstable.

• If surface features such as rocks, trees, or brush are visible above the snowpack in significant quantity, they will help anchor the snow. Once those features are buried, avalanche danger increases.

- If the rate of new snowfall is greater than about an inch per hour, avalanches are more likely to occur.
- If wind is present, the danger increases rapidly. In the absence of new snow, wind is the major contributor to instability. Sustained wind will push loose snow into gullies and slopes on the leeward sides, forming slabs.
- New snow is not necessarily deposited evenly on every slope, so be alert to variations in depth. When six inches of new snow builds up on a slope without sloughing, avalanche conditions are dangerous.
- Storms starting with low temperatures and dry snow, followed by rising temperatures, are a recipe for avalanches. The dry snow at the start forms a poor bond to the old snow or icy surface. On the other hand, if a storm starts warm, then gets colder, bonding is improved.
- Wet-snow avalanches occur most often during the first prolonged spring thaw. In the high mountains, however, wet-snow avalanche danger may exist throughout the summer.
- The art of avalanche avoidance requires constant vigilance. As you travel through the mountains, take note of old avalanche paths, especially those that show signs of recent activity, as those slopes will be most likely to slide again.
- If the snow cracks and the fractures travel for some distance, avalanche danger is high.
- If a slope is suspect, dig a snow pit through the snowpack on that slope and examine the various layers of snow. Take a handful of snow from each of the layers and try to form a snowball. If it holds together well, then that layer is probably stable.
- The safest routes follow ridge crests on the windward side below the potential fracture line of a cornice.
- On dangerous open slopes or wide couloirs, climb up and down the edges in a straight line. Switchbacks in the middle are likely to cause an unstable slope to slide.
- Traverse dangerous slopes or couloirs at the top, above the release zone. If you can't cross above the release zone, make an even longer detour if necessary and cross well below the bottom of the slope.
- If you must cross a suspect slope, only one person should cross at a time, with the others waiting their turn in a safe location and watching each exposed climber carefully. Don't assume a slope is safe because one person crossed it safely.

- Roped belays are only useful on small slopes. The force of a major avalanche will make it impossible to hold a victim.
- While traveling in dangerous areas, unhook the belly strap of your backpack to assure that you can quickly drop it if necessary. Wear your gloves and hat, and secure all openings in your clothing to help prevent frostbite and hypothermia should you be caught in an avalanche.
- If you're caught in an avalanche, get rid of your pack and all equipment and try to stay near the surface of the sliding snow by "swimming." Try to make it to the side of the avalanche.
- As the snow slows down, keep your hands in front of your face, trying to create an air pocket when the snow stops.
- If you are buried, you will survive longer, hopefully until your partners find you, if you don't panic.
- Members of a party should mark the spot where a victim was first caught and also the place last seen to aid them in the search.
- After locating and freeing an avalanche victim, treat for suffocation, shock, traumatic injuries, hypothermia, or frostbite, as appropriate.

"OBJECTIVE HAZARDS"

Falling rock, collapsing cornices and seracs, storms, hidden crevasses, avalanches, and weak snow bridges are often called "objective hazards," as though a climber can do nothing to avoid them. However, there are precautions that can be taken. And by accepting some responsibility for mountain hazards, aren't we more likely to be cautious, to try to do the right thing to minimize the risk?

We should cross the zones of rockfall only when the rocks are solidly in place, avoiding the morning thaw and evening freeze. We should allow enough time for new snow to settle and stabilize before we commit ourselves to an avalanche slope. We should rope up when snow hides crevasses, and unrope to move faster when that is appropriate. We should be prepared for freezing temperatures and storms. We should allow time to acclimatize properly, test our holds before putting weight on them, listen to our cautious side a little more, and avoid gambling recklessly.

And don't forget to drop a postcard to Mom once in a while.

Climbing into the Past

People have been present in mountain areas ever since the first hunters chased game up the primordial slopes. But early man did not settle in the higher mountains until chased there by enemies or circumstance. Viewed from afar, they were lands of impassable terrors, the hangouts of demons and unruly gods.

The connection between mountains and the supernatural has always been strong. The early Greeks placed their pantheon on Mount Olympus. To their way of thinking, the Pillars of Hercules, rocky gendarmes overlooking the Strait of Gibraltar, held up one end of the universe. Similarly, the ancient Chinese believed five mountains propped up the sky. High places have long been seen as holy. Moses received the Ten Commandments on Mount Sinai, and Buddha was born in the shadow of the Himalaya. Many great monasteries – the Potala in Lhasa, Tibet; the hospice of Saint Bernard; the cloisters at Mount Athos – are all well above sea level. When Christians look up at mountains, they feel a little closer to heaven.

Some date the birth of the sport of mountain climbing to 1336, when Francesco and Gerardo Petrarch ascended France's Mount Ventoux (6,273 feet). More often the chronology begins in 1492, when Charles VIII overcame the hostility of a church that viewed mountain climbing as heretical and ordered his chamberlain, Antoine de Ville, to scale Mount Aiguille (6,783 feet) in the Dauphine Alps near Grenoble. Most people assumed Aiguille was unassailable, but de Ville proved otherwise. After spending three days on the summit, he returned to write the first detailed account of what was probably man's first attempt to climb a significant mountain just to get to the top.

The Italian Renaissance provided a boost to climbing as well as art. In the sixteenth century even Leonardo da Vinci could be found clambering up the southern slopes of the Pennine Alps. The center of that climbing movement was actually across the Swiss border, in

Zurich, its leader Conrad Gesner, an eminent naturalist who resolved to climb at least one peak every year for his "mental delight."

In the New World, the first climber of any renown was Darby Field, who in 1642 climbed New Hampshire's Mount Washington (6,288 feet), the highest peak in the Northeast and site of some of the worst weather in the world. It was not weather, but superstition, however, that caused all but two of Field's Abenaki Indian guides to turn back before the summit. They believed the Great Spirit ruled from atop Mount Washington and would strike dead anyone who dared trespass on its upper slopes. Field, undaunted, not only made it to the top but returned a month later and did it again, this time with a half-dozen climbing converts. And thus the word spread.

THE ALPS

The highest mountain in the Alps, Mont Blanc (15,771 feet), has been summitted by thousands of people. But in 1760, no one had the courage to accept the challenge offered by Swiss naturalist Horace Benedict de Saussure. Make the first ascent of Mont Blanc, said de Saussure, and win a cash prize. It was twenty-six years before two Frenchmen took the dare and climbed the mountain. Buoyed by the confidence that it could in fact be done, de Saussure himself repeated the feat the following year—accompanied by his valet and eighteen guides. Some mountain scholars regard de Saussure as the first real patron of mountain climbing.

Despite the enthusiasm of men like de Saussure, not many embraced mountain climbing for the fun of it. Even those who lived among the mountains did not climb them. Many failed to appreciate their beauty, seeing them instead as mutations, deviations in the Divine Plan. Eighteenth-century travelers crossing the Alps sometimes requested blindfolds because their sense of harmony was disturbed by the sight of such wild irregularities in the earth's surface.

Meanwhile, the banner of adventure continued to be taken up by a spirited few—a lunatic fringe, some would say. By 1850, Mont Blanc had been climbed by fifty different parties. And in 1854, a Britisher on his honeymoon, Sir Alfred Wills, climbed the difficult Wetterhorn (12,166 feet). His achievement tapped some hidden spark in the Anglo-Saxon temperament and kicked off the so-called "Golden Age of Alpinism." Between 1854 and 1872, thirty-one of the thirty-nine major peaks climbed in the Alps were summitted by British mountaineers and their guides, who were usually Swiss.

The most famous, and tragic, climb of those years was Edward Whymper's 1865 ascent of the Matterhorn (14,685 feet) in the Pennine Alps. The Matterhorn, a breathtakingly beautiful obelisk of rock near the Italian border, was then thought to be invincible, for it had deflected numerous attempts to reach its summit, including seven by Whymper himself. Whether or not one agreed with superstitious natives who believed that a ruined city, located on the summit, was the home of demons and spirits of the damned, it was indeed the "last great problem of the Alps."

Whymper, 26, a sketch artist from London, finally solved the problem on his eighth try, when he led a party of seven to the top of the Matterhorn on July 14, 1865. They passed a pleasant hour on the summit, eating, drinking, and resting before they started down. The descent turned into a nightmare when the second man on the rope slipped, knocking the first man over and dragging the third and fourth violently down the mountain. The hemp rope snapped, sparing the other three members of the party, but dooming the unlucky ones to death. As Whymper later wrote:

"For a few seconds we saw our unfortunate companions sliding downwards on their backs, and spreading out their hands, endeavoring to save themselves. They passed from our sight uninjured, disappeared one by one, and fell from precipice to precipice on the Matterhorn Glacier below, a distance of four thousand feet. So perished our comrades!"

The outcry in Britain could be heard across the English Channel. Queen Victoria even suggested outlawing mountain climbing, but nothing came of it and the furor eventually subsided. Over the years, the Matterhorn has been climbed from every possible angle by more than sixty thousand people, including children, octogenarians, blind men, and a mountaineer who later became Pope Pius XI.

After 1870, with all the major summits in Europe having been trod by man, mountaineers began looking elsewhere for spectacular peaks to climb. In 1897, the British explorer Sir Halford Mackinder, with the aid of native guides, succeeded on Mount Kenya (17,040 feet). That same year, an expedition led by Edward A. Fitzgerald reached the top of Aconcagua (22,834 feet) in the Argentinian Andes, the highest point in the Western Hemisphere.

No longer did serious climbers go alone or with a friend or two. Success on higher peaks demanded elaborate teamwork, with roped parties moving up the slopes incrementally, establishing camps en route. Steeper, slippery routes required special equipment. The old-style iron-tipped pole (alpenstock) was replaced by the strong, light-weight ice ax. For better footing on ice, innovative minds devised crampons, sharp steel spikes that could be strapped to boots. Time eventually brought iron pitons for driving into ice or rock crevices. To a protective piton, a ring (carabiner) could be clipped, through which a rope ran.

THE HIMALAYA

The greatest test of man's ability to reach high places was also the hardest to approach. Besides geographical obstacles – Mount Everest is several thousand miles from London – there were political ones. Tibet and Nepal, the countries that are home to most of the high Himalayan peaks, had a long tradition of excluding Westerners. The first explorers climbers had to disguise themselves as Nepalese herdsmen, Buddhist pilgrims, or Tibetan merchants just to get across a border. Once in Nepal or Tibet, some disappeared, some returned to Europe with clandestine photographs, and a few traveled beyond the cities and towns to tiny communities in the high foothills, where they found herdsmen willing to help them climb a peak. Utilizing just such aid, W. W. Graham in 1883 went to the top of Mount Kabru (24,002 feet) in Nepal. Nobody would reach a higher summit for almost fifty years.

In 1904, Sir Francis Younghusband, a British colonel, entered Tibet, intent on forcing the Tibetans into discussions regarding British/Tibetan/Russian relations. On his push to the capital city of Lhasa, Younghusband and his 622 men engaged some natives in battle, killing hundreds of them while suffering no loss of British life. When they reached Lhasa, they learned that the Dalai Lama had fled to Mongolia, leaving a lesser lama to sign a treaty. Most of the concessions wrung from the Tibetans concerned trade and border disputes, but Younghusband, an ardent mountaineer, also wrangled permission for the occasional British expedition to explore the Tibetan Himalaya.

The opening of Tibet, plus improved transportation, encouraged more and more Western adventurers to find out just how formidable the Himalaya could be. If climbers survived the land and sea journey to Asia, then the approach on foot through steamy valleys and over mountain passes and up the steep glaciers, then intense cold and ferocious gales, they then confronted the rarefied air of high altitude. Many an accomplished Alps climber was beaten back in the Himalaya by the enervating effects of thin air. As George Leigh-Mallory said, the high-altitude mountaineer is "like a sick man walking in a dream."

Despite the substantial risks, there were plenty of adventurers in the twentieth century to whom an unclimbed peak was an open dare. Graham's altitude record was finally broken in 1930 when an international party organized in Switzerland summitted Jonsong Peak (24,340 feet). In 1931 it was rebroken by an English party that reached the top of Kamet (25,447 feet) in the center of the Himalayan chain. Then came Nanda Devi (25,660 feet), the highest peak climbed up to 1950. In the twenties and thirties, climbers attempting Mount Everest reached higher elevations, but they failed to top their mountain.

After World War II, climbers began to benefit from research aimed at, among other things, improving the efficiency and safety of high-altitude flight. Bottles of compressed oxygen were made lighter. Face-mask design was advanced, reducing the chances that oxygen flow would fail at a critical moment. Nylon rope replaced hemp. With many of the political and technical problems solved, the stage was set for success on the "eight-thousanders."

There are fourteen mountains in the world over eight thousand meters high, all of them in the Himalaya/Karakoram range. In 1950, when a French expedition led by Maurice Herzog had a go at Annapurna, the eleventh highest at 26,504 feet, none of the eight-thousanders had ever been climbed, despite twenty-two attempts.

Relying on hopelessly inaccurate maps, the French team took weeks to establish a base camp. The Western world followed their progress, joining in a mass countdown of the days left until the monsoon was expected to begin dumping massive amounts of snow on them. Even in pre-monsoon, storms relentlessly swept the mountain. In between snowfall and avalanches, the climbers and porters shuttled forty-pound loads, eventually establishing a string of camps high up the mountain.

On June 3 the weather cleared long enough for Herzog and Louis Lachenal to reach the summit. The eight-thousand-meter barrier was broken, but at an extravagant price. As they began their descent, the monsoon struck with a vengeance, forcing the two men to bivouac in a crude snow cave. Herzog lost his gloves and nearly died of exposure; at one point he was tossed five hundred feet down the mountain by an avalanche.

Back at Camp II he had to endure excruciating antifrostbite injections. He was carried on a litter for four weeks, delirious and near death, over glaciers and mountain passes, down into valleys, and back to civilization. On a train crossing the steaming Indian plains, the team physician amputated his gangrenous fingers and toes, tossing them out the window as they went.

The threat of dying or losing digits failed to deter the driven, however, and thirteen of the fourteen eight-thousanders fell in the next decade, including the two highest, Mount Everest (29,028 feet) and K2 (28,250 feet). Though K2 is generally regarded as the most difficult mountain to climb in the world, it was the conquest of Everest that got most of the attention.

Half a mile higher than Annapurna, Everest resisted more than thirty years of desperate human struggle to reach its summit. In 1921, a British party, with Tibetan permission, explored the northern approaches to Everest and found a route up the Rongbuk Glacier. George Leigh-Mallory, one of the great climbers of his time, along with two companions and several porters, reached the North Col, a saddle 23,000 feet up the mountain's northeast ridge.

The following year Mallory was back with a party of thirteen Englishmen and 150 porters. He retraced his route to the North Col, then went on to establish a camp at 25,000 feet, higher than man had ever set foot, but still more than four thousand vertical feet short of Everest's summit. Struggling on, Mallory and two companions eventually reached 27,000 feet before abandoning the climb due to frigid exhaustion.

Another team on that same expedition reached 27,235 feet, utilizing primitive oxygen equipment. The oxygen (called "English air" by the Sherpas) was of little use on the climb, but it saved the climbers' lives by keeping them from freezing to death in a storm. After resting below, Mallory made still another stab at the summit. He was stopped by an avalanche that killed seven porters and almost swept away the whole party.

Two years later, in 1924, Mallory and the English were back on Everest. The well-organized expedition used three hundred men to shuttle gear, eventually establishing Camp VI at 26,800 feet. From there, two strong climbers, Edward Norton and Theodore Somervell, attempted the summit, reaching the top of a stratum of sandstone called the "yellow band," just above 28,000 feet.

Next up was the team of Andrew Irvine and Mallory, who seems to have believed that it was his fate to climb Everest or die trying. Four days after Norton and Somervell's summit bid, Mallory and Irvine went for the top. N. E. O'Dell, who was hauling gear toward Camp VI sighted them as they crept up a rocky ridge, just below the last pyramid to the summit. They were "going strong for the top," he reported, but dangerously behind schedule. It was too late in the day for them to reach the summit and return to Camp VI before dark. As O'Dell watched, they disappeared into the mist.

That was the last anyone saw of either man. Nine years later, the next Everest expedition found one of their ice axes at about 28,000 feet. The fate of the two men has haunted mountaineers ever since – as has the question *Did they reach the top?*

Three more full-scale Everest expeditions followed in the thirties, but none reached the summit. In all, six British assaults on Everest between 1921 and 1938 failed, the last five ending in death for one or more climbers. After nearly two decades of struggle between Man and Mountain, seven climbers had reached 28,100 feet; none, with the possible exception of Mallory or Irvine, had been higher.

Was man capable of going higher? Some believed that an invisible barrier existed that would prevent anyone from reaching the top of the highest peak.

After World War II, Tibet lost its independence to Communist China, closing its borders to Westerners while Nepal was opening hers. That forced a change in the Everest strategy, for the mountain lies on the border of the two countries. The south face of Everest, in Nepal, was now available to be climbed, but in 1950 it was truly terra incognita. It took two years of exploratory reconnaissance and mapping of the Everest region before anyone would endeavor to climb the south face of the mountain.

By the time the British mounted their 1953 Everest expedition, the most massive climbing exercise in history, the mountain had already turned back seven assaults from major expeditions. Under the leadership of John Hunt, 362 porters were employed to carry five tons of gear 150 miles from the supply base at Darjeeling, in northeastern India, to the Everest Base Camp. At the higher elevations, succor was supplied by thirty-four mountain-tested Sherpas, the most accomplished of whom was Tenzing Norgay.

The climbers spent longer than usual acclimatizing to the altitude. They used supplementary oxygen more freely, both when climbing and sleeping. Moreover, they were supported not just by porters but by scientists, physicians, and oxygen-tank technicians. The result was another altitude record, as Tom Bourdillon and R. C. Evans were turned back just three hundred feet from the summit.

Following in their ice steps was a backup team of Edmund Hillary, a six-foot-three New Zealand beekeeper, and Sherpa Tenzing Norgay. After quizzing Bourdillon and Evans on what was ahead, they huddled in their tent at Camp VIII for an extra twenty-four hours, pinned down by a severe storm. Then the two men and their support team battled to a height of 27,900 feet and established Camp IX, which was nothing more than a tent on an icy, windswept ledge. The support team left Tenzing and Hillary to spend the night alone.

On the morning of May 29, 1953, after a breakfast of sardines, biscuits, and hot lemonade, they set out for the top. They passed the spot where one year earlier, Tenzing and Richard Lambert had been turned back. They climbed past the highest point attained by Bourdillon and Evans, past the south summit, and over a last steep cliff. Climbing carefully and using oxygen, they struggled up the razor-backed south ridge. They conquered the last three hundred feet by cutting steps in a wall of sheer ice.

Hillary has described his feelings upon reaching the summit: "My first sensation was one of relief. But mixed with the relief was a vague sensation of astonishment that I should have been the lucky one to attain the ambition of so many brave and determined climbers."

While Tenzing buried gifts for his Buddhist gods, Hillary took pictures. The photo that went 'round the world was of Tenzing, wearing an oxygen mask, brandishing a staff with the flags of Britain, Nepal, India, and the United Nations. After a fifteen-minute stay at the top, the two men descended.

As the years passed, a parade of climbers began ascending Everest. In 1971, a Japanese housewife became the first woman to reach the top, the British conquered the southwest face, and a Chinese expedition triumphed, reportedly without supplemental oxygen.

In 1973 a sixty-four-man Italian expedition was rumored to have spent $8 million in its quest for the summit. Rations included lobster bisque and petits fours. When one of their two helicopters crashed, the Italian army brought a replacement. Such opulence convinced some people that any climbing problem could be solved if only you threw enough money at it. Hundreds of people have now set foot on the top of Mount Everest; flags from dozens of countries have flown on its summit.

By the end of the seventies, almost all of the three hundred "seventhousanders" had also succumbed to the insatiable drive for bagging peaks. As a backlash to all that success, style began to take on a new importance. Climbers turned their attention to steep new faces of mountains already climbed, like the South Face of Annapurna, the West Face of Makalu, the Rupal Face of Nanga Parbat. In the ultimate triumph of *how* over *what,* Reinhold Messner and Peter Habeler made a pure alpine-style ascent of a new route on Gasherbrum I (Hidden Peak; 26,470 feet) in 1975. In 1980, Messner soloed Everest without supplementary oxygen. Since then, he has climbed all fourteen eight-thousanders.

Large, expensive expeditions continue to use traditional siege methods in the high mountains, but they are no longer on the cutting edge of the sport. The lightweight philosophy, first espoused by Eric Shipton in the thirties, draws ever more converts. The small, alpine ascent, without Sherpas or porters, is clearly the wave of the future.

YOSEMITE

When George Anderson achieved the first ascent of Half Dome in 1875, he used ropes and eyebolts. What separated his ascent from more modern techniques was the lack of a belay – a rope fed to the leader by a stationary second man.

Though there may have been climbers in the Sierra using belays before 1931, it was that year that Robert Underhill's article "On the Use and Management of the Rope in Rock Work" appeared in the *Sierra Club Bulletin.* Within two years, men were ready to attack the un-climbed – and. previously uncontemplated – big walls of Yosemite Valley. As the decade progressed, routes were put up on many high-angle faces, including Cathedral Spires, Royal Arches, Washington Column, and Lower and Middle Brothers.

In the thirties, the Sierra Club, already a major force in rock-climbing instruction, began to openly tout the unique joys of Yosemite climbing: the weather was consistently good; you didn't have to worry about avalanches ruining your fun; climbs were easily accessible, as were friends, wives, and restaurants when you returned.

Carabiners and nylon ropes, available just before World War II, did much to advance climbing standards. During the forties, the use of expansion bolts for direct aid (that is, to stand on by means of attached stirrups) further expanded the possibilities.

Even in the midforties, though, what Galen Rowell would call "the potential of Yosemite as the ideal locale for testing human limits on rock" was largely unrealized. Climbers in the Himalaya, in the Rockies, on McKinley, had long been testing themselves on multiday climbs in harsh environments. But in Yosemite, climbing was still limited to one-day outings. The biggest factor limiting rock climbs was the piton. The soft iron pitons imported from Europe before World War II were usually left in the rock, since removing them usually meant deforming them. Doing a long route on, say, El Capitan or Half Dome would have meant carrying several hundred pitons.

The beginning of multiday rock climbs arrived with John Salathé, a slightly-built Swiss wrought-iron worker. When he appeared in Yosemite in 1945, he was already in his midforties and less agile than many of his fellow climbers. His forte then was not tricky boulder problems, but rather the intricacies of piton placement, where his craftsman's affinity for tools gave him an advantage.

One day he was climbing a crack that narrowed to almost nothing. Upon closer investigation, he saw a blade of grass growing out of the minute crack. "If a blade of grass can come out," he thought, "a piton can go in." But when he tried to drive in an iron piton, it just bent.

Utilizing his knowledge as a metal worker, Salathé found a new piton material: high-strength carbon steel. He forged a piton out of steel drawn from the discarded leaf spring of a Model A Ford and returned to the tiny crack. As he later told the story in his heavy Swiss accent: "I took my piton and I pound and I pound, and it goes into the rock." Salathé, who Yvon Chouinard would call "the father of big-wall climbing," was now able to nail up hitherto hopeless cracks and thus avoid the need for bolts. Having made a dramatic breakthrough, he began to forge pitons in a wide range of sizes, emblazoned with the trademark of his Peninsula Iron Works, a P enclosed in a diamond.

The story goes that angels appeared before Salathé and advised him to scale three prominent rock faces. Accordingly, in the late forties, he pioneered the Southwest Face of Half Dome and the Lost Arrow from its base. In 1950, at age fifty-one, he and Al Steck summitted the dark, foreboding north wall of Sentinel Rock. Having satisfied the angels, he retired from big-wall climbing.

The next wave of pioneer climbers was led by Royal Robbins and Warren Harding. In 1955, the two men climbed together in a failed attempt to scale the Northwest Face of Half Dome. They hoped to return in 1956, but it didn't happen. In 1957, Harding organized his own group and arrived in Yosemite to find Robbins's party halfway up the 2,000-foot face. Robbins, along with Mike Sherrick and Jerry

Places like Overhanging Rock, Glacier Point, in Yosemite, have long beckoned the adventurous. (By Joseph N. LeConte, 1896, courtesy of Colby Memorial Library, Sierra Club)

Gallwas, went on to complete a five-day ascent of the Northwest Face of Half Dome, thereby establishing the first Grade 6 climb in North America.

A disappointed Warren Harding soon began fixing ropes on the "Nose" route of El Capitan. On November 12, 1958, after a twelve-day push (without coming down), Harding, Wayne Merry, and George Whitmore topped out on the "Nose." In all, Harding, utilizing a variety of partners, 675 pitons, and 125 expansion bolts, had taken forty-seven days over eighteen months to complete the climb. He and his team had fixed more than three thousand feet of rope from the bottom to the top of El Capitan, facilitating the many supply runs needed to accomplish the climb. Harding spent the last fourteen hours of the climb hanging in a sling, drilling twenty-eight bolt holes.

It was an impressive engineering feat, but was it really climbing? Many, including Royal Robbins, criticized the prolific use of bolts as overkill. "It was perfectly clear to us that given sufficient time, fixed ropes, bolts, and determination, any section of any rock wall could be climbed," Robbins wrote. "Siege climbing makes success certain, thus depriving alpinism of one of its most important elements: adventure." Two years later, in 1960, Robbins, Tom Frost, Chuck Pratt, and Joe Fitschen made the second ascent of the "Nose." The first continuous climb of El Capitan, it was accomplished without fixed ropes. Robbins's team had cut the time necessary to summit the route from forty-seven days to six and a half.

If the forties belonged to John Salathé, the late fifties and sixties belonged to Royal Robbins. In 1964, Robbins, Pratt, Frost, and Yvon Chouinard climbed the North American Wall on El Capitan, at that time the hardest big-wall climb in the world. The next year, Chouinard and T. M. Herbert scaled the Muir Wall, the first two-man ascent of an El Cap route. Not to be outdone, Robbins soloed the Muir Wall the following year, the first solo ascent ever of an El Cap route.

Great advances in rock climbing were in part linked to improvements in equipment. But they were also due to better-conditioned athletes. Before the late sixties, climbers did virtually no training for their sport. In fact, many relished the "climbing bum" image: unwashed, undisciplined, and unsober. It resonated well with the rebellious tone of the sixties.

In the seventies, with the arrival on the scene of rock jocks like John Bachar and Ron Kauk, climbing gradually came to be regarded as an athletic event rather than just rock play. Free climbing (moving up the rock without resting on protection) came into its own. Outdoor gyms were established. Athletic shorts and Lycra replaced tattered blue jeans; down vests replaced woolen sweaters.

That trend has only accelerated. Most top climbers today work out all year long. If weather precludes outdoor climbing, they move indoors, doing weight training or honing their skills on artificial walls.

The result has been a continued elevation of standards, and accomplishments, both in rock climbing and in mountaineering. Forty years ago, the high Himalayan peaks seemed as remote as outer space; today Everest's steep north face/Hornbein Couloir has been blitzed in forty hours round-trip, and the standard route was recently climbed in about twenty-three hours by a French guide wearing a throat microphone for a live telecast. On a single day in May 1992, thirty-two

Wilson S. Gould posed on the summit of Mount Gould in the Sierra Nevada, Kings River, 1896. (By Joseph N. LeConte, courtesy of Colby Memorial Library, Sierra Club)

people reached the top of the highest mountain in the world. Similarly, forty years ago, El Capitan and Half Dome were thought to be impregnable; but in 1987, John Bachar and Peter Croft climbed both of them in a single day.

As Galen Rowell writes, "Climbing is like the four-minute mile: once a barrier is surmounted, the impossible is oft-repeated. Yesterday's incredible feats are today's old classics." Yesterday, the world's best climbers looked up at El Capitan and said "No way!" Today it has been climbed by a high school student on spring break.

Tomorrow, who knows?

SOME NOTEWORTHY MOUNTAINS
1. Everest, Nepal-China 29,028 First ascent 1953 (British-Sherpa party).
2. K2 (Godwin Austen), Pakistan 28,250 First ascent 1954 (Italian).
3. Kanchenjunga, Nepal-India 28,208 First ascent 1955 (British).
4. Lhotse, Nepal-China 27,923 First ascent 1956 (Swiss).

5. Makalu, Nepal-China 27,824 First ascent 1955 (French).
6. Dhaulagiri, Nepal 26,810 First ascent 1960 (Swiss).
7. Manaslu, Nepal 26,760 First ascent 1956 (Japanese).
8. Cho Oyu, Nepal-China 26,750 First ascent 1954 (Austrian).
9. Nanga Parbat, Kashmir 26,660 First ascent 1953 (German-Austrian) In previous tries, twenty-nine people were killed.
10. Annapurna, Nepal 26,504 First "eight-thousander" summitted, in 1950 (French).
11. Aconcagua, Argentina 22,834 World's longest drop, over nine miles from summit to ocean bottom. First ascent 1897 (British).
12. Huascaran, Peru 22,205 First major peak climbed by a woman (Annie S. Peck of the United States in 1908).
13. Chimborazo, Equador 20,577 Attempted in 1802 by the explorer Humboldt; scaled 1880 by Whymper (British).
14. McKinley (Denali), Alaska 20,320 Highest on the North American continent; base-to-peak rise 18,500. First ascent 1913 (U.S.).
15. Logan, Canada 19,850 Second-highest on continent. First ascent 1925 (U.S.-Canadian).
16. Kilimanjaro, Tanganyika 19,590 Extinct volcano. First ascent 1889 (German).
17. Popocatepetl, Mexico 17,887 Sacred Aztec peak violated by Cortez's conquistadors, who climbed it in search of sulfur for gunpowder.
18. Kenya, Kenya 17,040 Extinct volcanic cone, almost directly on equator. First ascent 1899 (British).
19. Mont Blanc, Switzerland 15,771 Highest in the Alps. First ascent 1786 (French).
20. Matterhorn, Switzerland 14,685 Resisted many assaults; finally conquered in 1865 by Whymper and party (British).
21. Whitney 14,495 Highest in continental U.S. First ascent 1873 (U.S.).
22. Elbert, Colorado 14,431 First ascent claimed in 1847 (U.S.), but previously climbed by trappers and Indians.
23. Rainier, Washington 14,410 Volcanic peak bearing twenty-six glaciers. First ascent 1870 (U.S.).
24. Pikes Peak, Colorado 14,110 First recorded ascent 1820 (U.S.) Now has auto road to summit.
25. Grand Teton, Wyoming 13,766 First ascent 1898 (U.S.).

26. Wetterhorn, Switzerland 12,166 First ascent by British in 1854 sparked "Golden Age of Alpinism."
27. Etna, Italy 10,868 Highest active volcano in Europe—more than 260 eruptions in 2,500 years.
28. Olympus, Greece 9,550 Home of the gods in Greek mythology.
29. Washington, New Hampshire 6,288 Site of some of the worst weather in the world (a wind speed of 231 miles per hour was recorded in 1931). First peak in U.S. scaled by a white man, Darby Field in 1642.
30. Vesuvius, Italy 3,842 Only active volcano on European mainland. Destroyed Pompeii in A.D. 79.

Climbing Oddities

FEATS AND STUNTS

- In 1979, the team of John Roskelley, Ron Kauk, Bill Forrest, and Kim Schmitz spent three days ferrying seventy-pound loads up a 2,500-foot avalanche chute – just to get to the *base* of their proposed route on Pakistan's Uli Biaho spire. The team spent the next week climbing a 4,000-foot wall to reach the peak's 20,500-foot summit. On a scale that usually ranges from Grade I to Grade VI, the Uli Biaho route is rated Grade VII.

- Climbers Charlie Fowler and Mike Munger, bored one day, anchored one end of a 150-foot rope to a tree on top of Eldorado Canyon's Redgarden Wall in Colorado, tied the other end to themselves, and jumped off the lip of the overhanging cliff. Reminiscent of Errol Flynn, the feat earned them the instant recognition of the international climbing community – and business cards from quite a few psychiatrists.

- In 1985, Dick Bass and Frank Wells hired a guide to lead them up Everest. The first commercially guided climb of the mountain, it topped off an amazing achievement by Bass. In a twelve-month period, he had succeeded in climbing the highest peaks on all seven continents.

- In 1990, computer-science instructor Adrian Crane reached the highest points in all fifty states in a mere 101 days, beating the old record by three years. More recently, he summitted all fifty-four 14,000-foot Colorado peaks in fifteen days, beating the old record by twenty-four hours. On one day – July 17, 1992 – he topped out on six of Colorado's finest.

- On El Capitan, in 1980, Randy Leavitt completed a successful ascent of the difficult twenty-seven pitch "Excalibur" route, then jumped off the edge of the 3,600-foot cliff and pulled the rip cord of his parachute. Leavitt called his new sport "cliffing. "

- May 12, 1992, was a bad day for some Everest-lovers. On that day, thirty-two climbers trudged up the South Col route to the summit of the world's highest mountain. By far the highest one-day total ever, it included six people – five New Zealanders and one American – with desk jobs, guided clients who had paid at least $35,000 for their chance at the top.
- In 1992, unsung climber Ed Viesturs became the first American to summit the world's three highest mountains (Everest, K2, Kanchenjunga). The Seattle-based guide and nonpracticing vet has twice reached the top of Everest without supplementary oxygen. Said Viesturs of his anonymity: "There are so many people who go to Everest these days it's hard to get anybody excited. Sometimes I think, 'What do I have to do, climb it backward and naked?'"
- In the fall of 1992, Frenchman Pierre Tardivel climbed to the South Summit of Mount Everest, then skied down to base camp, covering

Joseph N. LeConte (right) *was part of the first party to summit Mount Williamson in the Sierra Nevada in 1903. (By Joseph N. LeConte, courtesy of Colby Memorial Library, Sierra Club)*

ten thousand vertical feet in two days. Besides breaking the altitude record for alpine skiing – 28,766 feet, a mark that will be broken only if someone rappels from Everest's 29,028-foot summit while wearing skis – he became the first person to climb up and ski down essentially the entire mountain. It was his fortieth first-descent on skis.

- In 1960, Warren Harding and Dean "Wizard" Caldwell spent twenty-seven days ascending the Wall of the Early Morning Light on El Capitan, the longest anyone had ever dangled from a rock wall. When Yosemite rangers threatened to rescue them for their own good, Harding responded with this note: "A rescue is unwanted, unwarranted, and will not be accepted." Ironically, the storms that had caused the rangers to fear for the climbers' safety actually saved them by refilling their water bottles.

- In 1974, Reinhold Messner and Peter Häbeler did the Eiger in ten hours. The previous best time on this dreaded wall in the Alps was almost twice as long. High on the Eiger's North Face, the two climbers met up with a party of Austrians, friends of Habeler's, who were on the third day of their climb. That evening, back down at the foot of the mountain, they got drunk with Clint Eastwood, who was there for the filming of *The Eiger Sanction.*

- In 1978, Reinhold Messner and Peter Habeler summitted Mount Everest without bottled oxygen, a feat many had believed impossible. Neither demonstrated any obvious brain damage. Explained Messner: "You don't know what will happen before it happens. It's like asking, 'Is your life worth your death?'"

- Herman Schaller, a guide, climbed the Matterhorn a record 233 times.

- In 1978, Ephraim M'Ikiara, 52, climbed up 17,022-foot Mount Kenya, barefoot and carrying only a thin blanket, a piece of hemp rope, a small package of food, and a leather bag containing a Bible. Coming upon a party of would-be rescuers, he muttered, "Was it you who showed me the way here?"

- A mountaineer who had a wooden leg climbed Mont Blanc, as well as five other mountains over 13,000 feet.

- In 1980, Reinhold Messner soloed Mount Everest.

- Christophe Profit soloed the north faces of three Swiss mountains – the Matterhorn, the Grand Jorasses, and the Eiger – in one day in 1985. He helicoptered from the summit of one peak to the base of the next.

- Also in 1985, Britons Nick and Dick Crane rode, pushed, and carried their mountain bikes to the top of Mount Kilimanjaro to raise money for charity.

- Seventeen-year-old Hugh Herr lost both feet to amputation in a January 1982 climbing accident; by August he was leading 5.11 climbs using prosthetic feet.
- Reinhold Messner, upon reaching the summit of Lhotse in 1986, became the first person to summit all fourteen of the world's eight-thousand-meter peaks.

MISHAPS

- In 1954, rescuers in Blons, Austria, had just dug out the survivors of an avalanche when a second slide reburied all twenty-five plus their rescuers. The only survivor of the second slide: a seventy-year-old woman, who endured fifty hours under the snow.
- Christopher Timms survived the longest fall in recorded history. On December 7, 1966, Timms slid 7,500 feet down an ice face on New Zealand's Mt. Elie de Beaumont and into a crevasse. His companion was killed, but Timms survived with only a concussion and some bruises.
- Since Edward Whymper and team first climbed the Matterhorn in 1865, at least sixty thousand people have summitted the mountain, including a seventy-six-year-old man and an eleven-year-old girl on the same day. The Matterhorn has also claimed at least ninety lives, including four guys who boasted in 1948 that they could get a cow to the top. They were found frozen to death.
- In 1933, Maurice Wilson, an Englishman recently converted to the benefits of fasting, decided that man's inability to reach the summit of Mount Everest was due to poor dietary habits. Eating less food, he reasoned, would leave more room for oxygen. Intent on proving his theory, he headed for the Himalaya. When the British refused to let him enter Tibet, Wilson disguised himself as a Sherpa and walked to Everest. He reached the Rongbuk Monastery on April 12, 1934, dressed in a mauve pullover, lightweight flannel trousers, and thin socks, prepared more for high tea than hiking in high mountains. Just as inadequate as his clothes was his expertise in mountain climbing. Fortified only with a rock-like faith, Wilson sallied forth into a fatal blizzard. The following year climbers found Wilson's body and his diary. Page after page documented his struggle with the mountain: "No food, no water . . . terrible cold . . . dead tired . . . must somehow go on . . . ."

- In 1951, avalanches and snowslides killed nearly four hundred people in Switzerland.
- Former gymnast Beverly Johnson was the first woman to solo Yosemite's El Capitan, in 1978. During an earlier ascent of El Cap, Johnson and her partner, Dan Asey, were startled by a climber zooming past them in the midst of a 2,000-foot fall. Asey turned to Johnson and said, "You don't see that every day. "
- Lori Kofhowski, a member of the University of Calgary's climbing-demonstration team, was attempting an ascent of the fifty-foot tower of the Alberta Pavilion at Vancouver's Expo '86 when she slipped and fell, crashing loudly onto the roof of the pavilion fifteen feet below and breaking her ankle. Thousands of Expo patrons looked on.
- In 1981, three years after he captured the climbing community's attention with his daring solo ascent of Mount Hunter, John Waterman set off to solo the east buttress of Mount McKinley. Reportedly into hallucinogens, he was trying to generate publicity for his fledgling campaign for president. Climbing without tent, sleeping bag, or dark glasses, and carrying little more to eat than flour and margarine (publicity for the world's starving), Waterman was last seen heading for a deeply crevassed section of the Ruth Glacier near the base of the mountain.
- On a single day in 1981, five people died in a fall on Oregon's Mount Hood and eleven members of a guided party were killed by an avalanche on Mount Ranier.
- Amid the tangle of existing ropes and hardware on El Capitan, Mark Smith and Richard Jensen established a new route in 1982 by drilling 145 bolt holes to ascend 1,700 feet of largely blank, unclimbed rock. A self-appointed "ethics committee" of resident Yosemite climbers, who disapproved of their tactics, said so by cutting down their ropes and defecating on them.
- Most people imagine climbing Mount Everest as a way of getting away from it all. But in the forty years since Everest was first climbed, climbers and Sherpas have carried hundreds of oxygen tanks up the mountain. The result is that the South Col, the main jumping-off point for the final push to the top, is a huge garbage dump, the snow dotted with yellow, red, and silver oxygen cylinders.

BUILDERING

- On May 26, 1977, toy maker George Willig attained instant notoriety with his shinny up the outside of New York's 110-story (1,377-foot)

World Trade Center. Authorities, who took a dim view of "buildering," decided to prosecute him. He was eventually fined a penny a floor, a total of $1.10, for his crime. On the up side, he was given a "lifetime" pass to the observation deck of the building. The next time he was in New York, however, he tried to use it and found out it had expired.

- Dan Goodwin set off on May 25, 1981, to make the first ascent of Chicago's 110-story (1,454-foot) Sears Tower, the world's highest building. Goodwin used suction cups and a homemade mechanical device that latched onto the building's window-washing tracks. Although he was clad in a rubber Superman suit, the Chicago cops failed to see the humor. In an attempt to discourage him, and others who might follow him, they blasted Goodwin with fire hoses and showered him with shards from plate-glass windows.
- In 1982, Michael Fagan scaled the walls of Buckingham Palace and chatted with the Queen Mother in her bedroom.

MISCELLANY

- Who is man's best friend at high altitude? The yak over the llama and the whiskey-toting Saint Bernard in a landslide. For the people of the high Tibetan plateau, the shaggy, ill-tempered relative of the buffalo is the key to life. The yak furnishes meat, wool, milk, butter, and transport. It is common for Tibetans to pay their rent or taxes in yak butter. Tibetan peasants spend their lives at the lonely task of herding yaks from one sparse pasture to another. For a year at a time they may be away from any village, living in tents made of yak hair, kept warm by fires burning yak dung. The national drink is tea laced with, yes, rancid yak butter. People drink thirty to fifty cups a day and worry about their health if they get less.
- More than a quarter of the earth's 56-million-square-mile land surface is three thousand feet or higher. Tibet, with an average elevation of about fifteen thousand feet, is higher than any peak in the continental United States.
- The community of Gartok, 15,200 feet high in northern Tibet, is credited with being the world's highest center of habitation.
- Measuring the height of large mountains is not a precise science. Consider the way the "official" height of Mount Everest was determined. Measurements were made from six places, with six different results, ranging from 28,990 to 29,026 feet. When all six were averaged, the figure came to exactly 29,000 feet. Believing that sounded

unscientific, the surveyors arbitrarily added two feet to make the official figure sound better. Today Everest has been upgraded to 29,028 feet.

- Although the earth's crust seems solid and immutable, it is actually quite malleable, even moving with the tides. The continents actually rise and fall about six inches every day under the influence of the moon.
- Mountains not only keep out people, but are an impediment to ideas as well. The innovations of mankind tend to reach mountain people late, if at all. Until well into the twentieth century, a remote tribe in the Caucasus Mountains, called the Khevsurs, still wore the same armor as crusader knights.
- There was an exodus of climbers from the granite walls of Yosemite Valley to the high country in 1977 when word spread that a plane carrying several tons of high-grade marijuana had crashed in the High Sierra. Though it was temporarily out of reach of the Drug Enforcement Agency, it was quite manageable for some Camp 4 climbers. Waves of them trekked up to the crash site, extricating bales of pot from the plane and a nearby frozen lake. According to *Outside* magazine: "When the climbers returned to the valley, they were noticeably better equipped. "
- In 1820, three climbers fell into a crevasse on a Mont Blanc glacier. Knowing the glacier's rate of movement, scientists calculated that the bodies would reappear at the melting terminus of the glacier in 1860. They reappeared in 1861.
- In the summer of 1956, a glacier at the foot of the Weisshorn ejected the perfectly preserved body of a man, later identified as Georges Winkler, a German climber who had fallen from the Weisshorn in 1888. It had taken sixty-eight years for the ice to carry Winkler's corpse approximately one mile from the upper glacier to the terminus.
- 1981: James Bond kills a villain with a well-thrown piton in *For Your Eyes Only.*
- *K2*, a two-man drama, opened on Broadway in 1983. It features two climbers trapped just below the summit who discuss the meaning of life while waiting for a rescue team that never arrives.
- A 1983 U. S. expedition to Mount Everest, led by Galen Rowell, used volunteer Americans as high-altitude porters (HAPs). Rowell calculated that back home, their HAPs earned, on average, $85,000 per year more than the climbers.

Quotations and Inspirations

Death is so close (when climbing). You could let go and make the decision to die. It feels so good.

— Jeff Achey

You are probably pretty confident that you could walk from here to the door without tripping. Climbing is the same for me.

— Jeff Achey

Soloing is serious business, because you can be seriously dead.

— John Bachar

If you take rock climbing seriously, sooner or later you will have that religious experience. You are going to be looking at God, saying, 'We're going to be lucky if we get out of here.' Your life is going to be in front of you and then you are going to realize that you would rather be grocery shopping.

— Ed Barry

You don't have to be crazy to climb mountains. But it helps!

— Jeremy Bernstein's dad

It is not variety that is the spice of life. Variety is the meat and potatoes. *Risk* is the spice of life.

— David Brower

Most men, if not all, have a spirit of adventure which needs an outlet. Many of the better-known sports . . . require a lot of money; but climbing needs nothing more than a pair of gym shoes and some old clothes to start with at least. One of the good things about climbing is that it is possible to enjoy it in any form, from messing about on small practice cliffs, to struggling up a huge Himalayan peak.

−Joe Brown

A popular misconception of climbing is that it requires great strength and nerve. If that were true then the strongest men would be the best climbers, which is not so. Strength is obviously an asset to a climber, but the most important thing is a combination of the mental ability to work out technical problems, physical suppleness and agility, and the right amount of confidence.

−Joe Brown

A long rock climb is a series of problems, each one different from the rest, which have to be solved by ingenuity of mind and versatility of body.

−John Buchan

I was fortunate to have the opposite of vertigo, for I found a physical comfort in looking down from great heights.

−John Buchan

High mountains are a feeling,
But the hum of human cities torture.

−Lord Byron

All climbers are a product of their first few climbs.

−Yvon Chouinard

Looking back up at our route late one afternoon when a bluish haze covered the west side of El Capitan, it seemed to have lost a bit of its frightfulness but appeared even more aloof and mysterious than before. It is far too deep-rooted to be affected by the mere presence of man. But we had changed. We had absorbed some of its strength and serenity.

−Yvon Chouinard

Play for more than you can afford to lose, and you will learn the game.

−Sir Winston Churchill

Let me assure you that any lady blessed with moderate health and activity may accomplish tours (in the Alps) with great delight and few inconveniences.

—Mrs. Cole, 1859

The sane friends of the mountaineer always regard him with mixed feelings, compounded mainly of good-natured tolerance and pity.

—J. A. Cory

Eventually . . . I came to climb, and the hills fulfilled their promise. I had discovered an extension of experience that moved and excited me beyond description; it was as exhilarating as a moment many years before, in a dusty classroom, when I first read Shaw's *Major Barbara*, and suddenly realized that it was possible to think for oneself.

—John Emery

I climbed to the limits of my ability because in so doing I could extend the limits of my experience. I could find out more about myself and about my friends when the situation was sharpened by difficulty

—John Emery

I was in the air long enough to think, 'Wow, this is really going to hurt.'

—Charlie Fowler, recalling his 400-foot fall off
the east face of Long's Peak. Fowler landed in a drift of fresh
snow and walked away unharmed.

Whatever you can do, or dream you can, begin it.
Boldness has genius, power, and magic in it.

—Goethe

Climbing is a glamour sport. People get into it because they think it takes guts but not a lot of skill.

—Richard Gottlieb, climbing instructor

Climbing is so straightforward. You either did it right or you cheated like hell.

—Richard Gottlieb

As I hammered in the last bolt and staggered over the rim, it was not at all clear to me who was conquerer and who was conquered: I do recall that El Cap seemed to be in much better condition than I was.
— Warren Harding, after the first ascent of El Capitan

Many years ago when I first started climbing, it really seemed like fun. I really enjoyed busting my ass trying to somehow get up something like Lost Arrow Chimney . . . or picking out a new route . . . but always feeling good about it. But suddenly it just seems like a drag. Maybe I should have stuck with sports car driving.
— Warren Harding

Such beauty . . . turns satisfaction to pure joy.
— John Harlin

The past was wiped out, all that mattered was the future; and the future lay over the snow-plastered, ice-glazed summit wall.
— Heinrich Harrer

Yes, we had made an excursion into another world and we had come back, but we had brought the joy of life and of humanity back with us. In the rush and whirl of everyday things, we so often live alongside one another without making any mutual contact. We had learned on the North Face . . . that men are good and the earth on which we were born is good.
— Heinrich Harrer

When adventure seems to disappear from around us, we will always know where ultimately to find it again – within ourselves.
— Maurice Herzog

Where there is the necessary technical skill to move mountains, there is no need for the faith that moves mountains.
— Eric Hoffer

The real thing is the mountains themselves, in wet or fine, whether the ice forms treacherously on the rocks, or the granite is sensuously warm to the fingers in the sun, whether you are crunching happily up in the early morning on the points of your crampons, or staggering horribly down in the afternoon slush of an August snowfield, whether you can see 100 miles or six inches, it is sheer joy to be in them.

—Quintin Hogg

Shaken by no wind, drenched by no showers, and invaded by no snows, it is set in a cloudless sea of limpid air with a white radiance playing over all. There the happy gods spend their delightful days.

—Homer, about Mount Olympus

A good scare is worth more to a man than good advice.

—Edgar Watson Howe

The greatest mistake you can make in life is to be continually fearing that you will make one.

—Elbert Hubbard

For this is what America is all about. It is the uncrossed desert and the unclimbed ridge. It is the star that is not reached and the harvest that is sleeping in the unplowed ground.

—Lyndon B. Johnson

The manners of mountaineers are commonly savage, but they are rather produced by their situation than derived from their ancestors.

—Dr. Samuel Johnson

Security is mostly a superstition. It does not exist in nature, nor do the children of men as a whole experience it. Avoiding danger is no safer in the long run than outright exposure. Life is either a daring adventure or nothing.

—Helen Keller

Something hidden. Go and find it.
Go and look behind the ranges—
Something lost behind the ranges.
Lost and waiting for you. Go!

—Rudyard Kipling

Climbers do not really conquer mountains; climbers conquer themselves.

—Ann E. Kruse

Mystery is essential to mountaineering.

—Voytek Kurtyka

We never grow tired of each other, the mountain and I.

—Li Po

There is no security on this earth; there is only opportunity.

—Douglas MacArthur

It (Everest) is an infernal mountain, cold and treacherous. . . . The risks of getting caught are too great, the margin of strength when men are at great heights is too small. Perhaps it's mere folly to go up again. But how can I be out of the hunt? It sounds more like war than sport, and perhaps it is.

—George Leigh-Mallory, in a letter written shortly before his disappearance near the summit of Mount Everest

Mountain scenes occupy the same place in our consciousness with remembered melody. It is all one whether I find myself humming the air of some great symphonic movement or gazing upon some particular configuration of rock and snow, of peak and glacier.

—George Leigh-Mallory

The one permanent emotion of the inferior man is fear—fear of the unknown, the complex, the inexplicable. What he wants beyond everything else is safety.

—H.L. Mencken

Every step (in mountaineering) is a debate between what you are and what you might become.

—George Meredith

The south saddle of Mount Everest is the world's highest garbage dump.

—Reinhold Messner (and others)

There are few human activities more beautiful to watch than a practiced rock climber in action – so delicate but so strong, so fastidious of
movement, apparently so effortless, presumably so unafraid.

– James Morris

The desert makes men solitary; the jungle seems to make them argu-
mentative; the sea makes them superstitious; but the mountains,
above all, make for gregariousness. I doubt if there is a more close-knit
freemasonry on earth than the company of climbers.

– James Morris

No longer may we talk of conquering the mountains – which, like
underdeveloped nations, must now be treated with a special and
rather sickly kind of obsequiousness. It is not them that we are conquering, but ourselves, in looking outwards we are only looking in,
and Life itself, the real zealots are quite likely to assure us, is only a
difficult serac.

– James Morris

The wilderness holds answers to questions man has not yet learned
how to ask.

– Nancy Newhall

Climbing would be a great, truly wonderful thing if it weren't for all
that damn climbing.

– John Ohrenschall

Go carefully lads, be careful; a single moment's enough to make one
dead for the whole of one's life.

– J. Pecoste

There are times in a young man's life that a great experience changes it.
Those two days on Half Dome were for me the divide between care-
less youth and serious manhood.

– A. Phimister Proctor, 1884

Summits are a place between heaven and earth.

– Gaston Rebuffat

I have never considered myself an exceptional, much less a super, athlete. I can only run a few miles, and twenty push-ups pretty much wipes me out. I'm much more into drinking beer, smoking dope, and having fun than some boring training regimen.

— Rick Ridgeway, K2 summiteer

There used to be so few climbers that it didn't matter where one drove a piton, there wasn't a worry about demolishing the rock. Now things are different. There are so many of us, and there will be more. A simple equation exists between freedom and numbers; the more people, the less freedom. If we are to retain the beauties of the sport, the fine edge, the challenge, we must consider our style of climbing.

— Royal Robbins

Perhaps if we can learn to face the dangers of the mountains with equanimity, we can also learn to face with a calm spirit the chilling specter of inevitable death.

— Royal Robbins

Siege climbing makes success certain, thus depriving alpinism of one of its most important elements: adventure.

— Royal Robbins

It was a joy to be climbing. Climbing was one of the best things — maybe the best thing — in life, assuming that one would never play shortstop for the Dodgers.

— David Roberts

We were within a stone's throw of a supreme test of our abilities. To apply one's best techniques, to suffer miserable wet cold conditions, to go on when every muscle ached, to forge up despite a strong logical inner will to go back down. But also to experience that heightening of sensory perception that such suffering induces and to experience the inner calm that springs from having accomplished an exhilarating climb.

— Doug Scott

Night's candles are burnt out, and jocund day walks tiptoe on the misty mountain tops.

— William Shakespeare

Thou hast a voice, great Mountain, to repeal large codes of fraud and woe.

— Percy Bysshe Shelley

The only true dignity of man is his ability to fight against insurmountable odds.

— Ignazio Silone

Supposing it was the regular thing for all mountaineers to use pitons on their climbs, would it not be a sign of the degeneracy of man? Would it not mean that he had no longer a desire to risk himself, no longer a spirit of enterprise and initiative?

— Frank Smythe

A wall built of unmortared bricks by a gang of untutored workmen.

— Frank Smythe, describing Mount Brussels in Canada

From one of our stations we saw more of this Karakoram country. . . . As far as we could see there was a turbulent ocean of peaks without so much as a glimpse of earth in repose. It hardly seemed possible that there should be so much of a disturbed landscape.

— Michael Spender

Mountain scenery is the antithesis not so much of the plains as of the commonplace. Its charm lies in its vigorous originality.

— Leslie Stephen

The majority of climbers are complete individualists. Dislikes and rivalries are common among them, and comparatively few go on climbing together year after year. Odder still, it is not unknown for two who positively dislike each other to climb together because the arrangement enables them to do the climbs they want.

— Lionel Terray

The ideal age for mountain climbers is between thirty-five and forty. . . . What counts is mature judgment and how tightly you are wound.

— Jim Whittaker, first American to summit Everest

Security is a kind of death.

— Tennessee Williams

Mountaineering is an intensely personal and private, almost sacred, experience. Therefore, the less publicity it receives, the better.
—Fritz Wiessner

Mountains are good adventure.
—Geoffrey Winthrop Young

Tell Webster's to change the meaning of insanity to 'John Bachar free-soloing New Dimensions!'
—Yosemite bulletin board

Embrace tiger, return to mountain.
—Tai-chi lesson

There are old climbers, and there are bold climbers, but there are no old bold climbers.
—Anonymous

A woman's place is on top.
—Official T-shirt of the 1978 American Women's Himalayan Expedition to Annapurna

There are many paths to the top of the mountain, but the view is always the same.
—Chinese proverb

One of the greatest advantages mountaineering has over other sports is that there is no danger of playing to the gallery, no question of exhibitionism. The greatest benefit comes from the impact, on the minds of students, of the symbolic aspect of mountaineering, the feeling of rising higher and higher, surmounting all obstacles. On a mountain, a mountaineer is always the gainer, even if he does not reach the summit. He has at least gained in the qualities which danger and nature in the raw sharpen. He learns to appreciate the value of physical exertion almost beyond human endurance, and above all the spirit of comradeship.
—The Himalayan Mountaineering Institute Bulletin, 1959

Glossary

AAC American Alpine Club. Founded in 1902, with headquarters in New York, it is responsible for representing American mountaineering interests.

abseil *(rappel)* To descend by sliding down a rope. Friction for controlling the descent is provided by wraps of the rope around the body or by a mechanical rappel device. The rope is usually doubled so that it can be pulled down afterward.

ACC Alpine Club of Canada. Founded in 1906, it is the national mountaineering club of Canada.

accessory cord Thin rope, from 3 to 8 millimeters, often used for making *slings (runners)*.

acclimatization The gradual process of becoming physiologically accustomed to the rarefied air of high altitude.

active rope The length of rope between a moving climber and another climber responsible for belaying the former.

acute mountain sickness (AMS) A condition characterized by shortness of breath, fatigue, headache, nausea, and other flulike symptoms. It occurs at high altitudes and is attributed to a shortage of oxygen; most people don't experience symptoms until they reach heights well above five thousand feet.

aid climbing The technique of moving up a rock face using artificial holds. *Slings* ropes, *nuts* and other paraphernalia are used for physical support, not just for emergency protection or belay anchors. (Contrasted with *free climbing.*)

aiguille A needle-shaped rock mass or mountain peak. Nearly one half of the high mountains in the French Alps are prefixed *aiguille.*

alpenstock A snow and ice tool; the forerunner of the modern *ice ax.*

alpine The highest biological life zone.

alpine style A method of climbing emphasizing speed and light weight, in which a mountain is ascended in a continuous push and climbers carry all necessary gear with them. (Contrasted with *siege style.*)

Alps The range of mountains extending across Western Europe, from the French Mediterranean coast to central Austria. The highest peak is Mont Blanc, 15,771 feet.

alternate leads A method of climbing rock or ice in which two climbers lead alternate *pitches* of a climb.

AMC. Appalachian Mountain Club. Founded in 1876, it is the oldest domestic walking, rambling, and climbing club in the United States.

amphitheater   A very large recess in a cliff face or a large oval area bounded on three sides by cliffs.

anchor   The point at which a fixed rope, a *rappel* rope, or a belay is secured to rock, snow, or ice by various means, such as an *ice screw* or other piece of protection hardware.

angle piton   A metal wedge with a V- or U-shaped cross section, designed to fit in cracks half an inch wide (baby angles) to four inches wide (bongs). Angles are very stable because they contact the rock in three places.

approach   The distance a climber must hike from the car to the start of a climb. An approach may take a few minutes or several days.

arête   A narrow, serrated ridge, usually separating two glacial valleys or adjacent *cirques.*

arrest   To stop a slip or fall, usually by employing an ice ax as a brake.

artificial climbing wall   A climbing surface made out of brick, board, stone, or a mix of polyester resin and sand that has artificial holds for climbers to work out, train, or learn to climb. Many are indoors.

ascender   A mechanical device, such as a *Jumar,* Gibbs, or Shunt, which works on a ratchet principle; the device can slide up a rope, but will grip securely when it gets a downward pull. It permits climbers to move up a rope while not sliding down. Ascender knots (see *prusik*) serve the same purpose.

avalanche   A sliding mass of snow or ice.

avalanche cone   The mass of material where an avalanche has fallen. Because the debris is compacted by the force of the avalanche, the cone remains long after other signs of the avalanche have disappeared. In places where avalanches are common, a cone may become a permanent feature.

backcountry   A wilderness area lying far from populated areas.

balaclava   A soft woolen hat, which can be worn as a cap or pulled down over the ears and the lower part of the face to give protection from wind and driving snow.

balance climbing   A technique used for climbing smooth rocks whereby a climber maintains a position of balance by careful choice of hand- and footholds.

bandolier   A chest loop for carrying climbing equipment.

base camp   The largest and lowest supply camp on a *siege-style* expedition. The other higher camps are numbered consecutively.

bashie   A soft, malleable aluminum blob, of varying size, that is hammered into a crack too shallow to take a piton.

basin   A circular or oval valley, or surface depression, the lowest part of which is usually occupied by a lake or traversed by a river.

bat hook   A device used for direct aid, invented by Warren Harding for use in shallow drilled holes on blank rock where bolts would otherwise be necessary.

belay   To belay is to tend the climbing rope, ready to immediately put enough friction on the rope to hold the climber in case of a fall. Friction is generated by the rope going around the belayer's body or through a belay device. Belaying is the primary safeguard in climbing, and its practice is universal.

The belay itself is the entire system set up to make belaying possible, including the anchor that holds the belayer in place.

belay device   Any of numerous small metal devices (*figure-8 descender, belay plate,* etc.) that force a bend in the climbing rope, creating enough friction to permit a belayer to hold a fall.

belay plate   A flat belay device with one slot (for a single rope) or two slots (double ropes).

bergschrund   The gap or *crevasse* separating the upper ice of a glacier from the mountain wall behind.

bight   A loop of rope.

big wall   A steep cliff or face, vertical or nearly so, that is one thousand feet or more from bottom to top.

biner   Slang (pronounced "beaner") for *carabiner.*

bivouac   A night out without a tent.

bivouac (bivy) sack   A lightweight, unfilled, waterproof nylon bag that can cover a sleeping bag, or a climber caught without his sleeping bag.

bivy   Slang term for bivouac.

bollard   A horn, or hump, of snow that can be used as an anchor.

bolt   A thin metal rod that is hammered into a pre-drilled hole in the rock to serve as a multidirectional *anchor.* Bolts, ranging in diameter from quarter-inch to half-inch were originally used to protect free climbers on otherwise unprotectable routes and to piece together crack systems on longer climbs. Because they are left in place for subsequent climbers to use, bolts remain controversial.

bolted route   A route that is entirely protected by bolts.

bolt hanger   A metal piece that is attached to the bolt, allowing a *carabiner* to be clipped to the bolt.

bombproof   Said of a hold or anchor that will not fail, regardless of how much weight or force is put on it.

bong (bong-bong)   The biggest *piton,* designed for cracks wider than a person's foot.

bouldering   Climbing large rocks close to the ground without ropes or protection. Excellent training for big climbs, it has become a sport in its own right.

boulder problem   A route up a boulder. The problem is usually named and rated, and can be top-roped or bouldered.

brake bar   A small aluminum rod that is used to create friction on the rope when a climber is descending by rappel.

bridging *(stemming)*   A climbing technique in which the climber pushes out to the sides with hands and/or feet, using opposing pressure against the rock. Often used in climbing *chimneys* or *dihedrals.*

bucket   A large bombproof hold.

bulge   A small overhang.

bumblies   Beginners, usually unsupervised, who have no idea what they are doing.

buttress   A section of a mountain or cliff standing out from the rest, often flanked on both sides by gullies or *couloirs;* somewhat wider than an arête.

cagoule   A long, pullover waterproof jacket.

cairn   A small pile of stones used to mark a trail, pass, summit, or some other feature.

carabiner   A metal, oval-shaped

snaplink about three inches long in the shape of a giant safety pin. Capable of holding a ton, carabiners are used for attaching the rope to anchors in rock or snow.

carabiner brake A configuration of four to six carabiners arranged to provide rope friction for rapelling.

cerebral edema Maladaptive response to high altitude in which there is excess accumulation of fluid in the brain.

chalk Light magnesium carbonate, powder or block, used by rock climbers to keep their hands dry and thus improve handholds.

chalk bag A bag, usually worn at a climber's waist, that holds grip-enhancing chalk.

chest harness Harness used in conjunction with a waist harness to attach a climber to the rope.

chickenhead Protruding knob on a rock face that can be used for a hold.

chimney A crack wide enough to accommodate a climber's entire body.

chimneying The method of climbing a chimney using the pressure of feet and back on opposing walls.

chock A manufactured chockstone; a piece of hardware, designed to fit securely in a crack or behind a flake, that serves as an anchor, attached to the rope by carabiners and runners. There are two basic types of chocks: wedges (such as a *nut* or *stopper*) and cams (such as a *Friend*).

chockcraft The art of using chocks to create secure anchors in the rock.

chockstone Mother Nature's own chock; a rock wedged in a crack or behind a flake, around which a runner

can be threaded and then clipped to a rope for use as an anchor point. Before artificial chocks, British climbers used to carry pebbles to place in cracks; later they used hexagonal machine nuts found on railroad tracks. Today there are two basic types of chocks: wedges and cams.

chock sling Wire, rope, or webbing that attaches to a chock.

chop To remove from the rock someone else's protection, such as bolts.

chute A gully or *couloir.*

cirque A steep-walled, bowl-shaped depression formed by erosion from a valley glacier.

classic routes Ways up mountains that have special character, historical interest, great difficulty, popularity – or a combination of any of these.

clawing A method of climbing ice whereby both hands and feet are used to drive sharp climbing tools into the ice, using them as holds. Usually, crampons with front-pointing spikes are worn on the feet, with an ice ax in one hand and an ice hammer in the other.

clean climbing Means of ascension which leaves the rock unscarred and undamaged after the climbing team has passed.

cleaning the pitch Removing all the protection hardware placed by the leader.

cliff A smooth, steep face of rock.

cliffhanger A *sky hook.*

clip in To attach oneself to the mountain by means of a carabiner snapped onto an anchor.

clove hitch One of the two main knots (other is the *figure-8*) used in the ropework system.

coiling The various methods of looping and tying a rope so that it can be carried, all requiring a certain amount of skill to avoid kinking.

col A saddle or pass between two peaks.

copperhead A malleable piece of metal used as aid; like a mashie, but for use in even smaller pockets and shallow seams.

cordee (French) A party of roped climbers.

cordillera A ridge or chain of mountains. Originally applied to the Andes, it now refers to the principal mountain range of a continent.

corner An outside junction of two planes of rock, approximately at right angles (Contrasted with *dihedral*.)

cornice An overhanging lip of snow that forms on the leeward side of a ridge or summit. As they are often fragile and difficult to see, especially from above, cornices pose special dangers to climbers.

couloir A gully often providing the main drainage for a rock face. Many couloirs are at least partially snow-filled; they're natural channels for avalanches, and a *bergschrund* often guards the entrance.

crab Slang term for snaplink carabiner.

crack A gap or fracture in the rock, varying in width from a thin seam to a wide chimney.

crag A low cliff, one or two pitches high.

crampons A framework of steel spikes that attaches to the bottom of a boot for gripping ice and snow. They usually have twelve points: ten pointing downward and two pointing forward beyond the front of the boot for very steep ground.

crater A circular depression at the summit of a volcano created by the extrusion of gases and lava; connected by a conduit to a magma chamber below the earth's surface.

crevasse A deep crack in the ice of a glacier, resulting from stress on the glacier as it moves over uneven ground. Crevasses range in size from narrow fissures to huge chasms, and may be covered over with snow.

crux The most difficult part of a pitch or climb (though some climbs have more than one crux).

cwm A deep, steep-walled, and usually snow-filled basin on a mountain.

day pack A medium-size soft pack, favored by day hikers, for carrying food, water, and other supplies; bigger than a fanny pack, smaller than a backpack.

deadman Any object that can be buried in the snow and used as an anchor point for attaching a rope. Deadmen can include snow *flukes*, ice axes, snow pickets, tent stakes, or plastic sacks filled with snow.

dehydration A depletion of body fluids that can hinder the body's ability to regulate its own temperature. One can become dehydrated during climbing if the fluids lost during perspiration and respiration are not replaced by drinking water. Chronic dehydration lowers a climber's tolerance to fatigue, reduces his ability to sweat, elevates his rectal temperature, and increases the stress on his circulatory system. In general, a loss of 2 percent or more of one's body weight by sweating affects performance; a loss of 5 to 6 percent affects health.

descender *(rappel device)* A friction device used for descending ropes (rappelling), the most common of which is called the *figure-8;* others include the *brake bar* and *carabiner brake.*

dihedral A high-angled inside corner where two rock planes intersect, shaped like an *open book.*

direct The most direct way up a route or climb, usually the way water would take to fall down the rock. The direct tends to be steeper and more difficult than ordinary routes.

direct aid The aid or equipment a climber puts weight on to progress upward.

divide The high country separating two river systems or basins.

double-dyno Two *dynos* in succession.

double-up To anchor two chocks close together for added protection.

down and out The correct position of a carabiner gate when it is connected to an anchor.

Dulfer rappel The method of descending in which a climber threads an anchored climbing rope between his legs, returning it to the front of his body, then wrapping it over a shoulder and holding it behind him with one hand. It is also called the Dulfersitz.

dyno A technique for reaching holds that seem just beyond the climber's grasp. The climber sinks slightly, then rises by pushing with the legs and pulling with whatever hand has the current hold, then reaches for the new hold with the other hand.

edging Using the sides of climbing boots to stand on thin rock ledges.

eight-thousander The term for a mountain higher than eight thousand meters (26,247 feet). There are fourteen eight-thousanders, all in the Himalayan or Karakoram ranges.

escarpment An inland cliff formed by the erosion of the inclined strata of hard rocks.

etrier A short, foldable ladder of three or four steps, with a small loop at the top for attaching to an aid point. It is usually made from metal rungs fixed to thin cord or from tape sewn or knotted to form loops for the feet. Most aid climbers carry two or three etriers. A climber who has moved up to the top of an etrier will lace another aid point, to which the next etrier will be clipped.

expansion bolt A bolt that expands and locks when screwed into a pre-bored hole in the rock. Used when a rock lacks cracks into which a *piton* or *nut* can be inserted. Bolts provide the safest protection, but alter the rock and change the character and degree of difficulty of a climb.

expedition An organized party of mountaineers, with a definite objective, who set out to climb or explore in one of the remote ranges of the world.

exposed A description of a climber's route when it is steep and hard with a big drop below it.

exposure A long drop beneath a climber's feet; what one confronts to the max when climbing a sheer face like El Capitan.

extractor A tool that climbers use to remove chocks that have become stuck in cracks; also called a chock pick.

face A wall of rock steeper than 60 degrees.

face climbing Using footholds and handholds on an open rock face.

face holds Edges and irregularities protruding from a wall, or the pockets sunk into it.

fall factor A numerical value indicating the severity of a fall. If protection holds, the most serious fall has a value of 2, and most climbing falls are between .5 and 1.0. Calculate the fall factor by dividing the distance of the fall by the length of rope between you and your belayer.

fault A fracture along which movement has occurred parallel to the fracture surface.

fault plane A fracture surface along which blocks of rock on opposite sides have moved relative to one another.

fell A hill or mountain. An obscure word, except in the proper names of hills in the northwest of England.

fifi hook A small hook designed to hold a climber's body weight on a placement while putting in the next placement.

figure-8 descender A metal rappel device in the shape of an 8. One of the holes is used to attach the device to a harness with a carabiner; the other hole is used to pass the rope through to provide friction for the descent.

figure-8 knot One of the two main knots (other is the *clove hitch*) used in the ropework system.

fill Sleeping bag insulation, usually either down or polyester.

finger crack A crack so thin only a climber's fingers will fit into it.

firn *(névé)* Well-consolidated snow reduced to a dense layer of granular crystals by alternate melting and freezing.

first ascent The first time a route has been climbed.

fist crack A crack the size of a fist.

fist jam A secure and painful (for the beginner) way of finding a purchase on a rock. In a fist jam, the climber shoves his hand into a gap in the rock and makes a fist, swelling the hand for use as an anchor point. The thumb is pushed into the palm to stretch the skin and create a wider profile.

fixed protection Anchors, such as bolts or pitons, that are permanently placed in the rock.

fixed rope A rope that a climber has anchored and left in place after a pitch is climbed so that climbers can ascend and descend at will. Most expedition climbing uses fixed ropes to facilitate load carrying and fast retreat over dangerous terrain.

fjord A long, narrow glacial valley at sea level; often flanked by steep mountains (such as Milford Sound, New Zealand).

flake A thin, partly detached leaf of rock.

flake To prepare a rope so it won't tangle when you are using it.

flapper Torn skin on the hand–the kind that flaps.

flaring crack A crack the sides of which flare out.

flash To climb a route on the first try, without falling or hanging from the rope. Many consider it the best style.

fluke A metal plate shaped like a shovel blade that is driven into the snow to form an anchor point. The blade has an attached wire to which a rope can be clipped. Any downward force on the wire serves to drive the blade deeper into the snow. A fluke is one type of *deadman.*

four-thousander A colloquial name for a mountain more than four thousand meters (13,123 feet) high in the Alps. There are about seventy-five such mountains.

fracture A break in a rock caused by intense applied pressure.

free climbing Climbing in which natural handholds and footholds are used. Hardware is used only for protection and not for support or progress. (Contrasted with *aid climbing.*)

free soloing Climbing without ropes, hardware, or a partner.

French free Resting on *protection* while otherwise *free climbing.*

friction brake A device such as a bar mounted on one or more carabiners that provides rope friction when rappelling.

friction climbing Ascending slabs using friction between shoes and rock or hands and rock, instead of distinct holds.

Friend An active (spring-loaded) camming device inserted into a crack as an anchor point. Designed and marketed by Ray Jardine in 1978, the Friend was a major breakthrough because it allowed climbers to protect roofs and parallel cracks with minimal time spent making the placement.

front pointing A method used to climb steep snow or ice by kicking in the front points of twelve-point crampons, often using an ice ax in one hand and an ice hammer in the other.

frostbite The freezing of body tissue; fingers and toes are particularly vulnerable.

frostnip Less severe form of frostbite.

frost wedging The opening and widening of a crack by the repeated freezing and thawing of ice in the crack.

gardening Cleaning a climb of vegetation and loose rocks.

gear freak A climber who has lots of equipment but not much knowledge.

gendarme A rock tower straddling a ridge, making progress difficult or impossible.

glacial budget The expansion and contraction of a glacier in response to accumulation and wastage.

glacial erratic A boulder transported by a glacier from its original source.

glacial groove A deep, straight scratch on a rock surface caused by the movement of sediment-laden glaciers over bedrock.

glacial ice Ice that has formed from *firn.*

glacial polish Smooth glistening rock produced by the movement of sediment-laden glaciers.

glacial striation A straight scratch on a rock surface, only a few millimeters deep, caused by the movement of sediment-laden glaciers.

glacier A mass of moving ice on land. Pushed by gravity and the pressure of more ice from above, it slowly carves its way down a valley or mountain slope until it finally melts or breaks away. Yosemite is an example of a valley that was sculpted by glaciers.

glacis An easy-angled slab of rock between horizontal and thirty degrees.

A *slab* is steeper and a *wall* is steeper than that.

glissade A voluntary, controlled descent of a snow slope by sliding. It is fun but potentially dangerous. A sitting glissade is performed on the seat of the pants; in a standing glissade, the soles of the boots are used like skis.

Gore-Tex The trade name for a material for clothing and tents that allows water vapor from the body to escape but will not allow liquid water droplets (rain) to enter. It has high breathability.

gorge A deep, narrow valley with very steep sides.

gorp A high-carbohydrate snack food made primarily from nuts and dried fruit; an acronym for "good ol' raisins and peanuts."

groove A shallow, vertical crack.

gully Steep-sided rift or chasm, deep and wide enough to walk inside.

Gunkie A climber who frequents the Shawangunks, a famous escarpment in New York.

hand traverse Horizontal movement across a rock face in which the body is supported mainly by the hands.

hangdogging Hanging on a rope, usually after a fall.

hanging belay A belay station on vertical rock that offers no ledge for support.

HAP High-altitude porter, often used to carry equipment for Himalayan expeditions.

harness A contraption usually made of wide tape sewn into a shape that is worn around the shoulders or waist and offers convenient loops through which to clip a climber's rope and gear. If a climber falls while roped onto a harness, the shock load is distributed over a wide area. The climber also has a better chance of remaining in an upright position, lowering the risk of head meeting rock.

haul bag A bag used for holding and hauling gear up a wall.

hawser-laid rope Rope made from three groups of filaments plaited together.

headlamp A light that is mounted on a climber's helmet or headband.

headwall The sheerest, often most difficult, section of a cliff or mountain, usually its uppermost.

helmet A hard shell that climbers wear to protect their head from falling rock.

hemoglobin The coloring pigment of the red blood cells that contains iron. It enables the cells to carry oxygen from the lungs to the tissues of the body.

hold A protrusion or indentation in the rock that a climber can grasp with fingers (handhold) or stand on (foothold).

horn A protruding piece of rock over which a sling can be hung for an anchor. Also: A steep-walled pyramidal peak formed by the headward erosion of *cirques* (such as the Matterhorn).

hypoglycemia A dangerous condition characterized by an abnormally low blood glucose level. It can be caused by medications like insulin (taken for diabetes), some illnesses, and severe physical exhaustion.

hypoxia Underoxygenation of the tissues.

hypoxic drive to breathe A measurement of how much one breathes when tissues are underoxygenated; it is an important predictor of how well a climber will do at high altitude.

ice ax   A tool with many uses: for self-arrest in a fall; for a personal anchor; for balance; for cutting or scraping steps in hard snow. The ice ax consists of a blade (adze) and pick mounted on a wood or metal shaft (the spike).

ice climbing   The act of climbing ice, often a frozen waterfall.

icefall   A chaotic mass of unstable ice resulting from a glacier traveling over steep, uneven bedrock. Also: a frozen waterfall.

ice piton   A piton that is hammered into the ice, specifically designed for that purpose.

ice screw   A threaded metal device with a pointed tip that is pounded, then screwed, into ice. It serves the same purpose as a piton in rock.

impact force   The tug a falling climber feels from the rope as it stops a fall.

inactive rope   Rope between any two climbers who are not moving.

jam crack   A gap in a rock that offers inadequate handholds but is wide enough for the climber to find purchase by inserting fingers, hand, fist, or feet.

jamming   Wedging fingers, hand, fist, or feet into a crack to create an anchor point.

jug   A large indented hold, a *bucket* Also: slang for the verb to *Jumar.*

Jumar   A trade name for a Swiss rope-gripping *ascender.* This device is so widely used for self-belay and for hauling on expeditions that the word has become a verb, as in "I Jumared up to the ledge."

kernmantel   Standard climbing rope in which the core (kern) is

protected by an outer braided sheath (mantel). The core is constructed of one or more braided units.

kletterschue   Climbing shoe.

knife blade   A long thin piton.

knife edge   An arête.

knoll   A small, rounded hill or mound.

lateral moraine   The sediment deposited as a long ridge along the edge of a glacier.

lava   Molten rock – magma – that has reached the earth's surface, often from an erupting volcano.

laybacking (liebacking)   Grabbing a vertical edge, often a flake of rock, then pulling with hands, pushing with feet, and walking the feet up almost alongside the hands. It is a strenuous but useful technique for *arêtes*, corners with cracks, and cracks offset in walls.

leader (or lead)   The first climber in a party of roped climbers; the leader of an expedition.

leader fall   A fall taken by the lead climber. The leader will fall double whatever the distance is to the closest *protection.*

leading through   The second climber continuing to climb through a stance, thereby becoming the leader. If both climbers are of more-or-less equal competence, this is an efficient way to climb.

ledge   A level area on a cliff or mountain, which may be grass, rock, or snow.

load capacity   The maximum load that a piece of gear can withstand.

loft   A sleeping bag's thickness or height when it is fully fluffed.

magma   Molten rock material generated within the earth.

manteling A technique in which the climber moves up high enough to push down on a ledge with both hands until the body is supported on stiffened arms. The climber then replaces one hand with a high-stepping foot and moves up to stand on the ledge.

mashie Same as a *bashie.*

massif A compact group of mountain peaks or high points, not necessarily a range or a chain.

maximal oxygen consumption (VO₂ Max) A measurement of the maximum amount of oxygen a person can transfer from the lungs to the cardiovascular system in one minute. Though generally predetermined by heredity, improvements can be made by engaging in a serious exercise program. It is a strong indicator of potential climbing performance.

medial moraine A moraine formed where two lateral moraines merge.

mesa A broad, flat-topped mountain bounded on all sides by steep slopes.

mixed route A route involving both rock climbing and ice/snow climbing.

monsoon The seasonal front of warm, wet winds that strikes the Himalaya around the end of May, bringing rain to the lowlands and so much snow to the high elevations that climbing is nearly impossible.

moraine A bank or ridge of loose rocky debris deposited by a moving glacier.

mountain An area of land significantly higher than the surrounding land.

mountain sickness A spectrum of maladaptions at high altitude, of which *pulmonary edema* is the most severe.

multiday climb A climb so long and/or difficult that it requires more than one day to complete.

multidirectional anchor An anchor that is secure no matter which direction a load comes from. *Bolts,* some fixed *pitons,* and some *chock* configurations are multidirectional anchors.

multipitch route A climb consisting of more than one pitch.

nailing Hammering a chain of pitons into a crack.

natural anchor A tree, boulder, or other natural feature that is well-placed and strong enough to make a good anchor.

natural line A rock climb that follows an obvious feature up the face of a cliff, such as a groove, a gully, or a series of cracks.

névé *(firn)* Well-consolidated snow reduced to a dense layer of granular crystals by alternate melting and freezing.

niche A small recess in a rock face, usually large enough to hold a climber.

nose A jutting protrusion of rock, broad and sometimes with an undercut base.

nut Artificial chockstones usually made of aluminum alloy and threaded with nylon cord. They are fitted into cracks in the rock and usually can be used in place of pitons, which can scar the rock. A climber using only nuts needs no hammer, since nuts can be lifted out of their placement.

objective dangers Mountain hazards that are not necessarily the result of flaws in a climber's technique, such as avalanches, rockfall, and crevasses.

off-finger crack A crack too

wide to finger jam, but too narrow to hand jam.

off-hand jam A crack too wide to hand jam, but too narrow to fist jam.

off-width Crack that is too wide to fist jam, but too narrow to fit the whole body into.

off-width protection *Chocks* that are wide enough to anchor in an offwidth.

on-sight To climb a route with no previous knowledge of its moves.

on-sight flash To climb a route on the first try without falling and with no previous knowledge of its moves.

open book A high-angled inside rock corner, a *dihedral*.

opposing chock A chock that is anchored in the opposite direction of another chock. In combination, the two chocks protect against a *multidirectional* load.

orogeny (orogenesis) The formation of mountains, especially through a disturbance in the earth's crust.

overdrive A piton is said to be overdriven when its effectiveness is reduced by too much hammering.

overhang Rock that exceeds ninety ·degrees.

palming A friction hold in which a climber presses the palm of the hand into the rock.

pass A deep depression between two mountains.

PDH. Pretty Darn Hard; extreme aid climbing.

pedestal A flat-topped, detached pinnacle.

peg British term for piton.

pendulum A sideways movement across a rock face by swinging on a rope suspended from above.

Perlon The German trade name for nylon.

pin Another name for piton.

pinkpoint To lead a climb without falling or resting on aid while clipping the rope to preplaced protection. The leader may have previously attempted the route (compare with *redpoint*).

pinnacle A partially detached feature, like a church steeple.

pitch A section of climbing between two stances or belay points. A climbing distance that is usually the length of a 150- or 165-foot rope, it is the farthest the leader will go before allowing the second climber on the rope to catch up.

piton *(peg, pin)* A metal wedge hammered into a crack until it is secure, used as an anchor point for protection or aid. Currently in the United States, pitons are used only when absolutely necessary, because repeated use damages rock. The first hard-steel pitons were made by John Salathé for use on the Southwest Face of Half Dome in 1946.

piton hammer A hammer designed and carried for pounding in and extracting pitons.

piton scar A groove in the rock caused by the placement and removal of a piton.

pocket A shallow hole – and thus hold – in the rock.

Portaledge A cotlike sleeping platform, suspended on a vertical rock face from pitons.

powder slide A small avalanche of powder snow.

powder snow Light, fluffy snow that has not thawed or been refrozen.

power Strength-to-weight ratio, and thus not simply dependent on size of muscles.

pressure hold A foothold or handhold used to maintain a position on a rock face by exerting pressure sideways and downward on it.

problem A climbing challenge. It is most applicable to shorter climbs, as in a "bouldering problem."

protection The anchors – such as chocks, bolts, or pitons – to which a climber connects the rope while ascending.

protection system The configuration of anchors, runners, carabiners, ropes, harnesses, and belayer that combine to stop a falling climber.

prow A rock feature resembling the prow of a ship, such as the "Nose" of El Capitan.

prusik A technique for climbing a rope – originally by use of a prusik knot, now also by means of mechanical *ascenders*. The knot, invented by Karl Prusik, uses a loop of thin rope wound around a larger-diameter rope in such a way that the knot will slide freely when unweighted, but grip tightly to the main rope when a climber's weight is applied to it.

pulmonary edema Abnormal accumulation of fluid in the lungs.

put up To make the first ascent of a route.

rack The collection of climbing gear carried by the lead climber, as arranged on a gear sling. (To rack the gear means to arrange it on the sling.)

rappel *(abseil)* To descend by sliding down a rope. Friction for controlling the descent is provided by wraps of rope around the body or by a mechanical rappel device. The rope is usually doubled so that it can be pulled down afterward.

rappel device *(descender)* Any of numerous devices (such as the *brake bar, carabiner brake,* or *figure-8 descender*) that provide rope friction for rappelling.

rappel point The anchor for a rappel; that is, what the rope, or the sling holding it, is fastened to at the top.

rating systems A term or number describing the difficulty of a climb. There are seven major rating systems, including the American (Yosemite) Decimal System, the British, French, East German and Australian Systems.

rat tail An excessively worn, unsafe climbing rope.

recessional moraine A pile of rocky debris left by a retreating glacier.

redpoint To lead a climb without falling or resting on aid, and while placing protection as the climb is made. A redpoint may occur after a climber has practiced the route.

rib A prominent, slender feature, more rounded than an *arête.*

rock-climbing boots Soft boots with flat rubber soles designed to grip rock.

rogue A climbing instructor who operates without permits.

roof An overhanging section of rock that is close to horizontal. Roofs vary in size from an eave of a few inches to giant cantilevers several yards wide.

rope Important element of the belay system. Modern climbing rope is 150 or 165 feet of nylon *kernmantel.* Single ropes range from 10 to 12 millimeters in diameter, double ropes 8 to 9 milli- meters. According to John Forrest Gregory in *Rock Sport,* the ideal climb- ing rope would have all the following qualities: low impact force, low elonga- tion under both impact force and low load, good handling qualities, light weight, water resistance, high ratings for holding falls, resistance to cutting and abrasion, and a low price.

roped solo climbing *Free climbing* or *aid climbing* a route alone but pro- tected by a rope. This is an advanced technique, requiring a lot of gear.

roping up The act of a party of climbers tying themselves together with climbing ropes.

route A particular way up a cliff that may have dozens of routes, each with a name and a rating.

runner *(sling)* A short length of nylon webbing or accessory cord tied or stitched to form a loop; used for con- necting anchors to the rope and for other climbing applications.

runout A section of a climb that is unprotectable, save with bolts (which may be discouraged).

rurp An acronym for Realized Ulti- mate Reality Piton, the smallest piton in the arsenal. A rurp, about the size of a postage stamp, fits in a fingernail-thick crack.

safety margin The amount of extra strength built into climbing gear. For example, a carabiner may have a strength rating of six thousand pounds, but it rarely has to support more than three thousand pounds. Thus it has a cushion, or safety margin, of three thousand pounds.

Sahib The term Sherpas use for Western climbers; literally, "master."

sandbagging Misrepresenting the difficulty of a climb, rating it easier than it really is.

sastrugi Wavelike sculpting of dry icy crust, formed by wind over open snow wastes. Where the full blast of the wind is unimpeded, as in Antarctica, these features can be quite dramatic and difficult to traverse.

scoop An indentation in the rock face, not as deep as a *niche.*

scramble An easy climb, usually without a rope.

scree A long slope of loose stones on a mountainside.

seam A crack far too thin for fingers, but big enough to accept some small chocks, pitons, or copperheads.

seam hook A small hook shaped like an anchor that can be set in thin cracks. Some seam hooks can be tapped into cracks with a hammer.

second The climber who follows the *lead.* While the lead might take a substantial fall, the second usually risks only a short fall, as the belay is from above. The second usually cleans the pitch.

self-arrest Stopping yourself during a fall, often with the use of an ice ax.

self-belay The technique of protect- ing oneself during a roped solo climb, often with a self-belay device.

serac An ice tower or pinnacle, often unstable.

seven-thousander A colloquial name for a mountain of greater altitude than 7,000 meters (22,966 feet). There are hundreds of them, all in the Hima- laya and central Asia.

sewing-machine leg Violent shak- ing in the leg resulting from holding a bent-knee position too long.

Sherpas Mountain people living in northeastern Nepal who are famous as high-altitude porters and climbing partners on Himalayan expeditions.

siege style A method of climbing a mountain by setting up and stocking a series of camps along the route in preparation for an assault on the summit. (Contrasted with *alpine style*.)

sit bag A cloth seat that climbers attach to the rock and sit in to make hanging from a wall more comfortable.

ski mountaineering The sport of climbing mountains on skis.

sky hook A tiny hook with a thin curved end that attaches to nubbins or flakes. Used when nothing else is available except maybe a bolt, it is precarious because only a climber's body weight keeps it in place.

slab Large, smooth rock face inclined between thirty degrees and sixty degrees.

sling *(runner)* A short length of nylon webbing or accessory cord tied or stitched to form a loop; used for connecting anchors to the rope and for other climbing applications.

smashie Same as a *bashie*.

smearing A technique of friction climbing used on steep, scooped holds, where the sole of the boot is squashed into the depression to gain the best hold.

snaplink The most common type of carabiner. Contrasted with screwgate.

snow blindness Temporary loss of vision caused by glare off snow or ice.

snow cave A hole dug in the snow or ice for the purpose of surviving a cold-weather bivouac. Sheltered from winds and most avalanches, it is far warmer than a tent.

snow goggles Dark glasses with both front and side protection to prevent snow blindness.

soloing Climbing alone, whether roped or unroped, aided or free.

spike A finger of rock.

spindrift Powder snow whipped by the wind.

sport climbing A type of climbing, often on artificial walls, emphasizing gymnastic moves and good protection.

sport rappelling Descending a rope in a fast, bouncy manner, with speed as the main goal.

squeeze chimney A *chimney* just wide enough to accommodate the body of a climber.

stance The position a climber is in at any given time, especially the position of the belayer.

stemming *(bridging)* A climbing technique in which the climber pushes out to the sides with hands and/or feet, using opposing pressure against the rock. Often used in ascending *chimneys* or *dihedrals*.

step-cutting Cutting steps in snow or ice with an ice ax.

step-kicking Kicking the feet into firm snow to create steps.

stirrups Direct-aid slings made into the shape of little rope ladders with aluminum steps. No longer used much in the United States.

stopper Wedge-shaped *nut*.

stuff bag A water-repellent or waterproof nylon bag with a drawstring, used for compact storage of sleeping bag, down jacket, etc.

suncups Depressions in the snow due to unequal melting,

swami belt Ten to twelve feet of one-inch or two-inch webbing wrapped around the waist in such a way that allows a climber to tie on to it with a rope.

taking in   Removing slack in the active rope from a moving climber.

talus   The weathered rock fragments that accumulate at the base of slopes.

tarn   A small high-mountain lake.

tarp   A waterproof sheet of material used for protecting exposed objects or people.

technical climbing   Climbing that requires hardware, harnesses, ropes, and specialized climbing boots. (Contrasted with *scrambling*.)

tension traverse   Direct-aid climbing in which a climber crosses a *traverse* with the aid of a tight rope from the side, using hands and feet on the rock to counterbalance the side pull of the rope.

terminal moraine   Rocky debris left at the end of a retreating glacier.

third-classing   Free-soloing a Class 4 or Class 5 route without protection.

till   Sediment deposited directly by glacial ice. It is neither sorted nor stratified.

tincture of benzoin   A solution of water, alcohol, and benzoin (resin from a tree in Java) that climbers can apply to their hands to provide a protective coating against rock abrasion.

toe-hooking   A climbing technique in which a toe is hooked around a rock edge.

top rope   A rope anchored above a climber, providing maximum security; sometimes called TR. (To top-rope means to rig a climb with a top rope or to climb a *pitch* using a top rope.)

trashie   A *bashie,* strung with

a nylon *sling,* that has been left on a route. The sling soon rots, and the metal blob turns ugly and useless.

traverse   To proceed around rather than straight over an obstacle; to climb from side to side. A traverse may be an easy walk along a ledge or a daunting passage. Protecting traverses is often difficult because a fall will cause the climber to pendulum, ending up off route even if no injuries occur.

trek   A long hike.

tunnel vision   Seeing only a small area directly in front. This is a common pitfall for the beginning climber, who, because of nervousness, may miss an obvious hold that is nearby but off to one side or the other.

Tyrolean traverse   A rope bridge connecting two points (with a backup second rope linked to the climber who is crossing).

UIAA   The Union Internationale des Associations d'Alpinisme, an international climbing organization founded in 1932 that coordinates and fosters mountaineering interests around the world.

undercling   A hold that permits the climber to grip the rock from below with the palms up.

unidirectional anchor   An anchor that will hold securely if loaded from one direction, but will pull free if loaded from any other direction.

valley glacier   A glacier confined to a mountain valley or to an interconnected system of mountain valleys.

verglas   A film of ice on rocks, too thin for crampons to penetrate, often caused by freezing mist.

volcano   A mountain formed by magma (molten rock) that is forced up through the earth's surface and ejected as lava in cone-shaped deposits. Most of the world's great volcanos are extinct, and all have been climbed.

waist belay A method of taking in and paying out a belayed active rope. The belayer passes the rope around his waist; the hand on the active rope side is the directing hand, while the hand on the slack rope side is the braking hand. (Also called the hip belay or body belay.)

wall A steep cliff or face, between sixty degrees and ninety degrees.

wand A long, thin stake placed along the climbing route so that even in stormy conditions climbers can find their way back along the route.

whiteout A condition of near-zero visibility caused by driving snow or fog merging with the white surface.

windchill The cooling of the body that results from wind passing over its surface – especially dramatic if the surface is wet. It is a more useful measurement of meteorological discomfort than is temperature alone.

zipper A series of poor aid placements, all of which can be expected to pop out, one after the other, if the leader takes a fall.

zone of accumulation The part of a glacier where additions exceed losses and the glacier's surface is perennially covered by snow.

zone of wastage The part of a glacier where losses from melting and breaking off exceed the rate of accumulation.

Organizations

Alpine Club of Canada (ACC), P.O. Box 1026, Banff, Alberta, Canada T0L 0C0; 403-762-4481, fax 403-762-3143. Founded in 1906, objectives of the ACC are the encouragement, practice, and promotion of mountaineering, as well as the preservation of the natural beauty of the mountains.

American Alpine Club (AAC), 113 East 90th Street, New York, NY 10028; 212-722-1628. The dominant advocate for American mountaineering interests.

American Hiking Society (AHS), 1015 31st Street, NW, Washington, DC 20007; 703-385-3252. Formed in 1977 to educate the public in the benefits of hiking; encourages hikers to build and maintain trails.

American Mountain Guides Association (AMGA), P.O. Box 2128, Estes Park, CO 80517; 303-586-0571. Offers accreditation programs for schools, certification programs for guides, and membership services for schools and guides.

American Trails Foundation (ATF), 1446 Glenmoor Way, San Jose, CA 95129; 408-446-4584. A group working for preservation and maintenance of trails.

Appalachian Mountain Club (AMC), 5 Joy Street, Boston, MA 02108; 617-523-0636. Objectives are to cultivate public knowledge of the environment and promote enjoyment of the outdoors throughout the northeastern United States. Maintains 1,400 miles of trails, twenty trail shelters, and an eight-unit alpine hut system.

Appalachian Trail Conference (ATC), Corner of Washington and Jackson Streets, P.O. Box 807, Harpers Ferry, WV 25425; 304-535-6331. Federation of trail and hiking clubs. Manages the Appalachian Trail, a 2,100-mile foot trail extending from Georgia to Maine.

The Mountaineers, 300 Third Avenue W, Seattle, WA 98119; 206-284-6310. Founded in 1906 for persons interested in exploring and studying the mountains, forests, and watercourses of the Northwest.

Bibliography

BOOKS

Annapurna. Maurice Herzog. New York: E.P. Dutton & Co., 1953. A gripping account of the first ascent of an eight thousand-meter peak.

Annapurna: A Woman's Place. Arlene Blum. San Francisco: Sierra Club Books, 1980. Close-up of the 1978 all-women expedition that scaled the treacherous slopes of Annapurna; two women of the second summit team were killed. Lots of photos.

Basic Rockcraft. Royal Robbins. Glendale, CA: La Siesta Press, 1971. Great coverage of all aspects of climbing, especially the all-important subject of protection. Goes into knots, belay techniques, harnesses.

The Big Book of Mountaineering. Edited by Bruno Moravetz. London: Barron's, 1978. As the title implies, this is a big book – not thick, just large, as though written for the visually impaired. The result is some BIG, bold, beautiful photographs. Also: some interesting articles by a variety of climbers, most of whom are European, on subjects ranging from thin air to the abominable snowman.

California Thrill Sports. Eric Fair. San Francisco: Foghorn Press, 1992. A superficial look at a dozen or so adventure sports, from bungee jumping to hot-air ballooning. Of limited value.

Climber's and Hiker's Guide to the World's Mountains. Michael R. Kelsey. Provo, UT: Kelsey Publishing, 1990. Information, maps, and black-and-white photos of every major mountain in the world, from the Vinson Massif in Antarctica to Haleakala in Hawaii.

Climbing: A Guide to Mountaineering. Raymond Bridge. New York: Charles Scribners, 1977. How to do everything from tie knots to dig a snow cave.

Climbing Back. Mark Wellman and John Flinn. Waco, TX: WRS Publishing, 1992. The life story of Mark Wellman, who lost the use of his legs in a climbing accident, then went on to climb El Capitan and Half Dome.

Climbing Big Walls. Edited by Mike Strassman. Merrillville, IN: ICS Books, 1990. How to go bottom to top, by a variety of authors. Everything from hauling and cleaning to living on the wall.

Climbing Ice. Yvon Chouinard. San Francisco: Sierra Club Books, 1978. Combination of how-to and history, with inspirational and instructional photos, by the master.

Climbing in North America. Chris Jones. Berkeley: University of California Press, 1976. A competently written history of the sport from 1492 to the seventies. Packed with intriguing photographs.

The Conquest of Everest. Sir John Hunt. New York: E.P. Dutton & Co., 1954. For those who like source material, this is top-flight. It's the story of the 1953 conquest of Mount Everest written by the leader of the expedition. Lots of photos and some cute little sketches.

The Crystal Horizon. Reinhold Messner. Seattle: The Mountaineers, 1989. The gripping story of Messner's 1980 solo ascent of Everest – without supplemental oxygen. Readable prose and a wealth of photos.

Dictionary of Mountaineering. Peter Crew. Harrisburg, PA: Stackpole Books, 1969. Dandy little dictionary, with a British flavor.

The Edge of Everest: A Woman Challenges The Mountain. Sue Cobb. Harrisburg, PA: Stackpole Books, 1989. The story of a fifty-year-old woman on an Everest expedition.

Eiger Dreams. Jon Krakauer. New York: Lyons & Burford, 1990. The mountain ramblings of a good writer; more about people than about rock and ice.

Eiger: Wall of Death. Arthur Roth. New York: Norton & Co., 1982. All about the mountain that killed the first nine men who challenged it. As of 1982, forty-three climbers have been killed on what may be the most dangerous mountain in the world.

Encounters With the Archdruid. John McPhee. New York: Farrar, Straus and Giroux, 1971. Three separate narratives: in each, McPhee, David Brower, and one of Brower's natural enemies adventure somewhere in the West and discuss the philosophy of conservation. Fascinating book by one of America's great writers.

The Games Climbers Play. Edited by Ken Wilson. San Francisco: Sierra Club Books, 1978. A huge anthology of climbing writings, everything from rock climbing to expeditions, from ethics to mountain rescue.

In the Throne Room of the Mountain Gods. Galen Rowell. San Francisco: Sierra Club Books, 1986. Alternating chapters on the 1975 K2 expedition, of which Rowell was a member, and historical tales of the second-highest mountain in the world.

The Last Step: The American Ascent of K2. Rick Ridgeway. Seattle: The Mountaineers, 1980. An account of the successful 1978 American K2 expedition that included three women climbers.

Meditations at 10,000 Feet. James S. Trefil. New York: Macmillan, 1986. A scientist gets out of the laboratory and into the mountains. Want to know where rocks come from? Or all about a mountain stream? This book is for you.

Men and Mountaineering. Edited by Showell Styles. New York: David White, 1968. An anthology of source material, some of which is fascinating, such as "Mallory's Last Climb" and "Night Out on Everest."

Men, Myths & Mountains. Ronald W. Clark. New York: Thomas Y. Crowell Co., 1976. The story of the exploration and conquest of the mountain world, from 1492 to 1976.

Moments of Doubt. David Roberts. Seattle: The Mountaineers, 1986. Twenty pieces of mountain writing, by a good writer, divided into adventures, profiles, and reflections.

Mountaineering: The Freedom of the Hills. Fifth edition. Edited by Don Graydon. Seattle:

The Mountaineers, 1992. Comprehensive instruction in all aspects of rock climbing and mountaineering.

Mountain Journeys. Edited by James P. Vermeulen. New York: Overlook Press, 1989. Harrowing stories of climbers and their climbs, including pieces by Galen Rowell, Maurice Herzog, John Muir, and Tenzing Norgay.

Mountain Passages. Jeremy Bernstein. Lincoln, NE: University of Nebraska Press, 1966. A philosophical look at climbing and mountains. Contains a lengthy profile of Yvon Chouinard.

The Mountains. Lorus J. Milne and Margery Milne. New York: Time Inc., 1962. The history, geology, and sociology of mountains, with loads of pictures.

The Mountains of California. John Muir. Berkeley, CA: Ten Speed Press, 1977. Pantheistic prose of the father of the American conservation movement.

The Mountains of Canada. Randy Morse. Seattle: The Mountaineers, 1978. Just color pictures and quotes, but what pictures!

Mountains of the Middle Kingdom. Galen Rowell. San Francisco: Sierra Club Books, 1983. As much as a mountain book, this is a paean to Tibet and a showcase for Rowell's photographs. Fascinating, nonetheless.

My Vertical World. Jerzy Kukuczka. Seattle: The Mountaineers, 1992. After Reinhold Messner finished climbing all fourteen eight thousand-meter peaks, Kukuczka did it too, mostly by new routes or in winter. He died in 1989 on the South Face of Lhotse.

Nandi Devi: The Tragic Expedition. John Roskelley. Harrisburg, PA: Stackpole Books, 1987. The story of the 1976 expedition to climb India's Nanda Devi; of Roskelley, who led a party of three to the summit; and of leader Willi Unsoeld, who supported the participation of his inexperienced daughter, named Nanda Devi for the mountain Unsoeld considered the most beautiful in the world.

Norman Clyde of the Sierra Nevada. Norman Clyde. San Francisco: The Scrimshaw Press, 1971. A narrative of Clyde's ramblings and first ascents in the Sierra. Some classic old photos.

One Step Beyond. Alan Hobson. Banff, Alberta: Altitude Publishing, 1992. Five rambling profiles of extraordinary Canadian adventurers, including Sharon Wood.

Risk! Steve Boga. Berkeley: North Atlantic Books, 1988. A collection of profiles of adventure athletes in a variety of sports.

Rock Climbing. John Barry and Nigel Shepherd. Harrisburg, PA: Stackpole Books, 1988. A great how-to book with more than seventy color photographs and thirty step-by-step diagrams.

Rock Gear: Everyone's Guide to Rock Climbing Equipment. Layne Gerrard. Berkeley: Ten Speed Press, 1990. Great reference guide, especially for beginners. Lots of diagrams, including a nice feature: a pictorial table of contents.

Rocks Around The World. Translated by Martin Boysen. San Francisco: Sierra Club Books, 1988. Mostly pictures, but what pictures! Dramatic and beautiful.

Rondoy. David Wall. London: Butler & Tanner, 1965. A harrowing tale of climbing in the Peruvian Andes.

Scrambles Amongst the Alps. Edward Whymper. Berkeley, CA: Ten Speed Press, first published in 1871. If you like source materials, this is for you. Prose is a bit difficult, but over one hundred incredibly detailed engravings (Whymper was an artist) make this compelling work.

Second Ascent. Alison Osius. Harrisburg, PA: Stackpole Books, 1991. The inspirational story of Hugh Herr, boy-wonder rock climber, who lost his feet to frostbite, but survived to climb again.

Spirit of the Age: The Biography of America's Most Distinguished Rock Climber, Royal Robbins. Pat Ament. Lincoln: Adventure's Meaning Press, 1992. The ups and downs of the man who owned Yosemite rock climbing in the sixties. Packed with photos.

To the Top of the World: Alpine Challenges in the Himalaya and the Karakoram. Reinhold Messner. Seattle: The Mountaineers, 1992. The capable writings of the man who brought "alpine style" to the top of the world. Ample photos as well as watercolors by Jean-Georges Inca.

A Treasury of the Sierra Nevada. Edited by Robert Leonard Reid. Berkeley: Wilderness Press, 1983. Dozens and dozens of short source pieces written by the people who came early to the Sierra, people like John C. Fremont, Jack London, Bret Harte. "Mountaineers" is only one of six sections.

The Vertical World of Yosemite. Edited by Galen Rowell. Berkeley: Wilderness Press, 1975. Fascinating compilation of source material that lays out the history of climbing in Yosemite; everything from A. Phimister Proctor's "An Ascent of Half Dome in 1884" to "Modern Yosemite Climbing" by Yvon Chouinard. Inspirational photos, both color and black and white.

Why I Climb. Steve Gardiner. Harrisburg, PA: Stackpole Books, 1990. Brief biographies of twenty-nine climbers, who attempt to answer the question *"Why do you climb?"*

PERIODICALS

Climbing, P.O. Box 339, Carbondale, CO 81623; 303-963-0372. The premier magazine of the sport. Covers all aspects of climbing.

Rock and Ice, P.O. Box 222295, Carmel, CA 93922; 408-625-6222. General information on rock, ice, and sport climbing.

Sport Climbing Connection, P.O. Box 3203, Boulder, CO; 303-442-5242. A new publication, devoted entirely to sport climbing.

Summit, 1221 May Street, Hood River, OR 97031; 503-387-2200, fax 503-387-2223. A quarterly with a nice balance between beautiful photos and good prose.

VIDEOS

Basic Rock Climbing, John Long. Vertical Adventures Productions, 818-883-4921.

Moving Over Stone, narrated by Doug Robinson. Ridge of Light Productions, P.O. Box 2906, Mammoth Lakes, CA 93546.